More Praise for *Activist Odyssey*

History comes alive in the author's probing, eyewitness accounts. Berkeley in the 1960s? Sylvia was there. Martin Luther King's March on Washington? Sylvia was there. The Vietnam War protests? Sylvia was there. The Zapatista rebellion in Mexico? Sylvia was there. All this is presented against the background of her rich and tumultuous personal life. Activist Odyssey *is a splendid book: instructive, inspirational and entertaining.*

— Stanley Krippner, humanistic psychologist, recipient of numerous awards, and author, *Haunted by Combat: Understanding PTSD*

A delightful read, this memoir is more than a personal story; it chronicles many important social struggles of our time. A fascinating resource for students of political and social movements, it's never dry since it's spiked with the irreverent asides of an accomplished woman and occasional scamp who steadfastly resists taking herself too seriously. As an activist who's participated in campaigns she describes, I can vouch for her accuracy in analysis and detail.

— Peter Bergel, community organizer, writer/producer/performer of guerrilla theater, and editor, *The PeaceWorker*

In Activist Odyssey, *she recounts her experiences with nuclear disarmament advocates in Berkeley, with Black Panthers in New York, and with Latin American solidarity activists in Nicaragua and Mexico. For Hart Wright, the political and personal have blended, sometimes productively, sometimes painfully. Written with grace and humor, her story takes many turns but it's marked by courage, candor and insight throughout. In my decades of teaching the history of American radicalism,* Activist Odyssey *would have been a welcome addition to my reading list.*

— Daniel Pope, Professor Emeritus of History, University of Oregon, and editor, *American Radicalism*

If Sylvia Hart Wright were a novelist she could have gotten several books out of her life story, and I would have enjoyed every one of them. Her political and personal adventures, her loves and lovers, her achievements and disappointments all make Activist Odyssey *a fascinating read.*

— Rosalie Calabrese, widely published and anthologized poet

Hey you, yeah you with the tattoos and the piercings—listen up! See that older lady with the twinkle in her eye? She's had a helluva life and now she's telling the inside story. Stormy relationships, she's had a few. And political activism? Well, just a little, from fighting for nuclear disarmament and against the Vietnam War to outing an FBI mole in the Black Panther Party to facing off paramilitaries and Mexican police to protect the leaders of the Zapatista rebels. She's written it all up in a brilliant, no-holds-barred memoir. Check it out, bet you won't be able to put it down.

— Jack Radey, military historian, former Berkeley activist,
and co-author, *The Defense of Moscow 1941*

Sometimes, like this morning, I was so absorbed that I forgot I had other things to do and just kept reading and reading to get to the end of one of Sylvia's many adventures.... Very lively, written in an easy, vivacious way that does not allow the reader to get bored. I also liked the mix of the political with the personal.

— Dr. Anabela Cardoso, diplomat, linguist, researcher,
and author, *Electronic Voices: Contact with Another Dimension?*

It certainly has kept my interest as I read it much too late into the evening.... We are fortunate to have a memoir that is insightful and candid, packed with adventure and passion—but it's much more. This is about social issues and activism, grassroots struggles in the U.S. and worldwide, and about solidarity and the dream of a world at peace. This book is not just good reading; it is worthwhile reading.

— Paul Dix, photojournalist
and co-author, *Nicaragua: Surviving the Legacy of U.S. Policy*

ACTIVIST ODYSSEY

Inside Protest Movements
Some of Which Worked

Sylvia Hart Wright

EnAvant Press

Activist Odyssey: Inside Protest Movements, Some of Which Worked

(This work was published previously under the title *Rough Flavors: One Woman's Activist Odyssey—Inside Protest Movements Some of Which Worked* ISBN 9781733012317)

Published in the United States by EnAvant Press
P.O. Box 10052 • Eugene, Oregon 97440
Copyright © 2020 by Sylvia Hart Wright
sylviahartwright.com

All rights reserved. Some names and identifying details have been changed to protect the privacy of individuals.

ISBN 978-1-7330123-5-5

Cover Design, Interior Layout & Publication Management
Long On Books • longonbooks.com

Front cover photo credits:
   Martin Luther King: U.S Embassy, The Hague on Visualhunt
   Pro-Choice Demonstration: PixelPro/Alamy Stock Photo
   Stop the War Now: State Archives of Florida
   Zapatista women:Juan Carlos Rojas/LatinoPhoto.org

Interior photos, back cover author photo:
   copyright © 2020 Sylvia Hart Wright

Publisher's Cataloging-In-Publication Data

Names: Wright, Sylvia Hart, author.
Title: Activist odyssey : inside protest movements, some of which worked / Sylvia Hart Wright.
Description: Eugene, Oregon : EnAvant Press, [2020] | Previously published as: Rough flavors. | Includes bibliographical references and index.
Identifiers: ISBN 9781733012355 (softcover) | ISBN 9781733012331 (hardcover) | ISBN 9781733012348 (ebook)
Subjects: LCSH: Wright, Sylvia Hart. | Women political activists--United States--Biography. | Women authors, American--Biography. | Protest movements--United States--History--20th century. | United States--History--1945- | LCGFT: Autobiographies.
Classification: LCC HQ1413.W75 W75 2020 (print) | LCC HQ1413.W75 (ebook) DDC 303.48/4/092 B--dc23

Truth has rough flavors if we bite it through.
– George Eliot (pen name of Mary Ann Evans)

*...I just want to be there, in love and in justice and in truth
and in commitment to others,
so that we can make of this old world a new world.*
– Martin Luther King, Jr.

CONTENTS

1 • Taking Our Chances in Mexico / 1

2 • High Windows / 17

3 • How I Got to Berkeley / 37

4 • A Peace Center and a Couple of Passions / 49

5 • "I Have a Dream" / 62

6 • Berkeley in the Tumultuous Sixties / 69

7 • The Free Speech Movement and the VDC / 76

8 • Panama: Introduction to the Third World / 87

9 • Getting Back on My Feet / 102

10 • Jordan and My Favorite Black Panther / 117

11 • Bill's Pet Panther / 126

12 • The Man Who Changed the Criminal Justice System / 139

13 • Rumblings about Abortion / 166

14 • The Harder They Fall / 174

15 • A Book, Some Insights, and a Giant March / 181

16 • Surprises / 189

17 • Bonanza in Panama—for Some / 198

18 • Nicaragua: A Rougher Taste of the Third World / 204

19 • The Man Who Gave Away a Fortune / 220

20 • Living on Less / 230

21 • Helping the Homeless / 241

22 • Solidarity in Seattle / 255

23 • On the Road with the Zapatista Caravan / 267

24 • Winding Down / 278

Afterword / 290

Acknowledgments / 293

Notes / 297

Index / 309

1

Taking Our Chances in Mexico

WHEN WE SIGNED UP TO BE international observers on that caravan, I never thought we'd land in the middle of a bloody disaster. I figured it would be fun—interesting and useful. Doing our bit for an honorable cause, something I'd done a lot. But from the beginning, some of our friends had doubts.

In those days I liked to fill our pretty little house by the river with people I cherished. Almost every year, when the season was dark and dreary, I gave a party around Valentine's Day. Charles, my husband, shared my pleasure. The two of us, veterans of other loves and marriages and loss, had met nine years before, in 1992. Here in beautiful, green and rainy Eugene, Oregon we were both working on a Quaker committee that was struggling to frame a statement on what an ethical economic system might look like. (Not as dry as it sounds if social justice is one of your passions.) We stayed with the committee till it petered out. Meanwhile we started to build a life together, building on what we'd learned during years of relationships, good and bad, and ramblings faraway and far apart from each other.

We'd been around longer than we cared to admit. Still we looked and felt much younger. Most of our guests were younger than we and politically progressive. Some had adventured with us to Seattle a little over a year before when, braving clouds of tear gas, we were part of a carefully rehearsed and oddly equipped crew that nonviolently blocked a crucial street corner, conspiring with tens of thousands of other peaceable activists from many parts of the globe to outfox the World Trade Organization and stymie one of their major meetings.

The WTO—not always as benign as it sounds. Too often a threat to the environment and labor rights. Favoring multinational corporations over consumers. But more about that later, many chapters later.

Back at the party, the bounty of food that Charles and I had put out in bowls and on platters and on a handsome cheese board made by a talented craftsman we knew had shrunken down to a few neglected morsels. A crush of happy campers were converging on the big, oblong baking dish that our friend Nancy had brought of her locally renowned apple-berry crisp, with vanilla ice cream to top it. Soon, stuffed, a few of our guests would thank us politely and head out—though most would stay to gab and debate and enjoy good company in this pleasant warm haven on a chilly night. Before anyone left, I raised my voice.

"Hey, guys, hey, everybody! I've got an announcement!"

The hubbub lessened a little. Across the room Charles, tall and lean with the confident look of a natural leader, was grinning at me, guessing what I had to say. "Dear friends," he shouted in his usually gentle baritone, "let the lady speak!"

"I've got an announcement," I repeated, my elation sizzling through the mostly hushed room. "Two weeks from now we're flying down to Mexico to help out the Zapatistas. We'll be international observers when their leaders travel to the capital. There's this American group we're meeting in Mexico City, then we go with them to where this caravan starts, this caravan we're going on."

We'd both been activists much of our lives. Each of us had lived and traveled in Latin America, both of us spoke some Spanish. Two weeks earlier I'd received an email inviting me to join this effort. Charles took a little convincing but soon he agreed to come along. We'd paid the Mexico Solidarity Network for the privilege of riding with the Zapatista caravan, taking our chances on whatever might come, doing the often lifesaving chore that human rights workers call protective accompaniment. (Often people threatened by death squads in oppressive Third World countries are kept safe by the simple presence of nonviolent volunteers from more powerful nations who stay with them vigilantly day and night.)

The Mexican state of Chiapas is in its southeastern corner. There, this militant faction of mostly Mayan Indians was demanding respect for their culture and customs, and authority over their traditional lands. There was oil under those lands of theirs, oil coveted by powerful interests, and because of that they had serious enemies.

I was picturing them, their heads sheathed with black balaclavas so that they and their relatives wouldn't be brutalized in retaliation. We'd seen photos of them and some videos too, since on New Year's Day, 1994, bands of scantily armed masked men overran five municipalities in this remote state not far from Guatemala. Within days, the army had forced them back into the high jungles from which they'd come. Since then they'd been mostly nonviolent, a political movement that spoke for the poor and disempowered.

Our guests looked startled by my announcement. One burly man I respected, outspoken and forceful, cocked an eyebrow at me skeptically—then took a swig from his bottle of beer and seeming to relent, shrugged his shoulders.

"This caravan of their leaders," I continued, "they're starting in San Cristobal and traveling through the country on their way to the capital. The new president of Mexico[1], he says he's not opposed to it. And he says he'll welcome internationals—hey, he used to be the head of Coca-Cola de Mexico—so I don't think we'll have any serious problems."

"Whew," said Sunshine, a teacher and a sympathetic sort, "I hope you're right."

A political science professor who kept up with all the news from Latin America leaned to his neighbor to say something about paramilitaries. He was talking softly but I caught his drift. Of course it was true. The Zapatistas were always being threatened, their villages were attacked.

An artist spoke up with a chuckle. He and his partner were great at making giant puppets for political demonstrations.

"You guys are gluttons for punishment. Seattle was excitement enough for me."

I smiled, remembering the thrill of taking on that challenge and winning.

"Guess it just whetted my appetite," I said.

Ruth published a counterculture paper in town. Now she spoke up in her firm, decisive way. "Sounds fascinating but Sylvia, don't forget, you'll have to send me progress reports."

"Sure thing," I agreed, "happy to do it," and made a mental note to keep a log.

TWO WEEKS LATER, STOOP-SHOULDERED UNDER BIG backpacks and a double sleeping bag, we weave our way through the Mexico City airport looking for the Aviacsa ticket counter. We know we've found it when we see a sprawl of scruffy young people sitting on the floor with worn packs, sleeping bags and duffels piled around them. Beside them are a few older folks, weathered and a bit untidy like us, standing or sitting on their luggage while three trim women in chic, sporty clothes hover nearby. Soon our leader, Tom, arrives and shepherds us to our flight to San Cristobal de las Casas, a picturesque mountain town near the border with Guatemala where the locals dress in intricately patterned, brightly colored fabrics they weave themselves. At least that's what I've gleaned from travel posters and old issues of National Geographic.

It's almost dark when we arrive there and start climbing toward the hotel where Tom has reserved rooms for us. Tom is a tall, big-boned man with a brusque, sometimes impatient manner. The narrow sidewalk is pieced together with jagged rocks perched irregularly about a foot above the stone-paved gutter. The women with stylish luggage on wheels are having a devil of a time tugging it up the sidewalk's endless steps. Charles does the sort of thing he's probably done all his life, he rushes back to help them, lifting their baggage and carrying it up the hill so those women can catch up with the rest of us. When he returns to me, he's trying not to sound winded. (Charles is eight years older than I.) Meanwhile around us, the moonlit night has turned surreal.

Across the street about a hundred Mayan Indians sit silent and almost motionless. They're small and brown-skinned. The women look stunning and improbable in multicolored handwoven skirts and vivid overblouses, handwoven or heavily embroidered. The men mostly wear jeans, leather boots, and unremarkable work shirts topped by denim jackets hanging open. Many of the women cradle babies in the colorful wide shawls called *rebozos*. Almost all their faces, both men and women, are covered with black ski masks or bright red bandanas.

A dozen yards further up the hill, standing shoulder to shoulder on the parallel sidewalks, two long rows of men and women much bigger and fairer than the Indians are dressed identically in white jumpsuits. Their two rows face each other, facing into the street. Suddenly with practiced precision they link hands, plunge into the gutter, and start chanting at the top of their lungs.

Zapata vive, la lucha sigue, sigue.
Zapata vive, la lucha sigue, sigue.
[Zapata lives, the struggle continues.]

"They're Italians," someone tells us. "They're welcoming the *Comandancia*. They call themselves Ya Basta."

I chuckle. Their name means "enough already."

"They raised hell last September at the meetings in Prague," he adds, gloating. He's one of those scruffy young men we met at the airport. "Of course, they weren't the only ones. The IMF and the World Bank, they shut down early. Lots of us were giving them flak!"

A new-looking white bus is slowly braking its way down the hill. Through one of its windows, a man in a black balaclava flashes a V sign at us. Other masked figures are seated near him. The Zapatista leadership! As the bus comes closer, dozens of their masked supporters brush past us. Stubby, determined men, they move quickly in single file, providing protective accompaniment[2] to the bus. Dazed and awestruck, I sense their commitment and their passion. As the bus and its cordon disappear from sight, I stumble on with our group into our hotel.

At eight the next morning, February 25th, we board two old buses the Mexico Solidarity Network has rented and join what I take to be our caravan. A multitude of vehicles—trucks, buses, cars—plus hundreds of indigenous on foot. More ski masks, more red bandanas, women with babies swaddled to their chests in shawls, carrying bundles.

We wave to pickup trucks full of campesinos wishing us luck and safe journey.

Que le vaya bien, que le vaya bien. Buena suerte.

"*Adiós,*" people shout. Folks on our bus start whooping as they see how vast our caravan appears to be—but soon many of our well-wishers turn away, heading back to their villages in the mountains. Our caravan, diminished but still forty or fifty vehicles strong—mostly buses plus some private cars and vans—rolls through foggy countryside.

The delegation that fills our two Network buses includes volunteers from all over the United States. Montana and Missouri, Florida and New York, Boston, Minneapolis, Berkeley, Ann Arbor. One comes from Canada, two from Australia. All but three of us are white, a few are gentle, black-clad young anarchists. Most of us have lived or traveled widely in the Third World. Elsewhere in the caravan are the Italians and other internationals, solidarity groups from other parts of Mexico, and supporters from Chiapas who are not members of the EZLN, the acronym for the Spanish name of the Zapatista Army of National Liberation.

Friendly police hold back traffic at an intersection so our cavalcade can move through uninterrupted. Lots of people watch and wave as we pass settlements, tiny shops, stands selling pottery. As we start descending out of the mountains we see fewer people in traditional costume. By 10:00 a.m. we're approaching Tuxtla. Ranks of mestizo supporters wave, flash V-signs, signal to us with thumbs up. Two boys shout, "Zapata vive, la lucha sigue, sigue!"

"You running low on water?" Charles asks me, shaking his almost empty canteen.

"Me too," I say and start rummaging in my daypack for the announcement the MSN sent us when we first signed up. On page 17 of the email I printed out I find the comforting sentence I remember reading. "We will carry sufficient bottled water with the delegation." I sit back, relaxed. Around 11 a.m we arrive in Tuxtla for a rally but there's little time for us to attend it. Tom alerts us to the song a performer will sing when the event is nearly over and we have to head back to the bus. Since there's no toilet on it, we have to find *servicios* as well as food and water, he says. Water! Again I dig out the announcement we received and walk forward to talk to our leader.

"Hey, I thought the Network was supposed to provide water."

Tom looks at me with irritation. "Where'd you get that idea?"

1 • Taking Our Chances in Mexico

I show him that line on page 17. He glares at me, then sends Josh, his assistant, off to remedy the situation. I suspect that he's decided I'm a troublemaker but, hey, if I were the passive sort, why would I sign up for a trip like this?

We search out bathrooms and buy food to go, careful not to get raw fruit or veggies that we can't peel and so might make us sick. Then we stroll down to the plaza just as the rally is drawing to a close. A row of *comandantes,* women as well as men, are standing on stage holding a big Mexican flag. Their poet of a leader, *Subcomandante* Marcos stands among them, identifiable by the pipe he smokes through a neat little opening in his mask.

Behind the balaclava that hides his face, Subcommander Marcos[3] isn't an Indian. He's a white, middle-class intellectual, educated as a boy by Jesuit priests steeped in the liberation theology[4] that, since the seventies, has been a powerful, controversial movement in the Latin American church. Liberation theology calls for serving the poor through action for social and economic change, not just occasional charity from a condescending privileged class. *Fourteen years later it will capture worldwide attention when Pope Francis, an Argentine Jesuit, voices its principles[5] in an encyclical.*

Now a big plastic barrel of potable water is stationed up front near the driver, equipped with a spigot so we can all fill our canteens and bottles whenever we like. That afternoon our caravan stretches out along the road. At 5 p.m. we catch up with a few vehicles that have been stopped and then released by four trucks of uniformed officers wearing body armor. Some of them carry assault rifles—not a heartening sight. One of the trucks is labeled Federal Preventive Police.

As we reach the outskirts of Juchitán, cheering, waving crowds line the road. A class of little girls in ruffled pinafores stands chanting "Marcos! Chiapas!" as a helicopter chug-chug-chugs overhead. Further down the road, Tom stations himself in the aisle to talk to us, bracing himself with his hands on the backs of seats. President Fox, he says, is trying to spin publicity about our caravan. Fox claims it's about reaching a peace agreement, not about yielding to Marcos' demands for the government to follow through on the San Andres Accords. The basic principles agreed to in 1996 by the Mexican government and the Zapatistas are:

Free all Zapatista prisoners.
Respect the culture and traditions of the indigenous in Chiapas.
Conserve natural resources within territories occupied by indigenous peoples and give them a greater role in determining how those territories may be developed.

That evening Charles and I share a table in a café with a courtly, middle-aged member of the National Congress from Guadalajara. He tells us he's one of a number of dignitaries, including observers from Uruguay and Argentina, riding in the first bus in the caravan, just in front of the Comandancia bus. Outside, I chat briefly with a young woman from Germany and overhear a couple in their twenties speaking French. It's great to know these *jovenes* are traveling with us. International activists like these young people, a year and a half ago, helped us block Seattle's streets.

The next morning we're slated to leave for Oaxaca. Tom shows up from a meeting of the caravan's guiding council and tells us that someone just handed a death threat to the Comandantes' bus from a well-known paramilitary group.

Here where the climate is warmer than in Chiapas, many folks along the side of the road are barefoot. Papaya trees grow along a fence and nearby, wild calla lilies are blooming. Our bus approaches clumps of children from several schools, dressed in contrasting uniforms, lined up eager to greet us. Their teachers wait behind them, alert. The kids are chanting and cheering, their faces full of excitement. The driver slows down. As our vehicle crawls by, they break ranks, run alongside, and reach their hands up toward us. They're irresistible. Those of us with window seats reach out to them. We trail our hands out our open windows to touch, touch, touch one small hand after another. It's thrilling, electric, an exchange of love. Then the driver speeds up and we have to leave them behind.

At 11 a.m., BAM! Our bus, equipped with two worn tires supporting each of its corners has a double blowout—but it's only carrying one spare. We all pile out while volunteers rush to put it on. In Oaxaca, a front-page headline in the local paper blares OAXACA TURNS

ZAPATISTA. But then the whole state of Oaxaca has been battered by the North American Free Trade Agreement. American grown farm products grown with pesticides and herbicides have been welcomed in by NAFTA and have put legions of its small farmers out of business. Many thousands of them, desperate for work, have been forced to cross the border illegally into the United States. Our rally in the main plaza draws 25,000 supporters and clearly they are not all displaced farmers. Earnest parents who look middle class carry on their shoulders little kids wearing tiny black balaclavas in sympathy with our cause.

That night we hear that national TV and other media are slamming our caravan. They claim foreign solidarity people like us want to strip Mexico of its resources. Lifelong progressives like Charles and me? Like all the other caravanistas hanging on through this crazy ride for Marcos and his peasant comandantes? Still we do what we can to change our image, we shift our more brunette riders to the window seats.

The next morning a couple of people visit us from the other MSN bus. Nancy, a sassy, bright Chicana journalist from San Francisco, leads an orientation session as we wait to depart. Mexicans are dissatisfied, she says, with the PRI, for 59 years the nation's ruling party. Despite its socialist roots and its bold name, the *Partido Revolucionario Institucional* (the Institutional Revolutionary Party) has steadily grown more conservative and corrupt.

The Mexican standard of living is in a downward spiral. Since 1982, Mexico's international debt has triggered pressure from world financial institutions[6] to follow stringent policies which the government has carried out, including privatization of much communally held land. In 1994, a peso crisis cut the value of the local currency in half and inflation soared, hurting the middle class as well as the poor. Formerly solid citizens lost their homes and businesses. Over the years, the government has ended subsidies for staples like milk and tortillas, and let prices soar on electricity, gas and heating fuel. Meanwhile education has been privatized, more and more children have been priced out of schools.

The economics lesson ends. A fellow sitting across the aisle launches into a story. "Folks around here take educating their kids seriously. When they slashed the school budget in one of these towns, the teachers and students went out on strike. So then in come the riot police and they make all these arrests. So then the community grabbed a bunch of police. They stripped them naked and tied them up in the plaza!"

Tom reappears and introduces the other newcomer to our group. "Jeff was thrown out of Mexico around the same time I was. That was a blow. I went to a *tiendita* for eggs and never got back to my delegation. Two men in sunglasses, cowboy hats and boots took me to the airport. One of them jabbed an M-16 in my back. Only time I ever had a private jet waiting for me."

Jeff says he, too, was shipped out on a private jet but first he was held in custody for three days. He's a slim man with short brown hair and an understated, matter of fact manner but there's an undercurrent of zeal in the way he speaks. "The minute I heard Fox was letting us internationals come back, I quit my job and I was on my way."

For three years, from 1995 till 1998, he worked with a group in Chiapas that was installing water systems. "Because that's what the indigenous wanted. That's what they still want: clean water, electricity, schools. Nothing fancy. Fifty-five percent of the power in Mexico comes from Chiapas"—probably, I surmise, from hydroelectric dams in their mountains— "but 75% of their villages don't have power. The PRI only gives water and power to the villages that support it.

"One day a village where we were working was having a fiesta. It was Good Friday, the anniversary of the assassination of Emiliano Zapata, a hero of theirs, a hero of us all, and suddenly the army attacked in force. They burned houses, beat people, jailed quite a few. Destroyed their cornfields, the school their community built, the mural they'd painted on one wall."

He pulls a battered picture postcard out of his pocket. He waves it around, then starts it passing among us on the bus.

"They thought they destroyed this mural," he says, "but we weren't about to let it be forgotten. We internationals, we talked to CNN and *The New York Times*, to people in Congress and the State Department. And this mural, it's been painted again in San Francisco and Mexico City, in Bilbao and Toronto and Madrid."

The postcard passes to Charles and me. It's bright and winning with simple images: Zapata and Marcos, flowers and butterflies, the schoolhouse they built and the Spanish word for peace. Charles hands it to the row behind us.

1 • Taking Our Chances in Mexico

Our bus drives on through mountainous, arid country, past organ pipe cactuses poking upward from gulches like abstract sculptures twenty-five feet high. Careful on our thin tires, our driver is taking a slow road instead of the toll road into Puebla. Burros amble beside us. Then the land gets flatter and greener with lemon orchards and adobe houses roofed with tile or corrugated iron.

At last another city, another rally. Thankfully this evening we don't have to rush around while the rally is on, buying food to carry back to the bus. We're staying in Puebla overnight so we can enjoy what is happening. As we stand in the crowd, an announcer bellows over the public address system, "International visitors, please come to the stage for security." The Comandancia must have received yet another death threat. Charles and I push our way in that direction, trying to be polite as we go, *"Con permiso, permiso, estamos internacionales,"* hoping our pale faces and foreign accents will ease our passage. When we get within ten feet of the stage, the press of bodies is too great for us to penetrate. But at least we can see the comandantes up close.

The stage is decked with white flowers and feathered headdresses. As always, a large Mexican flag hangs behind the Comandancia. On this warm evening, they wear several layers of clothing. Do all those layers, I wonder, hide bulletproof vests? In front they hold a smaller Mexican flag and a banner that calls for Liberty, Justice, and Democracy. When Marcos comes on stage, smoking his pipe, there's a palpable gasp around us. But first other commanders speak.

Two read speeches aloud from the kind of black and white mottled notebooks that youngsters use in primary school. A woman speaks about women's rights. A man who represents the indigenous of Puebla holds forth in both their Indian language and Spanish. They're not just concerned about economic issues, he says. They want respect for their dress, their music, their *curanderas* with their herbal knowledge.

At last Marcos speaks. I wish I could grasp all the poetry of his words but together Charles and I get the gist. We Zapatistas don't just represent the indigenous. We're for all of us. One Mexico, rejoicing in its diversity. We want to build a house for everyone, even our opponents. Dignity and respect must be the bridge. When he speaks about the misery of the indigenous, a chant rises from the audience of thirty-five or forty thousand. *No estan solos, no estan solos.* The verb form is all-encompassing: You and they are not alone, you and they are not alone.

BACK AT OUR BUS WE LEARN that the Italians of Ya Basta, our comrades on the caravan, have been abandoned by their drivers in Oaxaca. Paramilitaries told the drivers that these well disciplined rowdies in white coveralls were communists. They threatened the drivers with death as well as destruction of their buses so they dumped the Italians' possessions out on the sidewalk and took off without them.

A local university has offered to put up everyone on the caravan. That evening when we get there, it looks like a prosperous place with prosperous students, but where are we supposed to sleep? At 11 p.m. we stand like displaced persons in a fenced-in corral in semidarkness. We look around mournfully, searching vainly for porta-potties. Then Tom tells us we'll be bedding down inside the school's covered sports stadium and we won't have to leave until 6:30 in the morning. By midnight Charles and I have fallen fast asleep in an entry area on its second floor. But at 4:30 a.m., overhead lights flash on and announcements roar over the public address system.

We're leaving at 5:30, a mystery voice says in two languages, and breakfast is being served outside. In front of the stadium, indigenous women presiding over tall, steaming kettles dish out delicious hot rice and beans, plus rolls and hardboiled eggs. When we go back inside to get our things, a bagpiper—where did they ever find a bagpiper?—is pacing back and forth on the floor of the stadium blaring "The Minstrel Boy to the War Has Gone." By 5:45 we're all on the bus, ready to take off again. To shouts of *Vamanos!* We head out.

It's Wednesday and the caravan is growing, picking up more people and vehicles. For security, they move the internationals closer to the Comandancia. As soon as the two main buses pass us, we fall in behind them. The comandantes' bus and its companion vehicle filled with dignitaries look alike, they're new and white with slim blue and purple swirls on their sides. Surely they have toilets, I think enviously, and their tires aren't precariously thin. Still it's an honor to be chosen to accompany them so closely if only for a couple hours.

Along the route, police no longer hold back traffic at intersections to help us pass. The caravan is falling further and further behind schedule.

Nonetheless, our driver stops to finally buy the two more tires we desperately need for our bus. Soon we catch up to the caravan where it has stopped for a short rally. Further on, in a small town where we're just scheduled for a "wave-through," someone presents the driver with a gift for us all, a carton of food. Each of us gets a sandwich and an orange. The sandwiches are neat and tasty with ham and cheese plus thin layers of avocado and slivers of mild chiles. Something more makes them delectable. I sense that local women have prepared them for us with love.

That evening finds us in Tephé. The comandantes, decked with matching yellow wreaths hung around their necks like leis, stand in the plaza on a stage with an overhanging roof. Suddenly, although it's the dry season, a thunderstorm explodes. Rain crashes down on us, an avalanche of water. Charles and I take cover in an arcade from which we can watch the rally. People who have given up on it are still gaily chanting slogans as they run away through the storm. Eventually we slosh through ankle-deep water to a house down the road where Tom has arranged for seniors like us to stay.

That night the rest of the delegates sleep on the buses or stretch out on the floor of a public spa designed for day use only. When we show up at 6:30 a.m., we learn we won't be leaving as early as planned. It's Thursday, March 1st and the caravan is supposed to go into the state of Querétero, on its way to the town of the same name. The caravan is heading northeast, circling around Mexico City, following the same route the great revolutionary Emiliano Zapata followed when he led the Army of the South in 1914. The circle is a Mayan symbol full of meanings. Many along this route live on semi-arid land and work for poverty wages.

The caravan's organizers want to pass through the state of Querétero but now its governor is saying that all Zapatistas deserve the death penalty; he's threatening to arrest any caravanistas who enter the state. Tom goes off to meet with the guiding council, to figure out what the caravan should do. Meanwhile the rest of us settle around long wooden tables and sit on damp benches eating hot quesadillas and drinking coffee supplied by local women for a few pesos. After a while Tom comes back, buys himself a quesadilla and coffee, and between sips and munches tells us what's been decided.

"We're all going in. We're keeping the Comandancia in the middle of the caravan. If anyone stops the first buses, it won't be them."

One frantic evening he mentioned that he's trained himself to get by on three or four hours sleep a night when he's leading a group. This morning he looks exhausted. Back on our bus, he manages a catnap. I wish I could do the same but throughout this trip I've been running on adrenalin. Burning myself out. Can't sleep during the day and find it hard to fall asleep at night, lying with Charles's arms around me, sometimes listening to him gently snoring.

A few miles on, I see an unexpected sight. The Italians of Ya Basta are back with us. White twill arms and legs flap in a companionable way as a new bus the Italians have rented passes ours. They've hung their still damp coveralls out their windows to dry. An hour later the caravan slows. We're just crawling, crawling down a long incline. From my seat midway back I can see out the windshield up front. We must be coming into Querétero but the local cops are stalling us.

Four days ago when we started driving out of the eastern mountains, the steep, winding road was lined with our supporters, joyous to see us. Here in central Mexico, everything's different. We're on a highway now—newer, wider, better paved, straighter. But we rarely see allies waiting to greet us, just mile after mile of yellow-tan soil and very little green, just a scatter of brush and here and there a cactus.

We're at the border of the state of Querétero and the clamor of threats against us has been mounting. Still, over a thousand of us from many nations crowd buses and vans strung out along the road, and multitudes are waiting to welcome us at rallies, so the governing council has decided they won't just send in a couple of buses as an experiment— we'll all go in. If we can. If we can.

Our bus is creeping down a long incline. Two lanes go the way we're headed, but at the end of this incline another steep hill begins and what's happening there isn't pretty. One of these lanes is blocked by a police car parked across it; in the second lane, another is just creeping along so none of our vehicles, stuck behind it, can go any faster. They must want to make us disastrously late for the rally that's planned for the state capital. A couple hundred feet from the bottom of the hill we're on, all hell breaks loose.

BOOM ... BOOM. BOOM ... BOOM. "Get down!" someone shouts. BOOM ... BOOM ... BOOM. With each thunderous blast, the whole bus shakes. Someone must be shooting at us. Paramilitaries? But it's not just guns. What could it be—mortars?

Abruptly we stop rolling, we feel no more concussions. Cautiously we raise our heads. Then another voice shouts from up front, "Get out of the bus!"

I wonder if we're being summoned to be taken hostage or worse. But the order seems to have come from one of our fellow caravanistas and people are grabbing their daypacks and racing out the door. Once we're off the bus, no one grabs us. Instead men in all kinds of uniforms are rushing to surround us, not closing in on us but defining a space where too many things are happening.

I stumble forward, look around to get my bearings and see a big black Suburban parked at a crazy angle behind me with our now abandoned bus looming over it. Someone is calling my name but I don't respond. Four women push open doors on the car, wobble out, and limp past me. They're dressed more formally than any of us, in clothes that would look just fine in an office except that they're stained with blood. They seem dazed—but as they pass they seem to gain confidence and walk more quickly. They're heading for the Comandancia bus. Then I see Charles, he's calling my name and his voice is rasping with urgency.

He's one of maybe a dozen people who've started a protective ring around the comandancia bus, a human shield. The wounded women from the black car skirt our growing line to board the white bus as I join my partner in the cordon. Five, ten, dozens more join us. We're linking hands. People are streaming toward us from other vehicles in the cavalcade. In a few minutes we have the bus completely surrounded and a second ring is forming around us, all ages and sizes, men and women both. We're all bound together in common cause.

Meanwhile more cops—scores, maybe hundreds of men in three kinds of uniforms, local and national and I don't know what else—encircle a space like a football field. The road isn't a road anymore, it's a crime scene. An ambulance arrives from beyond the back of the caravan, screeches to a stop on the far side of the MSN bus we've abandoned, and moments later, its siren screaming, rushes back in the direction from which it came. It's eleven o'clock in the morning. A beautiful day, sunny, warm, and I don't know whether I'm going to live or die.

Ah well, I tell myself, I've had a full life. Guess I'll just have to take my chances. I've been in scary fixes before—somehow I've always muddled through.

Amazing numbers of photographers are spilling out of the caravan, poking cameras and video recorders between the policemen. I figure that's a good sign, we're a media event. No sign yet of the paramilitaries—maybe they've been scared off by all these men in uniform. More activists—a rumpled, determined lot, mostly young—join the cordon. Now it's five rows deep. Then a tow truck appears and hauls away the bus we were riding in. Nobody comes over to tell us what's happening. Suddenly we're homeless orphans.

"How're you doing?" Charles asks me coolly. No surprise there. He lived for years in a war zone in Nicaragua.

"I'm okay," I say with a shrug. Irony colors my voice. "Sure, I'm fine, I'm fine. You know I've always craved adventure."

But I can't help asking myself, how did I get to this improbable place? Me, sometime scholar, professor, author—a total New York City person once upon a time. I'm thinking of beautiful Oregon on the Pacific where I've lived for the past decade. Soon after I moved there I met Charles and fell in love with him at least in part because his life had been even wilder than mine. Wildly altruistic, wildly international, wildly trying to save the world.

And standing in the cordon in bright Mexican sunshine—high on adrenalin, alert and oddly calm—I sip water from my canteen and think of the great city that spawned me. New York on the Atlantic where I started out, a scared little kid in a tumultuous household that didn't quite want me, that was just scraping by. That's where I first learned that life isn't fair. The indignation I felt then still burns inside me—but so does the optimism of one who's survived and done pretty well.

I'm trapped by my beliefs, guided by my beliefs, that circumstances beyond their control can torment the innocent and twist them out of shape, can make it torturous for them to carry on. But sometimes there's a way, sometimes there's hope. And when good people help and the system works then, with luck, things can get better.

2

High Windows

My mother used to say she was a stick-in-the-mud. She'd say it with a contented smile. It seemed to comfort her that in all her life she'd never traveled three hundred miles from New York City where she'd been born: just south to Atlantic City with friends when she was a girl, north to the Adirondacks on her honeymoon, then north again many summers to Vermont where she had a small tribe of relatives.

When they married, my father hadn't traveled much further except for once during the First World War. While he was in the navy, he'd sailed to Bermuda on a training cruise but then the war had ended and he'd never gone further. While he was in the navy, too, he'd gotten to ride once in a plane. He wouldn't fly again until fifty years later when he took a flight down to Panama to help me because I was in trouble there.

My parents were good people. They were very bright, too, my mom and dad, though they hadn't had much education. My mother used to say that if she realized that the salesgirl at a five-and-ten had given her an extra penny in change, she'd walk back a block to return it so the girl wouldn't have to make up the shortage herself.

They were eager to stretch out a helping hand to others worse off than they. After I was born, a cousin from Vermont came to stay with us until she could find a job in the city and make a life on her own. For a while after she moved out, she'd come back and visit us. (She couldn't call ahead, we didn't have a phone.) By then I was four or five. She'd talk with my mom in the kitchen for a while. Then my cousin would play games with me as others rarely did—clapping-hands games, hide and seek.

I loved it when this cousin came over. But then my playful cousin stopped visiting and it seemed to me that only Aunt Edna, my mom's rich older sister, ever knocked on our door and was invited in.

My parents were good people but life had pushed them out of shape. Both spoke openly of having been poorer than we were when they were kids. But what I would only much later piece together from subtle clues was that my dad was the son of an alcoholic; my mother had been sexually abused. Under their often charming facades, they were deeply damaged. Little wonder that when I was a child, our home was not usually a happy place.

Mom swore by the Golden Rule, I'm sure she tried to abide by it. But her screaming rages wore us all out. Each evening after my dad came home from work at one low-paying job or another, she'd put a hearty dinner on the kitchen table for him—grudgingly, grudgingly. Then she'd gripe at him, yelling about things that had happened years before. Many decades later, I can still hear her.

"You were making good money when I married you. You were a salesman, a top salesman," she says. "Well, it suited you, good-looking man with the gift of gab—but you never had a head for business. *You* had to go into business for yourself. Had to be a big shot. Some big shot *you* are!"

"You know damn well I had a partner. I thought he understood the business."

"Your dimwit of a partner, no more sense than you. And Joe and Edna doing so well, you could have been a salesman for them."

"You *know* I couldn't work for Joe, your two-faced baby brother. All smiles but he never listened to a thing I said. Just a kid but he thought he knew it all."

"Well, maybe he *did* know." My mother's voice turns belittling, "You're good with numbers, I'll give you that. But Joe, he's got a good, practical head on his shoulders.

"God gimme strength!" she wails.

Another night her shouts explode from the kitchen. "Crazy man, crazy man! When your veteran's bonus[1] came through we could hardly pay the rent. Hiram had just broken his glasses. I'm worrying how I'm gonna buy him new ones—then your bonus comes through, your veteran's bonus from when you were in the navy and you looked like such a mensch to me. God, what a fool I was to marry you!"

My mother takes a breath as if remembering the look of my dad in uniform during the First World War, then she starts again, "Hundreds of dollars like manna from heaven—and you use it to pay back your *cousins,* your rich cousins in Chicago that you never see. *They* didn't need the money, your *family* needed the money. Crazy man, crazy man!"

I hear a loud bang. My mother has probably slammed a pot on the stove but the kitchen door is closed and our family doesn't eat together. She serves us each separately. Maybe that's her way of keeping my dad from acting like the head of the family and, when my big brother comes home from school, of giving her closest attention to Hiram—his unusual name chosen just because it goes well with our surname, Hart. Hiram's her only boy and her hope for the future.

"*You're* the one who's crazy," my dad shouts back at her. "I'm an honest man. I pay my debts. You should respect that. The kids should respect that. What kind of people do you come from, that you wouldn't pay your debts?"

"Oh, God gimme strength," my mother wails again.

In our living room, my teenage brother is reading a book. Bernice, four years older, is doing a solo foxtrot to dance music on the radio. I go from one to the other asking, "Are they really crazy? Is one of them crazy?" My brother acts like he hasn't heard me. Bernice, slim and pretty, just shrugs and keeps on dancing.

When Edna came over, she and my mom would huddle together at the kitchen table. The kitchen door was closed, everyone else left them alone while she shared news from their other relatives. Probably she also advised my mother, probably she gave her money. As the eldest of seven siblings, she took responsibility.

Edna and her much younger brother Joe, with little formal education, had made a fortune as book publishers. They were our guardian angels when bills piled up after my mother had pawned her diamond engagement ring, a relic of more prosperous times. They lived not far away but in classier parts of the borough, worlds apart from where we lived.

In those days my family lived in a neighborhood at the northern tip of Upper Manhattan. It was white working class and lower middle-class, a mix of Irish and Jews and miscellaneous others. My parents had been born Jews, they considered themselves Jewish but they had few ties to the Jewish community. They never went to synagogue, they didn't speak Yiddish, neither of them had ever gone to Hebrew school. They didn't celebrate Chanukah, they didn't own a menorah. They barely observed other Jewish holidays or customs.

All my parents' immigrant forebears had come to this country before 1890, before Ellis Island was where newcomers came ashore. In the 1930s my parents were poor relations in a big extended, nonobservant family where some had prospered greatly. My mother's shame and grief about how far they'd fallen permeated our home.

Aunt Edna was ten years older than my mom. As a girl she'd been well off. Their father ran a small garment factory of his own though, after his wife died when Edna was eighteen, he settled in with another woman and paid less mind to his first family.

Edna was daring and ambitious. Blue-eyed with curly brown hair, she was striking in a strong-nosed, strong-jawed way. At a time when Jews rarely married outside their community, she married a gentile, an older man, a doctor at that. My mother was skeptical about the wisdom of what Edna had done.

When she described her big sister's marriage, she used a Yiddish expression she had to explain to me: *hoykhe fenster,* high windows, as if her big sister had stood on tiptoe to see into a forbidden, grander world that would never let her in. Edna had a son by Dr. Williams but her husband turned out to be an alcoholic and the marriage didn't last. They got divorced—scandalous in that era—then Williams died and Edna, now a struggling single parent, called herself a widow. She worked as a bookkeeper for a publishing firm. Then she took over a small bookstore, a few steps below street level near Columbia University.

And here the plot thickens. Columbia bought the building. They wanted to raze it and build on the site so they offered bonuses to tenants as inducements to leave. Most of them took the money and left but

Edna held out. Her lease had another seven years to go. Columbia was impatient so they raised their offer. When my aunt told my parents that she'd decided to accept, my father with his socialist inclinations and an amateur economist's insight protested, "Don't you dare give in yet, make 'em pay through the nose! It's worth a lot more to them than it is to you."

So she did. And for years thereafter in my parents' fights, my father would take credit for the riches that later flowed to Edna and Joe because the fat sum that Columbia gave her when she finally vacated was the capital she and her brother used to start a prosperous business together. But luck and wit also played a part in this.

The company where Edna had worked as a bookkeeper published obscure medical texts thick with Latin phrases. By the time she closed her shop, their books had grown outdated and they were going bankrupt. Here Joe comes into the picture. His mother died when he was barely four. He and his still younger brother Harold were handed over to their childless Aunt Mary whose husband owned a small department store out west in Phoenix.

In Arizona Territory, not yet a state, they moved in privileged circles. One of the kids they knew there, Barry Goldwater, would in 1964 be the Republican candidate for president. (Barry's father owned the biggest department store in town.) Mary was a cold and selfish woman. Life with her must have been less than rosy, still living in a prosperous mercantile family schooled them in the vagaries of the business world and gave them a taste for living well.

When Joe was twelve, Mary hauled them back to New York and dumped them on what was left of their family. In those days Joe was cross-eyed. At school where he was the new kid, his classmates called him Cockeye, so often he played hooky and spent the day reading in the library instead. As soon as he got older and landed a job as a postal clerk, he saved money to have surgery that straightened his eyes and made him good-looking. Edna told him about the publishing company where she'd worked and the scarcely readable tomes still sitting in their warehouse. A couple of those books were guides to sex. In dryly technical Latin terms they described for doctors an ambitious range of erotic practices and "perversions."

My Uncle Joe got a wild idea. At fire sale prices, using Edna's windfall, Joe bought up their stock of these dusty books along with the metal plates that in those days could be used to print more copies. Then he sent brochures about them to a mailing list of Catholic priests. Yes, Catholic priests. Obviously they were undaunted by Latin. He invited them to buy these books to help them—but of course!—counsel their parishioners. Joy was unconfined. Joe and Edna made heaps of money.

They used this capital to launch more orthodox ventures, publishing classics no longer covered by copyright. Joe's years hanging out in libraries had not been wasted; he was a widely read, cultivated young man. And through his stepfather in Arizona he had valuable connections. Throughout the Depression their company, Illustrated Editions, put out handsome, inexpensive copies of classic novels, many of them with their original illustrations. Around the country, Macy's featured them in its stores.

From time to time, cartons of my aunt and uncle's wares would appear on our doorstep, to be shelved in bookcases they also supplied. They gave us an encyclopedia, too, plus coffee table books on art and interior design. As a little kid I hungrily studied the pictures in these volumes, they transported me to realms of gracious living and high style.

I WAS BORN IN THE HEART of the Great Depression. Much later my mom would tell me that I was an accident. While my father said he'd welcomed me because, though he was broke then, "If Joe could have another child, so could I!"

After I was born my mother worried about me. She didn't think I was pretty. My nose wasn't pert like her short, straight one, my features weren't perfectly symmetrical like hers. And at first my skin, much fairer than hers, burned and grew prickly with heat rash under summer sunlight. Still I was strong and graceful. By the time I was five, at Aunt Edna's suggestion, she'd started sending me to an excellent ballet school, though classes just once a week were all we could afford.

Looks mattered a lot to my mother though she lacked the feminine wiles to keep them up. As a girl, she'd been a beauty. "At Hebrew Technical School"—she always spoke the name proudly, respectfully—"everyone thought I was so beautiful. Sometimes my girlfriends did my homework for me! Still when I came to graduate, the teachers chose me to be salutatorian. That's second best," she'd explain. "Probably if I'd studied, I could've been valedictorian!"

This fragment of a high school had been set up to train poor, bright Jewish girls in two hasty years to do office work. There she'd learned typing and shorthand and more than enough English to write business letters. But not much more. She'd gone on to what she considered a comfortable job, her looks and intelligence had opened doors for her. She felt assured of happiness—but then her luck had changed.

After my father failed twice in business, she put on too much weight and didn't cut her curly hair to keep up with the styles. Depression crushed her. After I was born, Bernice took care of me more than my mother did. When my father came home from work, he'd kneel beside the bathtub to scrub my dirty diapers.

A lesser man might have blasted her for the slatternly way she kept the house or might have turned his back on her in the desperate days of the Depression and left us all behind. But I guess he felt guilty for not making her life easier. And he'd always loved his wife far more than she loved him.

My mother ruled our apartment but the way she maintained it made it a slum. A few years before, when my folks had been on "home relief," New York's early version of welfare, social workers had criticized my mother's housekeeping and given her low marks. When the family applied for good housing for the poor subsidized by the city, they were turned down for the same reason. My mother remembered these failures with shame—still she couldn't change.

For modesty's sake, sagging, dust-laden curtains hung at our windows over the landlord's white oilcloth shades with a pull cord dangling. But no pictures hung on our walls, no rugs or carpets cushioned our floors. Our furniture was mismatched, drab and ugly. My mother couldn't bring herself to spend money on what she considered nonessentials. "There's more to life than material things" she'd say.

Was that why she didn't own a nightgown or pajamas? She slept in her slip and taught me to do the same. And she'd go through our wastebaskets, looking for oddments that she thought might prove useful later or to which she might assign some sentimental value. She'd stash these questionable treasures in paper bags and a couple of small cartons that she crowded into our few closets or set to stand in a corner. This hoarding she fondly called "my saving ways."

Worst of all, in our kitchen an ample supply of roaches paraded over the walls and climbed the legs of our chipped kitchen table to be swatted away before they reached the top. We struggled to keep them out of our other rooms. Those legions of roaches humiliated me. I'd never seen their like in the movies or in the few apartments I'd seen aside from our own. I never dared to bring classmates home and that made me act like a loner. Kids in grade school called me stuck-up though I yearned to have friends.

IN HIS YOUTH MY FATHER HAD been a wiry amateur wrestler and boxer. He'd been raised in Yorkville at the turn of the twentieth century when it was Manhattan's immigrant German neighborhood. One of his legs was scarred from an accident with a hatchet he used to chop firewood for his mother's stove. His father was a sickly man, a sometime cigar maker, with a thirst for more beer than he could afford. Often he'd send my dad to fetch a pail of beer from the local tavern. *My father, like my mother, didn't drink. We never had anything alcoholic in our house.*

A few blocks away from Yorkville's tenements lay Park Avenue and Fifth Avenue where some of the richest people in the nation lived in lavish marble mansions.

"Sometimes," my dad would recall with a bitter smile, "when the daughter of the house came out, they'd lay a red carpet, a *real carpet* out across the sidewalk for her to walk to where her carriage was waiting, her carriage with its footmen or, later, her car with its chauffeur."

Meanwhile, because my father's family could barely afford his keep, at fourteen he left the public school where he'd won prizes for boyish achievements in math to deliver laundry to households more prosperous than his. Eventually he took a few college courses at night. He thought of going on to law school—in those days boys who, like him, had left school after eighth grade could do that—but his plans didn't work out. He became a self-taught economist and a democratic socialist who cherished the classic Marxist dream, "From each according to his ability, to each according to his need." He taught me that motto when I was a little girl—along with the law of supply and demand.

2 • High Windows

FORTUNATELY ON ISSUES OF SOCIAL JUSTICE my parents shared common goals. They belonged to no activist groups—no clubs, no cells—still they loved to discuss current events. When they did, they didn't scream at each other. Instead in rousing discussions, my parents would grapple with politics and ethics and the human condition and we kids were welcome to join in. My mom was a Roosevelt Democrat, more of a skeptical realist than her husband who tended to focus on socialist principles.

Somehow our household rumbled on. Once in a while when the weather was fine, my mother sat downstairs with other women from the building but she never invited them to our place. She didn't make friends with other mothers nearby. I never visited another kid's house on a play date, I rarely saw anyone else's home. A Girl Scout troop met in the school across the street but my mom never signed me up for it. I never went away to summer camp though free options were available.

One day at the beach, when my father started teaching me how to swim, my mother erupted in something like a panic attack so he never tried again. (Thanks to the gym program at my high school, I would finally learn.) Still we three kids had a roof over our heads, we ate healthful food, and nobody beat us or molested us. Classical music often played on the radio and our home was full of books. In their own eccentric way our parents did their best for us. Only when we visited relatives, did I see other ways to live.

My Uncle Harold's parties were treats for me, like trips to an enchanted world, sparkly and fun. Harold, my mom's youngest brother, was a man for whom vaudeville had died too soon. Lean and bouncy with light brown hair, he looked like Bob Hope. Probably he'd have made a pretty good song-and-dance man with his whiskey tenor, his long ski-jump nose, lots of enthusiasm and a yen to please. He'd stand by their little upright player piano, belting out golden oldies like "Yessir, That's My Baby" and "You Made Me Love You" while magically, untouched, in ever changing patterns the keys of the piano bobbed up and down. And sometimes Uncle Harold would hoist me up onto his shoulders. No one else ever did that for me.

Whiskey flowed generously in Harold's big living room. Shot glasses and cocktail tumblers glittered on tables, not too high for me to reach. As I wandered underfoot at those parties bustling with my aunts and uncles and cousins, I helped myself to the few drops of booze left in those glasses—nobody tried to stop me, nobody seemed to notice—and they added to my sense of euphoria there.

My mother started suffering from what she called rheumatism. It was hard for her to use her hands, to bend or kneel. Sometimes Bernice volunteered to sweep or mop the floor. My mother didn't object but she never taught me to do the same. "I can't worry," she'd say, "about material things." She filled herself up with cheap comfort food. Then the extra weight she put on slowed her down still further.

When I was seven, Bernice ran off and got married to a bold and masterful fellow—very unlike my father—she'd met at a boathouse on the Hudson River where some older kids from the neighborhood hung out. That's when my mom told me that Bernice wasn't really my sister at all. She was another cousin my family had taken in; my rich aunt and uncle had paid for her keep.

Her mother had died when she was an infant. Her father was a successful musician but he couldn't take care of her because usually he was on the road playing trumpet in a big dance band. Relatives sent his tiny child to stay temporarily for a fee with three unmarried sisters. "Temporarily" lasted five years.

These sisters were Catholic, they raised Bernice to be Catholic too. They taught her to be a well-mannered little thing who knew how to dust and sweep and who kept her ruffly dresses clean and neat. Only after my parents had been married three years and my brother was a wild two-year-old toddler did they take this ladylike niece of theirs into their helter-skelter home. Much later Bernice would tell me that when she moved in, she clutched for her protection and consolation a little card with an image of the Sacred Heart of Mary and babbled to anyone who would listen about the Baby Jesus.

This must have discomfited my parents but they never punished her for it. Gradually she adapted, still she hung out with kids from the local parochial school. When I was born she cherished me as no one else did. Bernice followed her own leadings—and sometimes the rest of the family went along. In a home that made no mention of Chanukah, she taught me to believe in Santa Claus.

2 • High Windows

AFTER MY MOM LOST HER OWN mother at eight, she'd been left nearly un-parented. She just "growed like Topsy," she used to say, like the neglected slave child of *Uncle Tom's Cabin*. Her two oldest sisters were left to cook and look out for their siblings' welfare while they themselves were still in their teens. "But of course, they had their own lives to live. My sisters weren't around a lot," she recalled. "They got jobs, they got boyfriends ... then they got married and moved away."

Mom would turn sad-faced and silent remembering things she wouldn't tell me about. Much later I'd realize that an odd older brother of hers, Arthur, had routinely molested her when no one was around to protect her—until he too got married and moved to Vermont. There he, his wife, and their two sons lived next door to their more propserous cousins, my Aunt Sadie and Uncle Jake. Before I was born, my family sometimes traveled north in the summer to stay for two weeks with Sadie and Jake. They did so once more when I was five but I never saw the inside of my Uncle Arthur's ramshackle home—my mother warned me sternly never to go there—and my family never visited Vermont again.

Always when that ne'er-do-well uncle visited New York my mom, who kept up with all her other relatives, refused to see him. In time I'd forgive her for whatever failings she may have had as a mother and a housewife, thinking of how damaged her own childhood had left her.

WHEN MOM WAS IN HER EARLY teens, unprotected and unguided, she was profoundly influenced by an English teacher she adored, a maiden lady who, between lessons in grammar and the fastidious use of words, taught her to love the poetry of the New England Transcendentalists. That teacher became a surrogate mother for her. (All her life she would gravitate to older women who mentored her.) The high-minded poems by Longfellow and Whittier that my mom memorized for her teacher became the basis of her convictions. Often she'd recite those poems aloud. That's one way she passed on her personal creed to me, an unrelenting Protestant ethic.

> *Lives of great men all remind us*
> *We can make our lives sublime,*
> *And, departing, leave behind us*
> *Footprints on the sands of time....*

> *Let us, then, be up and doing,*
> *With a heart for any fate;*
> *Still achieving, still pursuing,*
> *Learn to labor and to wait.*

Still she hardly monitored my homework, she never urged me to excel. She just assumed I'd do well enough and, in the unchallenging neighborhood schools I attended, I was usually the best student in my class. It helped that, in a home with few toys, there was an abundance of books to read—though most had been written for adults. As a little kid I immersed myself in beautifully printed volumes from Illustrated Editions like *Alice in Wonderland* with the original drawings by Sir John Tenniel, *Oliver Twist* with pictures by Cruikshank, *The Adventures of Tom Sawyer,* and a wealth of other estimable works. These classics enriched my vocabulary and my mind.

WHEN I WAS EIGHT, I SCORED so high on an IQ test at school that two women came up from Columbia University to test me at home, one-on-one. Nothing much seemed to come of this except that later I learned that I'd scored high in the genius range—probably much higher than my brother. And since I was a girl, this was a problem for my family. An embarrassment better forgotten.

Not long after Bernice moved out, our family—no longer being subsidized by relatives for her keep—downsized to a three-room apartment. In its one bedroom, I shared a double bed with my mother while my brother slept in a single bed on the other side of her. *Was she trying to protect me from the kind of abuse she herself had suffered?* My father slept in the living room. These arrangements mortified me. I had a recurring dream where, beside the door that opened into our bedroom, a door appeared into another room. When I woke, downcast, I would realize it was only a dream.

I went on reading the books in our living room. The zinger was that my relatives had published collections of romantic poetry and translations of French novels that were arguably more risqué than a sheltered little girl should have been reading. But nobody stopped me, nobody seemed to notice. I never read about the Bobbsey Twins or Nancy Drew. Instead I delved into stories about courtesans in Classical Greece and

19th century Paris. I never planned to become a courtesan. Still I imagined growing up to please a man and make him happy, far happier than my tormented father. Something in me sensed that if my mother didn't forever push him away and undercut him, he'd be easier to live with and would garner more success.

When I was ten, my Uncle Joe's wife Bessie invited us to join them, their two daughters, and other guests for Thanksgiving dinner. They'd moved to a new address in one of the classiest parts of Manhattan. It was the only time in my childhood I'd see the way these relatives lived.

Wearing our best, we visited them in their 12-room, two-story apartment overlooking Central Park. It was plush with antique furniture, oriental rugs, and my uncle's collection of unusual old clocks. Their dining room was manorial: huge, high-ceilinged, and paneled with gleaming dark wood. One of my cousins invited me to her bedroom upstairs to see the latest pretty clothes she'd gotten.

Her family had recently acquired a live-in butler and cook, an African-American couple, both of them college graduates, far better educated than their employers. Still in those days of fierce job discrimination, the two had settled for positions as high-class domestics. Given my family's political bent, I was not unaware of the barriers they faced. This choice spared them from living in a ghetto while letting them save money for a nest egg.

The butler served us meticulously from the left and cleared from the right. I tried not to show my confusion as he came by time and again, politely offering to spoon dainties onto my plate from porcelain tureens. I struggled to not make a fool of myself in this household so different—so much more privileged than my own. Though I don't think I consciously envied my rich relatives. I'd been brought up to be poor but proud.

Back home my mother, who would never hear criticism of her brother Joe, blamed her sister-in-law for their ostentation. "*Nouveau riche, nouveau riche.* Who does she think she is? The queen of England, with a butler, no less! Who does she think she's fooling? She's nothing but an okay-looking girl from the Bronx, none too bright, who made herself a lucky marriage."

AROUND THIS TIME MOM ANNOUNCED TO the family that she'd converted to Christian Science, a religion that had sprung up some sixty years earlier in New England from Transcendentalist roots, though I doubt that she ever noticed this connection. She was convinced her new religion had cured her of the "rheumatism" she'd been suffering from for years. What was more, it delighted her that this new faith of hers had been founded by a woman. Much later, browsing through an encyclopedia, I would run across an article that reported there was a form of rheumatoid arthritis that appears in midlife, lasts a few years, then spontaneously goes away.

Though my mother had terribly high blood pressure, she refused all medical care and didn't take me to doctors. If I needed a medical certificate filled out for school, she'd take me to Uncle Joe's physician; he'd check me out and sign the form. If I got sick, my mother prayed for me and thought positive thoughts: God is good, God is love, God doesn't send illness. I stayed home until I got well.

Each day, stretched out on the couch in our living room, my mother read and reread the Christian Science text, *Science and Health with Key to the Scriptures,* and faithfully referred to her King James Bible as her weekly study guide decreed. She subscribed to the *Christian Science Monitor* and piles of newspapers she couldn't bear to part with gathered dust around the house along with her bags and cartons. Each Wednesday and Sunday she went to services.

My brother graduated at 19 from the City College of New York with a bachelor's degree in physics. Though World War II was still raging on, Hiram was deferred from military service so he could work at a company that manufactured binoculars for the war effort. Now he was making money but he didn't move out. Even if he'd wanted to, there was a housing shortage in the city. Hiram could no more find a place of his own than our family could expand from our cramped three-room apartment. Still he brought home *The New York Times* instead of *The Daily News* and bought season tickets for three—my father not included—to an excellent concert series where world-class artists performed at bargain prices at a public high school in Lower Manhattan. Once in a while he'd splurge and buy the three of us second balcony seats to Broadway shows.

2 • High Windows

My father reached out to Hiram in other ways. He encouraged him to save his money and, as my brother's savings grew, my dad, mostly self-taught in economics and the vagaries of the stock market, spent hours doing research for him in the Forty-Second Street library, that grand marble edifice in midtown Manhattan whose stately facade is graced by two majestic, unthreatening stone lions. In those days before the Internet and copy machines, my father would come home with sheets of paper covered with laboriously copied statistics on corporations whose stocks he thought might rise. Soon he and Hiram were discussing price/earnings ratios and growth rates, book value and long-term debt—while I, the pesky little sister, listened in. Soon my brother was making money in the market.

I GRADUATED FROM SIXTH GRADE A year early because, like my brother, I'd skipped semesters. That spring I went out of my district to attend an enriched junior high program which would cover three years' work in just two and a half. Here I felt more isolated than ever. Most of the other kids in my classes had known each other for years. They went to parties at one another's homes and the next day they'd talk about them at school. I was the outsider, I wasn't invited.

It wasn't because I was Jewish—most of them were Jewish too. Many of them had been born in Germany or Austria and had come to this country, fleeing the Nazis, when they were four or five. They came from middleclass homes a notch or two better off than mine.

I wished I could ask other girls to my place to break the ice but that was hardly an option for me. When the class split into teams, I was always the last one chosen. For no clear reason, they nicknamed me Fish Face. And when kids called each other at night, I was left out because my family still didn't have a phone.

For what seemed like forever I was miserable. But then life started getting better. First, I managed to improve things at home a bit. Our bathtub like countless others had a shower fixture overhead but none of us dared to use it because we had no shower curtain. One day I used my allowance to buy one—though it turned out that one wasn't enough. It took two curtains to surround our freestanding tub, not to mention the little rings to hang them up. To my surprise my mother didn't resent my interference. Instead she placidly sent me off with more money to buy what we needed. Thereafter, though my mom still took baths, the rest of us took showers.

When I was twelve my father finally landed a reasonably steady civil service job, sorting mail as a substitute postal clerk on railroad trains. So he could learn which route he'd be traveling each day, at last we had to get a phone. Then together my father and brother bought a car.

By now my rich uncle's bank was sending monthly checks to an account my mother kept secret from my dad. (Recently Joe and Edna had launched Avon Books, the second company in the United States to publish mass market paperbacks with glossy, vivid covers.) At twelve I had a radiant soprano voice and my mother had long since decided that, since I was no beauty, I should at least be accomplished. She didn't seem to notice that I'd been growing taller and curvier without losing the dancer's verve and posture I'd always had. As I neared my teens, wolf whistles from strangers started assuring me that I was attractive.

Mom took me to the preparatory division of the Juilliard School of Music for an audition. They accepted me—but they said I was too young to study voice so I should just minor in piano and study subjects like music theory and harmony and chorus. No pressure. I started attending classes there on Saturdays.

Juilliard Prep was fun. I was no musical prodigy though there were many of them at this school, kids who, since they were barely out of diapers, had practiced three or four hours a day under the ambitious tutelage of their parents. Happily, I fit in with other girls in my classes— and, since I lived further away from Juilliard than they did, I didn't feel obliged to invite anyone to my apartment.

We ate lunch together at the school and roved around the dignified neighborhood it was then in near Riverside Drive, singing what we called "fake Bach"— rambling, improvised fugues. My new friends were artsy types from well-to-do families and, for the most part, I could keep up with them.

My Aunt Edna started inviting me to accompany her to shows at Radio City or, when I was particularly lucky, at the Metropolitan Opera where she had season tickets. She didn't try to woo me away from my possessive mother. Her manner was cool and calm, almost formal, yet that too was a gift—a soothing alternative to mom's hair-trigger mood swings. Without fuss or comment she gave me access to her world where comfort and culture were taken for granted. I'd take the subway downtown to meet her in her comfortable but unpretentious apartment in a tall building on lower Fifth Avenue, just above Greenwich Village. Often she socialized, my mother whispered—not quite approvingly—with bohemians there. In time Edna would be a role model for me.

My ordeal in junior high ended. In high school no one made fun of me or called me names. I made good grades though often more diligent kids outshone me. I didn't care. I was giddy with poetry and unaccustomed hormones. That spring I met a tall, skinny boy named Marty who was a year ahead of me at another school. We met at a neighborhood Y that sat plopped on a hill across the way from the George Washington Bridge. By then I was fourteen, virginal but seething. We walked halfway across the bridge and felt it tremble beneath us as breezes swept up the Hudson to whip our cheeks and hair. We stood slightly out of the wind to kiss and hug, then walked back to the Y.

The next time I saw him, he led me into a park that nestled by the river. We sat beside a little old lighthouse, we cuddled together. That night as he walked me home, rapture coursed through me. When my apartment door closed behind me, I wanted to hide but I had no room of my own to hide in, to savor my startling new sensations. In the living room, my father sat slumped in our faded old armchair, silently smoking his pipe. Faintly from behind the kitchen door, I could hear my brother telling my mom in endless detail about his day at work. So for want of a better place, I sat on the couch and hid my face in a pillow, drunk with soaring emotions and inchoate desire.

Marty was the first boy I ever loved. He was smart and exciting and, like me, he was full of ideas about politics and where the world was tending. He belonged to a leftwing political club; often I sat in on its meetings. Afterwards we'd go for a walk or a soda or we'd just hang out. Meanwhile my mother took to keeping the living room tidier so I could venture to bring Marty and other boys home.

Back in high school, to my astonishment, I was nominated and elected to minor offices in two clubs. In my senior year I never applied to any out-of-town college — though probably my parents or school counselors should have urged me to. I expected, like my brother, to go to one of New York's free schools—at least they were free then. But as I was finishing twelfth grade, the strategic largesse of a government program changed my life.

Each year the State of New York offered four-year scholarships, good for use in any in-state college, to thousands of new high school graduates who scored especially high on a competitive test. Only after I won a New York State Regents Scholarship did I discover that, by scoring sixteenth in Manhattan, I'd won a scholarship to Cornell University as well.

That fall I went away to Cornell while Marty remained in the city. Moving to the elite precincts of an Ivy League campus, over 200 miles from home, I escaped the tumult of my parents' fights in my family's cramped and crazed apartment. At holiday breaks Marty and I got together but the rest of the time we went out with other people and soon we grew apart. For the next two years at Cornell I dated sedately but I never fell in love, I never coupled off. In that era when most coeds married young, many girls in my dorm got engaged. They waved their left hands under our eyes for us to ritually admire their rings. They had talked with their beaus about how many kids they wanted and how they wanted to live. Hearing them, I knew I didn't feel ready. Cringing from my parents' example, I had almost no idea how I'd live with a man.

Early in my senior year I met Herb Goldstone, an English professor in his thirties. He had bright red hair that I liked, he was tallish and slim. I thought his hawk-nosed face with its oversized jaw was far from handsome. I didn't love him, his presence didn't excite me. But I was an English major, I dreamt of being a novelist, so we found lots to talk about. He never stopped acting detached and professorial, still he started talking about marrying me.

I dreaded the thought of living with my family again. Even if I found a job after I graduated, my parents would never approve of my leaving home to live with roommates and I couldn't muster the self-confidence to imagine opposing them.

They'd moved by then to a six-room apartment in the West Bronx. At last I had my own room with my own bed and dresser. But my parents still had screaming fights and my mother's sloth and craziness still sullied the place. When one foot of a couch broke, they propped it up on a couple of books and no one thought to have it fixed. And each time I came home from college, the apartment had grown dirtier and there were more roaches. My mother refused to have anyone come in to clean. Bags of oddments my mother treasured leaned against the walls and yellowing *Christian Science Monitors* were stacked nearby.

So I married Herb Goldstone though I was pretty sure that this marriage wouldn't last. I just wanted *to have been married* so my mother wouldn't insist that I live at home. Still I tried to get along with this icy, distant person. I applied for a part-time job at the university and they assigned me to work in the library. At home I patterned myself after June Allyson in the movies or Donna Reed on TV. I didn't rant and rave like my mother, I gave in to sex with Herb though I didn't desire him. I started to learn how to cook and keep house, determined not to be the negligent slob I'd always felt my mother was. But trapped in Herb's unrelentingly cerebral company, I felt miserable, stultified.

One month my period didn't arrive on time. Desperation racked me. I didn't want his child, didn't want to be tied down to him. At last my period came but I lived in fear that the next time I might not be so lucky. Still I never told Herb how unhappy I was—until I decided to walk out on him. He showed little reaction as, broke and too timid and inexperienced to set out on my own, I moved back home. Soon he took charge of our separation. He had our marriage annulled—easier then in New York State than getting a divorce—and I went back to using my maiden name.

For many months I felt too confused and drained to look for work or go back to school. I wanted to go for therapy—but my controlling mother didn't approve. One evening she timidly ventured to my brother, "Aunt Edna thinks maybe Sylvia should maybe apply to law school." (For years she's treated Hiram as the man of the house..) But instantly he sneered his disapproval so she dropped the subject.

Instead, I studied voice and took ballet lessons, as if I were sixteen again. Then I sang and danced in the chorus of a Gilbert and Sullivan company that put on shows off-off-Broadway; this was fun but I performed for free. At last at my brother's suggestion, I applied for a job at the New York Public Library. After I'd worked in a branch for a while, my boss urged me to go for a degree in library science. As soon as I could support myself, I left home for good.

I'd learned some hard lessons. I wasn't June Allyson or Donna Reed and I didn't want to live like the unadventurous housewives they portrayed. Never again would I sleep with a man I didn't desire. I'd earn my own money and pay my own keep. I didn't crave lots of possessions—I'd hardly been pampered as a child. I just longed to be free to go where my spirit led me and make my own life.

3

How I Got to Berkeley

THE SUMMER AFTER I GOT PROMOTED to senior librarian, I signed up for a tour in Mexico. The year before I'd finished my master's degree in library science. I'd fallen into the field almost by accident and I thought of it as a portable skill, a way to earn a living wherever I chanced to go. It was an easy, civilized way to spend my time, still I longed to move on. To go new places and figure them out. To gain insight into other people's lives.

So there I was in an exceedingly foreign country that dazzled with unfamiliar sights and sounds and smells. Our tour leader led us to respectable tourist destinations. We stayed in comfortable hotels but the water that came from our bathroom faucets wasn't safe to brush our teeth with. (Carafes of safer water were supplied by servants whose obsequious manner made me uncomfortable.) Our leader warned us not to eat food from street vendors, no matter how tempting, or any fruit we couldn't first peel. And everywhere were people who didn't speak our language and didn't look like us; they were brown, part Indian, mestizo. Too often they looked desperately poor. And only too often, small barefoot children crowded around us begging for money.

We zigzagged across the north-central part of the country in limousines and trains, shepherded by our bilingual, long suffering guide. To Monterrey where we had lunch in a beautiful plaza paved with blue tile;

to Saltillo where we saw serapes made and, inevitably, were invited to buy them. West we traveled to Guadalajara, a gracious city I loved for its grand colonial buildings and music and parks and no end of tempting crafts for sale at startlingly low prices. I rubbernecked and shopped with the rest of our genteel herd, mostly middle-aged women, until we got to Mexico City. On our second day there, I met another girl about my own age in the lobby of our hotel. Soon we were telling each other the most private things.

Louellen was from Oklahoma. She was a natural blonde but not especially pretty; her small features looked crammed together in the center of her round, soft face. Still her expression was sweet and vulnerable. She seemed eager to find another American girl to talk to and hanging out with her was a welcome change for me from dealing with the placid older ladies on the tour.

At first Louellen told me that she'd come to the city on vacation with her husband of four years but he'd had to rush home on business. It wasn't true. She changed her story after I told her that I'd been married myself but it hadn't worked out. I'd left my husband and gone back to using my maiden name and now I was single and living with a roommate.

So then this blonde girl from Oklahoma told me that her family had lots of money from oil wells on their property. Money wasn't her problem, something else was. She'd met her husband, Mercer, in college; they'd worked together on campus shows. She'd played bit parts, sometimes she made costumes. But Mercer was good looking, Mercer had style. Once he even played a romantic lead—but that wasn't what he wanted to do. He wanted to be a stage designer; he was carrying a double major in art and drama. He wasn't coarse and countrified like she felt her family was. So she married Mercer and ended up mostly supporting him as they floated around from one regional theater to another—but he never made love to her much. Then two weeks ago, she'd discovered why. He was having an affair with a man, an actor in the company.

"I feel like such a dummy," she said, "I bet everyone else knew all along but, of course, nobody told me. Whew! And now I can't bear the thought of having his hands on me. I feel like such a fool. So anyhow I told him I needed time to think and I flew down here. But what's there to think about?"

I told her I often worked with men like that in library branches. They didn't call themselves "gay" yet, at least not to me, but now and then one might whisper that some movie star with a rugged image was actually "queer as a three dollar bill." Usually they were easy to get along with and kind of fun—though of course, they were all different. One big, ruddy-faced Southerner was great at throwing obstreperous teenagers out, walking them politely but firmly to the door. Another fellow, a lean kid from Brooklyn, always noticed what lipstick I was wearing and whether I'd bought new shoes. But, of course, I'd never been married to one.

Louellen laughed ruefully. "I don't want to go home yet but I sure don't know how I'll manage to stay. God's truth is, I'm running out of everything but I don't feel up to shopping."

The town she came from was real small, she said. Drivers here flirted with girls by practically running them down, only at the last minute veering away. Since Louellen was blonde and a novelty, lots of men aimed their cars at her. She could barely muster the courage to cross Mexico City's broad boulevards by herself. But mostly, she said, she needed to find an American style drugstore or a five-and-ten; she was running out of hairspray and Tampax and toothpaste.

"Oh, that's no problem," I told her. The day before, my tour group had passed a nearby Woolworth de Mexico on the way to lunch so I walked her over. Louellen was thrilled. The next day we went to a museum together and I dropped out of the tour.

In those days librarians at the NYPL got five weeks vacation so for the moment I felt gloriously free. My new girlfriend and I signed up with the travel agent in the hotel lobby for day trips. He arranged for us to travel out to the pyramids and to go to Xochimilco to cruise among floating gardens.

I found a bookstore and bought a guidebook in English. Following its lead we took cabs to University City with its bold architecture and to Chapultepec Park, grand and historic. We shopped for silver jewelry and ate in mid-priced restaurants the book recommended. Everywhere we went, Mexican men looked at us admiringly.

One afternoon Louellen told me she'd met two nice guys from Texas and how would I like to double date? Of course I said yes. I was high on freedom, high on how far my dollars went, and high on my sense that just being a curvy young American with light eyes and skin and no chaperone made me some kind of sex goddess to a panting throng of Mexican men.

Soon I found myself sitting in some nightspot drinking margaritas with Louellen and the fellows she'd just met. My new girlfriend seemed to be in her element, talking excitedly with these men about "claiming races." Whatever they were. It turned out that they were events where people with bundles of cash went where all the horses were for sale. You could buy or sell a racehorse that way—if that was the sort of thing you did. Hey, I was really out of my league with these people.

My date and I got up to dance. He was a lot older than I was and though he tried to act pleasant there was something nasty about him. I sensed that to him I wasn't a sex goddess, just a young librarian from New York, a young librarian without much money who should play up to him and maybe sleep with him because he was rich. When he pulled me close, crushing my breasts against his chest, I felt revolted and pulled away. This holiday of mine was spinning out of control. Someday, I thought, maybe someday soon if I'm lucky I'll come back to this fascinating country with a man I can trust and love.

I quit drinking margaritas and switched to ginger ale. The next day I made reservations to fly back home. Back in New York, restlessness still tormented me. I wrote away for applications to work abroad as a librarian for the government. Maybe I'd get a job in India or Burma or Turkey, somewhere faraway, somewhere totally different. The application forms were slow in coming. I saved money, promising myself that if nothing else came along, next year I'd go to Europe on vacation.

Meanwhile my girlfriends and I got on the city's party circuit. One weekend, my roommate and I went to some crowded, noisy blast where I met some guy I would only go out with once and she met Robert, an engineer with a difference. He had a quick, irreverent sense of humor, alert brown eyes and the even features of a young Robert Downey Jr. He started coming over to our place to see my roommate once or twice a week. I thought they were getting along fine but then she told me that things weren't clicking between them, maybe he'd be better for me. He'd asked her about me, he wanted to take me out.

Robert Nadler was full of wild ways of looking at the world that made him a festival to be with. The first time I went out with him, he seemed to be on the brink of exploding, fired up and tormented by reckless energy much like my own. I started thinking that each time we made love I was helping him drain off some of that crazy-making turmoil inside him so we could get around to other things, like going to off-Broadway shows and smoky jazz clubs where dark musicians hunched into their instruments and spattered the sounds of brass and sass against the walls. We were co-adventurers, young and rootless in our hearts, but I was his earth mother. Once in a while when we were alone together, he drifted into baby talk.

Robert's background, like mine, was Jewish but he was totally non-observant. Both of us had chosen to move in bohemian circles where labels like that didn't matter a lot. Within weeks of the first time I dated him he was insisting that I make dinner for him practically every night at his place. Robert lived in Greenwich Village, not a long subway ride from me, so sometimes I'd stop at my place first to pick up clothes for the next day and maybe food, and sometimes I'd go direct from work. Soon I was virtually living with him, which was daring at the time but seemed kind of inevitable.

I loved him and he needed me and that felt great. He decided he wanted to marry me and that sounded pretty great to me too. I told him how much I'd liked Mexico; it was cheap and different and could be lots of fun. So we started making plans to quit our jobs and go live there for a year. We'd both saved some money and we wouldn't need much.

Robert started growing a beard, I let my shoulder length hair grow longer. Mechanical engineer that he was, he tuned up his VW. We got married at City Hall. As soon as we could pack our things and pick up our final paychecks, Robert and I took off for a year of freedom. At last, I thought, I'd have more time to write fiction, something I'd been dabbling at for years. Meanwhile my new husband would go scuba diving and skin diving—two of his passions—and maybe get himself a boat. On the way, he would do all the driving, I hadn't gotten a driver's license yet. But that didn't matter because Robert loved to drive, could drive for hours and hours and never got lost, or almost never.

We zoomed south in a blur of highways, diners and mid-priced motels and crossed the border in Laredo. We saw shacks and stunted people, the look and smell of poverty. I'd seen it all before, the last time I'd been in Mexico. When I tried to talk about it to Robert, he said, "Don't give me a hard time. They don't know any better." So I swallowed those thoughts though they troubled me because I loved Robert and we were having fun and I could go new and exciting places with him.

We set out for Monterrey, surrounded by mountains, where the streets as I remembered them were paved with beautiful blue tiles. When we got there it turned out to be a sooty, industrial city with blue tiles only where the tourists went. On we headed to Mazatlán, 500 miles away on the Pacific coast.

We got on a road that cut west and south across serious mountains. For mile after mile it was a slender shelf that tipped and swerved atop gaping ravines. Sometimes we could see a white fog of clouds below us in valleys, sometimes stretches of pavement had slid down a cliff. (Parts of the road washed away, people told us, each year during the rainy season.) Robert sped on, heading toward the coast where he'd heard the swimming and diving were great.

We came to a stretch where a forest fire was raging somewhere high above us. The air was musty, hard to breathe; ash and cindery branches littered the road. Robert sped on. At last we left the fire behind us, the road started dropping down, down. The vegetation changed, we were driving through jungle. The air grew steamier, then we reached the coast. By now it was May.

We set up housekeeping in Mazatlán, then a town of 50,000. (Now it's a city of almost half a million.) Robert who spoke more Spanish than I did, found us rooms in a middle class private home. The *ama de casa* was very proud of her new American refrigerator. She invited me to share it. It was usually pretty empty except for the Jell-O she liked to make. The water we drank came from a giant *jarafe*, a monster jug delivered to us every few days and parked in the hallway just outside our door.

3 • How I Got to Berkeley

Armed with my pocket Spanish-English dictionary, I shopped for food daily, as the lady of the house did, learning to buy eggs sold without cartons and carry them home rattling against each other precariously in a paper bag. One time when I bought cheese cut from a wheel in the market, both of us got terribly sick for a day. After that it was strictly packaged Kraft de Mexico cheese for us. Still I was settling in, enjoying the challenge of learning new ways of life.

I started writing a new short story. Robert found a place that rented scuba gear. Because of his beard, now a bushy brown presence, kids in the neighborhood nicknamed him Fidel. They'd call out to him in the friendliest way. Smiling, Robert waved back. (Castro, bold and colorful, was one of his favorite people, quirky as Robert's politics were.) But after two weeks in Mazatlán, just as I was beginning to feel comfortable there, Robert got antsy and told me the place was creeping him out. I tried to talk him out of moving on but he resisted loudly.

"I'm so fuckin bored. Jesus! If we stick around here another week I swear to God, I'm gonna be climbing the walls!"

I was terrified of turning into a scold like my mother so I backed off and turned sweetly compliant. Soon we packed up and took off again. This time we headed north to California.

Robert had decided that, aside from New York, the San Francisco area was the only place where he could bear to live. We checked out the City Lights Bookstore, fabled meeting place of beatniks, and lunched at the Coexistence Bagel Shop in the heart of North Beach. Then Robert shaved off his beard and started looking for a job. Shaved off his beard—my God! At first I thought, who is this stranger I'm living with? He'd started growing it right after we started dating; without it he looked entirely different. But still I kept loyally hanging onto his shirttails, wondering where he would take me next.

This time he didn't quickly find the kind of job he wanted. Not to worry, he was fussy. In those days, American industry was booming and engineers like him were in great demand so it was commonplace for them to recklessly ditch one job for another. After three weeks in California we headed back east.

We found ourselves an apartment in Brooklyn Heights, then each of us found a job, though mine was just part-time. Robert was an only child; he liked having me at leisure to focus on him. In my free time,

I thought, I'd do my creative thing. Though in those days I was mostly enjoying being his wife, enjoying making him comfortable.

Making him comfortable—that was what I liked to do with men. Anything so I wouldn't be like my mom. In Robert I'd found someone I could laugh with and explore the big bad world with. And to help make that happen, I was determined never to nag him or tear him down. I tried to cook the foods he liked and be his sexual playmate as best I knew how.

It was late spring of 1960 when we got back to New York. Once we'd settled into our new place, we started taking the subway over to Manhattan to dig jazz at the Blue Note in the Village and at the Five Spot, east of it, near Cooper Union. We saw The Fantasticks at the unpretentious start of what would be its 42-year run. Robert passed on to me his dog-eared copies of Henry Miller and William S. Burroughs while I pressed D. H. Lawrence on him. Come summer we went sailing with friends of his on their boat and sometimes all of us partied together.

Winter came on, Jack Kennedy was elected. At first Democrats like us rejoiced; the Cold War seemed to slack off a bit. New civility and charm graced the White House. But then came news of the Bay of Pigs invasion. Cuban émigrés who opposed Fidel Castro had left their new homes in Florida to make what they thought would be a surprise attack. They expected that the locals would rise up against Fidel. But it didn't work out that way—they got slaughtered or captured. Soon word leaked out that this action had been planned under the previous administration. The C.I.A. and U.S. ships and planes were involved. Meanwhile at the United Nations, our ambassador Adlai Stevenson was doing his best to deny all of the above—and that, Robert and I found particularly galling.

Stevenson had run for president as a Democrat in 1956. He was a courtly, professorial man who intellectuals thought was the soul of honor. That summer while I was in library school, I'd worked as a volunteer in his campaign. Now I felt betrayed. Besides, I'd seen Cuba briefly with my own eyes. Two years before Castro and his ragtag army rode into Havana, I'd spent my Christmas vacation there. (Or at least I called it a vacation—another mission had impelled me there. More about that later.) Cuba's dictator, Fulgencio Batista, was still in power though everyone knew Fidel was holed up in the mountains, preparing for a push into the capital. Armed men patrolled Havana's streets and I hated the look of them. Most of them were barely medium height by U.S. standards but they were grossly overweight. Their cheeks and bellies bulged. They looked greedy and brutal and smug, as if they knew they inspired fear and that was the way they liked it.

I took a tour of Havana's more sedate points of interest; these included its medical clinics. There I met fresh-faced young doctors and nurses and I asked them what they thought about Fidel. They chose their words carefully—what else would I expect? They lived under a dictator—still I saw their faces glow with idealism and hope.

So I couldn't help thinking of Castro as a good guy, even if he had confiscated U.S. corporate property: sugar plantations and processing plants, tourist hotels and Mafia-controlled casinos. I'd heard that under international law that was okay. Robert didn't see it that way, still he admired Fidel. Flamboyant rebels looked good to him. So one day the two of us made protest signs, strung them on cords we could hang around our necks, and took off to demonstrate outside the United Nations. (It was illegal in New York to carry posters on sticks—a holdover from days when sticks had been used as weapons.)

The New York cops didn't let us get close to the U. N. tower but they shepherded us to a plaza where protestors could make their feelings known. We marched in a meandering circle with maybe eighty others, none of whom we knew. Off to one side, a man held a camera aimed at the marchers. He focused on getting mug shots of our faces and we guessed that he was F.B.I. because though by then the McCarthy era was beginning to wane, American civil liberties still left much to be desired. Every time I circled past the man with the camera, I would raise my sign to cover my face. I did it out of sheer perversity. If he really wanted to get my picture he could shoot me from the side—and probably did.

After a while a familiar figure joined our circle. It was the famous writer Norman Mailer tailed by four newsmen, two of them with cameras of their own. He only demonstrated for about ten minutes, but he made a statement, he stuck his neck out. Nobody from the government ever tracked us down. Our lives went on about the same as ever.

Come June, Robert bought an oversized foam surfboard with pretensions; it boasted a tiny mast and sail. We stored our micro-yacht at his parents' house in Flatbush and sailed it in quiet waters nearby. Sometimes we hung out in the back of a local shop that sold handmade sandals and belts made to order where the owner, an amiable young craftsman, let local part-time beatniks like us congregate. Sometimes we got stoned. When one nickel bag we bought turned out to be full of seeds, I planted a batch in a long, narrow window box and set it on a table that looked out on a courtyard. Several took hold and grew like weeds which of course was what they were. I thinned them down to four. These grew straight and tall and pretty while they screened the view.

But then Robert got antsy again and started answering ads for engineers in the San Francisco Bay Area. He was looking for a job where he could combine his technical skills with his salesman's wisecracking personality. Eventually he found something he thought would suit him.

For me, the pot I'd been growing was my most pressing problem. Was it ready to harvest? A few years later there'd be handbooks on every paperback rack telling hippies all they wanted to know about the care and feeding of marijuana plants but this was 1961, and the era that's called The Sixties hadn't really begun.

I pulled off the leaves and dried them as best I could. We had half a dozen friends over from the sandal shop crowd. We tried to turn them on but our homegrown crop didn't make anyone high—just awfully sleepy. That night six people sacked out on the pale red shag rug in our living room. Then Robert and I packed up yet again and headed west to San Francisco. By now it was September 1961.

At first we stayed in a motel. From there each weekday morning Robert drove across the Bay Bridge to his new job many miles east in Contra Costa County. Evenings we explored the city. One night in some small dinner spot we heard a pretty girl named Grace Slick belt out "They Call the Wind Mariah" and the sound of her voice stayed with me until a couple of years later when she stormed into the spotlight with the Jefferson Airplane. The City by the Bay was our playground—but then Robert announced that it wouldn't work for us to look for an apartment there. Each morning a traffic snarl at Ashby Avenue in Berkeley across the bay slowed his commute to his job further east in Walnut Creek. His new boss wanted him to buy a house in the sprawl of suburbia where he worked. "Hell, no," he told me, "We'd rot out there." But maybe, he thought, the university town at the gateway to Contra Costa would do for a while. So just past Ashby we found an airy, sunny apartment, larger and cheaper than what we'd had in New York.

So that's how I got to Berkeley—where I finally got to feeling like a grownup. Where I started to figure out who I really was while around me history erupted big time. Ah, sunny Berkeley in the fall of 1961. Very clean in those days when much of the town and the campus was new and where everywhere green things seemed zealous to grow. Palm trees and evergreens, stands of bamboo, flowers and vines I'd never seen before plus relatives of plants I remembered from the East. One day as I wandered down a residential street I sniffed a familiar scent and ran into a giant geranium bush. Till then it had never occurred to me that geraniums grew anywhere but window boxes. Now I too started digging in roots, taking hold.

The town was full of beautiful people, young and bright and proud to be there. In those days the university was free to anyone who'd lived in California a year, provided they could meet its high academic standards. Even graduate school was free and Nobel Prize winners taught there. And compared to New York, rents were low for pleasant housing. Paradise on the Pacific, that's how it seemed to me.

I put a Positions Wanted ad in the local paper. I was bored with libraries and wanted to tackle something else. What I ended up with was a job as the only paid employee of a trade association with headquarters in Oakland. It represented companies like Hertz and Avis that rented or leased out cars and trucks in California. The industry was huge—but we were minute. My boss had organized a handful of firms around the state, most of them tiny independents struggling to compete with the giants, or franchised by them. They paid the association minimal dues. My desk was in a grungy office I shared with two older women, in a glorified shed on one edge of a great expanse of parking lot. The good part was that I got to create my own job and soon my pay for twenty hours a week was as much as a secretary made working full time in San Francisco. Phil, the association's president, filled me in on what we were about.

Not long before, Hertz, the biggest firm in the industry, had been part of General Motors but in those days of strict government regulation of corporations, GM had been forced to divest itself of this subsidiary so it wouldn't overpower competitors in the rental business. Now Hertz tried to keep a low profile.

Phil owned maybe a hundred trucks which he rented out to individuals or businesses for a day or two or maybe a couple of weeks. He was a picture perfect small businessman— congenial, middle-aged, backbone of America—a perfect front man for a giant corporation. Now, he told me, the association needed more information. It had been set up to represent the industry whenever legislation that might affect them came up. But they seemed to have no clue about what was coming up.

With my boss's encouragement, I contacted the state capital. Soon we were swamped by a flood of flimsy pamphlets that legislative committees rushed out on newsprint to list the bills they had pending. We also subscribed to the *Sacramento Bee*, the capital's main paper, which I was supposed to skim for news. The *Bee* was quite a good, liberal publication. Bless its little black and white heart, it also had great comics and recipes. For a while I got to earn my salary by mostly sitting around the office reading. Then I started writing a newsletter for the association.

Meeting the deadlines I set for myself helped me shake off my tendencies toward writer's block. It felt good to be something of a professional writer, though I sure wasn't creating art or working for social change. For three years I'd earn my keep working in Oakland part time. Meanwhile I'd get involved with a group in Berkeley that would change my life.

4

A Peace Center and a Couple of Passions

IN DECEMBER 1961 I WALKED INTO a place that called itself a peace center. This was the second such resource in the country. A hand lettered wooden sign that said TURN TOWARD PEACE hung in front of a small frame house. I walked in and asked lots of questions; the group's goals and concerns turned out to be much like my own. This was an era of international threat and counter-threat, an era when the United States was setting up ever more military bases encircling the U.S.S.R. and elsewhere, and inflaming anger and fear around the globe by testing nuclear weapons in the atmosphere. TTP argued for policies that would lessen the Soviets' fear of us while making it clear during this the McCarthy era, that it was not a Soviet tool.

I'd grown up in a family where money was tight. Thrift, I figured, was a virtue even on a national level. So why were the world's two superpowers expending inconceivably vast sums of money—while polluting the air with murderous radiation—when both sides already had stockpiled more than enough[1] to destroy and maybe vaporize the planet many times over?

Two years before, I'd responded to an ad in *The New York Times* by joining the Committee for a Sane Nuclear Policy. (This would later be known simply as SANE.) Founded by a coalition of liberal intellectuals, religious leaders, scientists and traditional pacifists, bolstered by Eleanor Roosevelt and the chairman of the board at General Mills, it dared to speak out against weapons tests. Its size and impact were modest but at least it was a rare voice for moderation. Was Turn Toward Peace really doing something, I wondered, that might help turn things around?

Its headquarters looked oddly cozy, furnished with a hodgepodge of donated desks, tables and chairs. Café curtains in a woodsy print fluttered at the windows. Faded rose cushions topped window seats. Everywhere else it was awash in paper and files. Cabinets and bookcases filled the walls; in-boxes were stacked on shelves above a phone.

People gave me pamphlets to read and explained how Turn Toward Peace had come to exist. The year before, when the East Germans had flung up the Berlin Wall and many in the world had feared that total war would break out, a Quaker intellectual had spoken out at a crisis meeting in New York.

"Why do we only organize in response to crises?" this man, Bob Pickus had asked, "As people of goodwill we should be working *all the time* to counter the threat of international conflict. We should be planning long-range programs, digging in for the long haul."

A few leading liberal figures endorsed his ideas. A modest amount of funding came his way. He used it to establish two centers on the West Coast to promote what he called "American initiatives" toward a more peaceful world, independent acts that wouldn't require prior Soviet agreement. Concrete steps toward disarmament, growth toward world law and a sense of world community, economic planning for a peaceful world, and support of just demands for revolutionary change where people's rights were trampled by dictatorships.

Pickus, whom everyone called "Pick," was raising important questions and suggesting small steps toward turning the tide. All of this sounded pretty gutsy in 1961. He'd collected around him a tiny underpaid staff and a band of oddball volunteers to spread his gospel in churches and unions and civic groups. Soon I was his newest oddball volunteer.

It was fun hanging out at the peace center. The folks I met there tended to share my opinions and be around my age. It was a great place to talk politics and hear about the latest movie and share scuttlebutt about things happening elsewhere in town. First I typed and stuffed envelopes, then Pick entrusted me with the task of starting a newsletter

4 • A Peace Center and a Couple of Passions

for Turn Toward Peace. In it I listed the actions of local affiliates of national groups that thought much as we did: the Committee for a Sane Nuclear Policy, peace fellowships affiliated with Methodists or Jews or Unitarians. The Catholic organization Pax Christi and the War Resisters League, United World Federalists, the United Nations Association, and others. I listed the programs they were holding in town: guest speakers and panel discussions, vigils and picnics. We also used our newsletter to alert activists to potential speakers who would soon be visiting the area and to anniversaries coming up that might spark public interest in a future event.

Now I was writing two parallel publications—though I just got paid for writing one, that Oakland trade paper that meant virtually nothing to me. The peace center became my home away from home. Its little band of activists became my tribe while Pick became a mentor for me. A pot of coffee was always brewing in the kitchen and sometimes I brought in apples or a bag of fresh donuts from a shop down the street. Almost every day around noon, one older volunteer brought in a stack of sandwiches on close-grained whole wheat—tuna fish one day, egg salad the next—welcome gifts to the more impoverished members of our ragtag crew. Nothing could have seemed more sedate than my routine there—but soon it would spawn turmoil in my life.

Much of that unrest had to do with a man named Bob Martinson. At first he was just an unlikely presence at the edge of my perception. Handsome in a sharp-featured Nordic way, prematurely gray at 33, and far taller than anyone else at the center, he was a lean, ectomorphic man whose shoulders looked almost too broad for his slim, long legged body.

We didn't work together, Martinson and I. (Though a few called him Bob, people at the center and elsewhere in Berkeley usually used his last name instead.) Mostly I worked on the newsletter. He did research and drafted position papers and wrote articles that appeared in socialist journals and now and then, *The Nation*. People at the center said he could be a stunning speaker, that when he was still a grad student on campus, he'd often held forth at the Free Speech Plaza. He'd been flamboyant and charismatic—but that was not the person I was coming to know, a brooding man whose nearsighted blue eyes usually seemed to be peering at documents.

I picked up scraps of gossip about him. He'd run for mayor of Berkeley once as the Socialist Party candidate; he'd lost but managed to get 18% of the vote. Less than a year earlier he'd gone south as a Freedom Rider and had been imprisoned in Mississippi for almost six weeks. There was even some play he'd starred in on campus not long before. When a great French director, Jean Renoir, had come to the UC campus to stage something he'd recently written, Bob had played a German general unwillingly serving under Hitler. His acting got rave reviews. (He'd dabbled in theater for years.) Renoir wanted him to turn professional and perform the role again, maybe in New York but he hadn't pursued it. The reason he would give me much later was that he could never succeed in movies because his eyes were too deep set to photograph well.

So what was he doing here at Turn Toward Peace? I wondered. He looked to be just one more perennial grad student drifting around Berkeley, "ABD," All But Dissertation, a PhD candidate who'd long since finished his course work in sociology but never completed the required thesis, a brilliant drifter who'd never get anywhere.

(In fact, a dozen years later he would soar to towering acclaim as a scholar—only to have his conclusions used to help create a national disaster.)

He was married to a fellow Freedom Rider, a light-skinned, very young black girl, tall, willful, very bright. Then I heard that he'd separated from her but that didn't concern me. I was busy being Robert Nadler's wife. I figured that Robert and I would stay together always. Until my plans for our life together started conflicting with his.

In those days, doctors used to say a woman should have her first child by the time she was 30. I was turning 29; I figured it was time I got pregnant. But my husband didn't want us to have kids. And he didn't want to stay in Berkeley either, he said, he wanted us to move back east. While I was getting hooked on the place, I felt I was finding myself there, and it just so happened there was this extraordinary long-legged radical I was getting to know who was no longer living with his wild teenage wife.

Robert moved out—though for a while he'd come back to our apartment on absurd errands, picking up a misplaced tie, looking for skindiving gear I knew he'd collected weeks before. I guess he thought

4 • A Peace Center and a Couple of Passions

I'd back down and agree to live on his terms. But now my emotions were otherwise engaged. I didn't care what my husband did, I didn't miss him.

Pretty soon Martinson and I were a couple. He took me to Berkeley parties where beautiful, laidback young people danced to music played by their talented friends, and little kids, unattended but doing fine, prospered underfoot and a few older folks mingled and everyone was smiling. At least that's how it seemed to me at the time. And sometimes we went to picnics or meetings where we got into political wrangles that were spirited and fun. We debated with friends or clumps of folks we'd just met. Each of us showed off what we knew and what we'd been thinking about, we speculated on where the world was tending. And then Bob and I would leave and make love and that was the best part. But we were still legally bound to other people and for the present, that was fine with me.

I couldn't figure Martinson out, I wasn't even sure I wanted to. I knew he was almost unimaginably gifted. As a child living near Palo Alto, his IQ had torn through the top of the Stanford-Binet. But there seemed to be a hollow place inside him where confident drive and a true sense of self should reside.

When he wasn't operating in bookish mode, his mannerisms were ostentatiously bold and manly, still often when we lay face to face in bed together, he would wrap his long limbs around me like a clinging, needful child. Then I would feel protective, like an earth mother trying to make him whole and give him peace. And when he slept, often his lips pursed and he made odd sounds.

One morning I asked him about them. He averted his eyes. They were suckling noises, he said, a throwback to infancy—that's what some psychotherapist had told him. Noises he made because when he was a child he hadn't had nearly enough love from his mother. But then he'd been born when his mother was only sixteen, probably she'd never wanted to have him. Only later would he share more of that story with me—and I would never know it all.

That spring I was twenty-nine—and I'd still never been to Europe! Most of my New York girlfriends had traveled there. When first I met Robert, I'd been saving for a trip across the Atlantic. Instead he and I had pooled our resources to move to Mexico but we hadn't stayed south of the border long. When we split I still had some savings stashed away so in May I got a passport and started making reservations. I signed on with a group, Servas (the name was Esperanto for "service") that helped traveling peace activists stay briefly for free in European homes. I talked my boss in Oakland into giving me two months off without pay and made tentative plans with a New York girlfriend to meet her in France and ramble around with her part of the time—but whether or not that worked out, I was determined to do my Grand Tour before I turned thirty.

I told friends in town about the vacation I was planning. Some thought I'd take the money and buy a car instead. But Martinson believed me. One evening in July after he'd come over for dinner, Bob said why didn't I take him along with me. Take him along! When even with my new copy of *Europe on Five Dollars a Day,* I was far from sure that I'd have enough money when I got back to the States to pay my rent until my first paycheck came through in the fall.

He pranced around my living room and made sweeping gestures with his long arms and his long fingered hands. "Oh you New Yorkers, the Atlantic's just a pond to you. Hey, I'm older than you but until I hitched a ride down to Mississippi, I'd never been east of Chicago."

I laughed. That Freedom Ride hadn't been much of a vacation for him. When I met him he was working at the California Department of Public Health, analyzing data for a study of alcoholism treatment programs. But recently his hours there had been cut and soon the study would end. He wasn't sure he'd be able to find another job till fall.

"Take me along," he said again.

"No way I could do it. I wish I could. But I can barely afford...."

He didn't seem to hear me.

"Europe. Imagine! So much history there. I could hunt up my Swedish relatives. We could...."

I was sitting in a plush covered armchair I'd bought secondhand. It was deep cranberry red, my favorite color. My mail, still unopened, lay on a table beside me. I fingered a letter nervously, not knowing what to say. And then he did an extraordinary thing.

Bob came and knelt before me. He pressed one neatly trousered knee hard against my leg, hidden under a floral print skirt. I almost reached out to stroke his thick gray hair but instead I drew back. For this was an

4 • A Peace Center and a Couple of Passions

actor's gesture. I wondered what role he'd practiced kneeling for, what fantasy was playing out in his mind. Years later, I would read the script of *Carola,* Jean Renoir's play, and find that in it the general he played knelt twice to his lady and the second time he begged her to come away with him.

I knew he'd had a breakdown after his father died. And I'd noticed that, though everyone said he was a breathtaking orator, the director of the peace center never sent him out on speaking gigs—afraid, I guessed, that Bob would say something that might get the center in trouble. His instability frightened me. That evening in July, some part of me pushed him away. Early that August I took a plane by myself to New York, visited friends and family, then flew on to Europe the cheapest way, via Icelandic Airlines. During the next seven weeks I would visit ten countries and have more than my share of escapades and encounters.

Travel they say is broadening. It's also often exhausting and scary. The girl I'd planned to tour with just showed up for one long, pleasant lunch in the Copenhagen airport; then we went our separate ways and once again, I was on my own. Often I'd arrive in a railroad station and take a tranquilizer before I figured out what I should do next. Still I had entree to two Americans living in Europe. A longtime girlfriend of mine from Juilliard Prep was now married to an Englishman; a successful American artist who lived in Paris was an old Navy buddy of another friend of mine.

My Servas hosts, too, were welcoming and eager to converse for hours. Staying in their homes I learned volumes about local politics, economics and customs. They also told me lots of practical things, like where to buy shoes when mine threatened to fall apart as I walked miles each day in that summer's seemingly endless rain—which that year Northern Europeans were blaming on Soviet and American nuclear tests in the atmosphere. But I found it hard to adjust to each new household, to my hosts' children and pets, to their unpredictable schedules, the noise they made when I needed to sleep, their widely varying diets and manners. Often it was a relief to pay for a modest hotel room where I could be simply, gratefully alone.

I had one misadventure that, with respect to my education, turned out to be a blessing in disguise. Shopping in Florence one day I met a nice young Italian who offered to give me a lift back to my hotel, up and down this hill town's narrow streets, riding on the back of his motorcycle. In my characteristic take-a-dare fashion I said "Why not?" and hopped on although I'd only ridden a motorcycle once before. Barelegged and ignorant, I burned my right leg badly not once but twice on its scorching hot exhaust pipe. This led to my experiencing European "socialized medicine" in three countries. Good thing.

My Florentine escort took me to a first aid station located in little more than a kiosk. There a doctor cleaned up my wounds, bandaged them and—in French, our one common language—explained how I should take care of them in the future. No charge, no paperwork. The only problem: though I understood that I should wash them from time to time, my high school French failed me when he used the word *savon* (soap). I blundered on, not knowing exactly how to treat my burns, till I got to my next stop, Paris.

Here I looked for another doctor. As I took a pair of slacks into a dry cleaner, I mentioned conversationally, *"Je cherche un médicin."* The man at the counter looked alarmed. Given his Gallic turn of mind he seemed to assume that if I was looking for a doctor I must be pregnant. No, no, I explained, using the most idiomatic construction I ever carried off in my travels, *"Je m'ai brulé le jambe."* (I to me have burned the leg.) He exhaled with relief and directed me to a local *médicin*. This man was cagy when I asked him what I owed him, whatever I thought appropriate was what he suggested. I still hadn't figured out what *savon* meant and didn't have the commonsense to ask him to explain. Nonetheless, by the time I reached London, my leg was clearly healing and all I needed to find was a place to buy fresh bandages.

It was a Saturday evening. Lots of shops were closed but folks in the lobby of the hotel where I'd just checked in chorused that I should go to Boots in Piccadilly. There, stumbling out of the underground to meander around what was then a crowded, razzle-dazzle Times Square of a plaza, I managed to find a chain drugstore which stayed open all night and offered clinic services as well. There a motherly nurse took me in hand, explained at last what *savon* meant, tended cheerfully to my leg and sent me on my way. No charge except for the cost of the bandages. Ah, the horrors of socialized medicine. Ever since then, I've felt sure that its demonizers were either liars or badly misinformed.

4 • A Peace Center and a Couple of Passions

AT LAST I RETURNED TO BERKELEY. When I got back, much in Martinson's life had changed. He'd gone back to his wife. He'd found a new job, this time for an institute with ties to Berkeley's School of Criminology. It gave him professional status he'd never had before. I didn't run into him at the peace center anymore but he'd call me and come by my place when he could. Often he'd come by when I didn't expect him. He'd fill my doorway knowing that when I saw him, I'd melt and let him in. Then we'd talk. He'd tell me about ideas and issues that he'd been thinking about, he'd tell me about what he'd been reading lately. And he was so brilliant and such fun to talk to. And inevitably we'd end up in bed.

Nonetheless I saw other people. Briefly I dated Chick Callenbach, a friend of Bob's who'd been one of his most ardent campaign workers when he ran for mayor. Chick's day job was editing *Film Quarterly,* a magazine published by the university, and his real first name was Ernest. Sixteen years later, Ernest Callenbach's novel *Ecotopia* would become an international bestseller, would gain him lifelong fame and would help to spawn the environmental movement. But just then he had other concerns.

His wife had committed suicide. He was looking for someone to parent his fearful, clinging little daughter but the chemistry between us never worked. No matter—I was still crazy in love with Martinson. He'd hunt me down. He knew where I bought groceries after I got off work. He'd corner me there, blocking my way down an aisle. And my heart would stop at the sight of him. Then he told me that Rita wanted to have a child, that because she hadn't gotten pregnant as quickly as she wanted, he was taking some treatments.

"Her mother's Creole," he told me one evening over a goblet of wine at my place. "Her mother could pass for Spanish or Italian, something like that. Mediterranean, not black. Rita's never forgiven her mom for marrying a man with Negroid features. "

"Because her skin's pretty light."

He nodded.

"So I guess that's where I come in," he said with a hint of sarcasm. "It's not like she's that crazy about me. She sleeps around, she always has."

"But if anyone could give her a white child, you could?"

I wondered how much of what he told me was true. Didn't a married man always tell the other woman nasty things about his wife? I'd broken up with my husband because I wanted to have a child. Now that Bob actually had a decent job and was beginning to seem stable, I, too, was aching to have a child of his.

Then he told me that he was moving. Los Angeles was Rita's hometown and she was down there already, staying with her parents. He'd been transferred there and some friends were giving him a farewell party. He seemed to be deliberating as to whether it would be all right for me to come but then he gave me the address and I tacked it to my bulletin board.

When that day rolled around, I didn't feel brave enough to go to Martinson's farewell party. Around this time I had a buddy in town named Donn Bayard.[2] Donn was a few years younger than I. He'd been named for Donn Byrne, a poet and writer of the early twentieth century, very romantic and picturesque.

Donn was a sweet guy but he wasn't especially romantic. Mostly he was exhausted all the time because he was working his way through a master's program in anthropology and also trying to have a life. He figured he could get by on five hours sleep a night but the strain of it showed. The most fun thing about him was that he shared a house with two friends he'd known since prep school, where he'd been a scholarship student, and every Sunday afternoon they held an open house with lots of beer and conversation for anybody who showed up.

So that's where I headed, pretending that I wasn't coming apart. As I sipped my second beer I mentioned, as casually as I could manage, that I was thinking of going to a party that night but I wasn't sure I wanted to. Donn and his housemates asked if they could come along so I ended up attending with these three as my honor guard. It just so happened that these guys were giants, conspicuously younger and taller than Martinson. Donn was 6' 5" and the fellows he roomed with were around the same height so it must have looked like I was making a point, putting Martinson down, in a manner of speaking. It was good for my ego, it made it easier for me to face my vagabond lover.

That night he barely said hello to me and I was not the sort of girl who made a scene. I almost felt guilty to be in love with him at all; in the circles we moved in it was politically incorrect to compete with the African-American Freedom Rider he'd chosen to marry. That night someone at the piano played union songs and other old political ditties from *The People's Songbook*. I knew most of the words and sang along with spirit. Sometimes, soprano that I was, I improvised a descant. Then the pianist defected and a girl put on dance records in another room. Donn and I did the twist together, then I danced with other guys, some of them led me through lindy hops.

The California lindy was different from the version I'd learned in New York. Migrating west, the dance pattern had shed a beat but I loved to dance and accommodated easily to my partners. I probably looked like I was having a high old time. All this leaping around made me forget for a while to grieve the sorry state of my relationship with Martinson but the fact was, when the evening was over I felt like shit.

AFTER BOB MOVED DOWN TO L.A. with Rita he still visited Berkeley once in a while on business. Now and then he sent me typewritten letters, never very long, that sketched out what he was doing and how he was feeling. "Work is work is work," he said. Clearly he felt unfulfilled. But at least now he had a position with some professional dignity. One evening he breezed by my place, helped himself to a salami and cheese sandwich from fixings he found in my fridge, then shared with me the latest salty gossip from Southern California. "There's this man named Pusey who's in charge of the local meter maids. You know what they call 'em?"

I shook my head.

"Pusey's pussy posse!"

We both laughed. It was the kind of earthy male humor he knew he could share with me. I still cherished the dream that someday I'd write The Great American Novel and how could I hope to do that if I didn't know how men talked among themselves when genteel young ladies weren't around? For that reason I'd always been attracted to men who often treated me like one of the boys. Nonetheless I sometimes acted as his errand girl.

He sent me a receipt for some laundry he'd left behind in town. I picked it up dutifully and left it for him at an office at the university where he could pick it up. Twice he enclosed checks, paying me back in installments $50 I'd lent him months before. Then there was the night he came by when I was watching the tube, watching some mindless detective show with a dashing hero, filling that last couple of hours before I meant to tuck myself into bed alone. Except here was Martinson looking so pleased to see me.

He sat down with me on a black plastic couch that I'd bought in Woolworth's, all straight lines, minimalist modern. I'd dressed it up with colorful pillows. He shoved them aside, put one long arm around me and sighed contentedly. After a few minutes he asked, "You really want to watch this?" So I turned off the TV and we talked for a while and then we made love.

He didn't have to leave until the next morning. That night as we lay together he told me that Rita was five months pregnant and very excited about it and he was kind of excited too.

I felt as if he'd slapped me. Cringing, I pulled away from him.

"So what are you doing here?" I asked him.

"What am I doing here? Well, that's a good question. A perfectly good question. And one that you have a right to ask."

I turned my back on him. "Oh god, you make me so mad!" I was too upset to look him in the eye.

"Well, I wouldn't be surprised if she walked out on me once she has the baby. She's not that wild about me, you know. And she's still in college. Wouldn't surprise me if she dumped the kid on her mom and went off on her merry way."

So maybe I still had a chance with him. But did I really want to try to make a life with him, unstable and habitually promiscuous as he was?

We fell asleep but after four hours I woke up again, seething with grief and desperation. For years I'd wanted to have his baby, still I'd never made any demands on Bob. That's how I was with a man if I loved him, I did my best to make him feel confident and happy. And you really can catch more flies with honey than vinegar as the old saying goes, but this man filled me with longing. So I let Martinson sleep and I made myself chamomile tea and then I tried to sleep on my living room couch but all I could do was toss and moan. And then he left and I went to work but the grief and desperation remained.

My companions in the large office where my desk sat were two pleasant older women, a bookkeeper and a secretary who worked for my boss's rental business. They'd been kind and understanding during the first months I struggled through my breakup with Robert Nadler and then went back to using my maiden name. They knew that now I was on my own.

That morning I skimmed as best I could through the latest batch of notices I'd gotten from Sacramento, copies of every bill proposed in the legislature in the past couple of days. I set a few aside and discarded the rest. I glanced at the copy of *Business Week* my boss routinely passed on to me so I could summarize items of interest in my newsletter for his trade association. After a while its headlines swam before my eyes. Then I crossed my arms on my desk, lay down my head and started to cry.

I cried and cried. Charlotte brought me water. Ellie touched my shoulder gingerly and asked me did I want to talk about it? They looked alarmed. After a while, I stopped crying and poured out at least part of the whole sorry tale. I didn't tell them about my lover's politics or mine, I didn't say he'd slept over that night, but I told them he'd gone back to his wife and now they were going to have a baby.

"He's not good for you," said Charlotte.

Ellie said, "Someone better will come along but first you've gotta show this man the door."

"I know," I said and for a change I meant it. And that was the end of my first affair with Martinson.

5

"I Have a Dream"

IN THE SUMMER OF 1963, PEOPLE on the left were talking about a March on Washington for Jobs and Freedom. It wasn't a new idea. It had first been proposed in 1941 when the United States was gearing up for the Second World War. In those days African-Americans were frozen out of jobs in defense industries and, in the armed forces, segregation ruled.

The nation's one major black union leader[1]—A. Philip Randolph, organizer of the Brotherhood of Sleeping Car Porters—and Walter White, the head of the National Association for the Advancement of Colored People,[2] met with President Roosevelt. They demanded that war industries stop discriminating against blacks and that the U.S. military be desegregated. Otherwise, they threatened, 100,000 blacks would march on Washington. Roosevelt issued an executive order that forbade employers with government contracts from discriminating on the basis of race, creed, color or national origin. So they called off the march.

Unfortunately, this order didn't last past the end of the war. Southern racists blocked passage of such legislation on the federal level. The American civil rights movement fought back using a variety of non-violent tools. A lawsuit against the school system in Topeka, Kansas culminated in the Supreme Court's historic ruling, *Brown v. Board of Education,* which outlawed segregation in public schools. The

Montgomery Bus Boycott, sit-ins, local marches and Freedom Rides all forced changes in repressive and humiliating practices—but pushback from segregationists was brutal.

In the South, black churches were bombed, activists were beaten or murdered. No one was punished for these crimes. This was the climate in 1963 when once again a March on Washington was proposed. Though I'd been more involved in the peace movement than in the battle for civil rights, I decided that this time I'd put my body on the line.

I arranged to fly to the New York area where I could stay with people I knew. First I stayed with a girlfriend of mine who'd invited me to visit her in New Jersey where she was studying for a PhD in biochemistry at Rutgers. Elvira and I had met three years before when we were both employed at the Sloan-Kettering Institute. I'd felt I needed a break from libraries, so I'd taken a job as part-time secretary to a research professor who ran a small graduate program on the side. Elvira was one of his research assistants.

We were almost the same age, both married but childless, with master's degrees. We had the same high energy level and the same quirky, skeptical sense of humor. How could we not become friends? But of course I should mention that Elvira despite her freckled face had the sepia skin and rounded features that in those days labeled her "Negro."

By 1963, like me, she'd split up with her husband. She was sharing an apartment with a fellow doctoral candidate, a white girl. The two of them made me comfortable on a couch in their living room. Elvira had no intention of joining me on the march and I respected her decision. Everything this friend of mine did, brilliant and achieving as she was, was a political act, a witness to her right to equality. She told me about some of the barriers she faced: a professor at Rutgers who questioned her ability at every step, the places where she was only admitted because gatekeepers assumed that she was a servant. Staying with her I learned from her—but I had to connect with a group that was heading for that big demonstration in Washington.

A few phone calls put me in touch with a major New York union. The Amalgamated Clothing Workers still had a few empty seats on buses they were sending down to Washington. So that's how I ended up before dawn on August 23rd in the heart of Manhattan's garment district. Two matching buses, chamois colored with deep red accents, were parked at the curb on Sixth Avenue.

The woman who'd signed me up over the phone had advised me to bring three sandwiches and something to drink. Berkeley party person that I was, I brought along a six-pack of beer to share. This raised disapproving eyebrows. The woman who was checking off the names of people getting on the union's buses wouldn't let me bring it along—I had to leave it on the sidewalk. When I finally climbed onto their last bus it was practically full with a multiracial mix. The majority of the passengers were women, mostly older than I and broad in the beam, I guessed, from sitting at sewing machines all day. I squeezed into an aisle seat beside a middle-aged black woman who told me her name was Ms. Hooper. Soon, like Ms. Hooper, I closed my eyes and slept for a while.

When I woke up, it was light and our bus was somewhere on the Jersey Turnpike rolling south through what seemed like a lot of traffic for 5:30 on a Wednesday morning in August. It was hardly a surprise that cars and vans were rolling south with us on this wide, multi-lane highway but I wondered why there were so many buses as well.

Lots of the passengers were African-American. I checked the license plates on their vehicles: New York, New Jersey, a scattering of New England states, now and then even one from Canada. Couples and families in cars. Beside me, Ms. Hooper stirred, blinked her eyes, and started staring out the window like me. A big green bus passed by us bearing a banner on its side. Together we read it off with delight.

FREEDOM NOW!!!
MARCH ON WASHINGTON FOR JOBS AND FREEDOM
Jubilee A.M.E. Church — Boston, Massachusetts

Through its windows, a mix of dusky faces, mostly middle-aged church ladies plus some teenagers and an occasional man, looked at us through its windows and smiled. We smiled back. And the buses kept coming. It was easy to guess that most of these buses were heading to Washington, just like us.

About a third sported banners on their sides. They proclaimed to the world that they were carrying members from a church in Harlem or

Trenton or bringing members of the NAACP. Two matching blue-and-yellow buses passed us filled with hospital workers. Now and then we passed travelers from mostly white groups, from proud congregations of Unitarians and Methodists, Catholics and Jews. A few waved at us and we waved back, thrilled to be on this pilgrimage together, heading for ... we didn't know just what.

At the Philadelphia interchange a new herd of vehicles crowded onto the road bearing meat cutters and coal miners, social workers and teachers, and God knows how many other people making their move to stand up and be counted, to vote for positive social change with their physical presence in the nation's capital.

As our vehicle rolled on, I napped again. When I woke we'd crossed into Delaware and were heading west to the Maryland border. By now our procession of buses had become a huge, prophetic cavalcade that spoke of something remarkable to come. Cattycorner from me, across the aisle and behind me, a white couple had a portable radio. The man turned it on and started fiddling with the dial but all he got was static and a blur of pop music. "Here, gimme that. Let me try," said the woman, grabbing it unceremoniously from him. After a few more seconds, she managed to find a news report coming through loud and clear.

" ... and as many as a hundred thousand are expected to descend on the nation's capital today for what's being billed as the biggest civil rights demonstration ever. The metropolitan police department will be bolstered by 2,000 National Guardsmen and 2,000 specially trained marshals to protect the city from violence. Four thousand Marines are on standby alert. Citizens without legitimate business in the area are advised to stay away from...."

The woman flicked it off angrily, "Assholes!" she said. "Totally clueless."

"My land, my land," Ms. Hooper said, "now isn't that a disgrace. As if we're a pack of animals don't know how to behave ourselves!"

"Shows how much they understand about nonviolence," I agreed.

"And about Dr. King," a woman added from somewhere in front of us. "Just know how to beat you with a stick and sic *dogs* on you, that's all they know."

"Ignorant. Ignorant people!"

A phrase from the broadcast kept ringing in my ears. "A hundred thousand," I repeated, "I wonder if that's right."

"That's what The Man's hopin for," a deep male voice said, chuckling. "They's hopin it'll *just* be a hunnerd thousand. But just you look at this crowd, just you look at this crowd a-comin and comin. *Two* hunnerd thousand, that's a helluva lot more likely. That's what I'm bettin on."

People started singing civil rights songs and hymns. Some of them I knew, some of them I didn't. When I could, I sang the words, sometimes I hummed along.

By then, we'd been traveling five or six hours. I pulled out my second sandwich—I'd eaten my first for breakfast. Since I'd left my six-pack of beer behind on a Manhattan sidewalk, I didn't have a thing to drink. Ms. Hooper offered me a swig of her apple juice. Finally our bus, braking, rumbled off the highway and the driver started slowly working his way into the center of Washington, D.C.

Down shabby ghetto streets he steered, streets that looked nothing like the boulevards lined with imposing marble buildings that news reports on TV chose to show. They were lined with dingy row houses with two or three steps out front. This morning those steps were crowded with people in all those hues that Americans then called "Negro," from palest octaroon to melanin-drenched blue black. Poorly dressed people, their shoulders hunched, sat watching our cavalcade of vehicles pass by. And their faces were something to see. Their faces were transfigured. They were glowing as if all the lights of heaven were shining from our caravan. As if in us they saw God's messengers. *Precious Lord, take my hand, lead me on.*

The white woman with the radio said what I was thinking, "I can't believe the way they're looking at us. You'd think we were on our way to free the slaves or something."

Dark eyes reached out to us, astonished by our numbers and oh, so grateful. We waved and grinned back through the bus's windows. Probably most of these people sitting on their stoops hadn't planned to go to the rally. They'd felt too defeated, down deep in their souls, to make the effort. Now something magical sizzled between us till the air was alive with hope and an exchange of love.

5 • "I Have a Dream"

That day our bus carried a tiny fraction of the 250,000—yes, the quarter million strong—who demonstrated in the capital at the Lincoln Memorial in a massive Amen for the sisterhood and brotherhood of all. I could tell you that that day we heard powerful speeches. And moving singers. And telegrams read from the stage sent by famous people who hadn't come themselves but who wanted the world to know that they supported our goals. They wanted the world to know that they supported such daring things—at least they were daring *then*—as integrated schools and a national minimum wage and fair employment practices and government guarantees of the right to vote. This giant assemblage of ours, steeped in the principles of nonviolence, was wondrously polite and gentle and I was proud to be there, showing my solidarity as a white in a multitude that was four-fifths black.

But the program went on too long and sometimes the sound system faltered and there weren't nearly enough portable toilets and there wasn't any shade. Alas for me, I wasn't wearing a hat and I'd brought nothing to drink and, though somewhere at the far edge of this vast demonstration there might have been vendors selling sodas, I dreaded joining one of those block-long lines for a port-a-potty so I tried to hold out. And then I started getting woozy from heat exhaustion. Once before, after a day at the beach in Mexico with Robert, I'd gotten sick this way. I should have recognized the symptoms: a brutal headache, nausea, trouble thinking straight.

So by the time Martin Luther King made his famous speech, I could barely take it in. Since then, of course, like everyone else, I've heard it quoted dozens of times. "I have a dream," yes, "I have a dream." What they don't mention is what, in melodious, preacherly cadences, Dr. King said before that.

One hundred years after Lincoln freed the slaves, he said, "the Negro lives on a lonely island of poverty in the midst of a vast ocean of material prosperity.... America has given the Negro people a bad check which has come back marked 'insufficient funds.'" We've come here, he said, "to remind America of the fierce urgency of now."

Still he urged his people to "forever conduct our struggle on the high plane of dignity and discipline." And he took note of the earnest palefaces like me in the crowd, saying, "The marvelous new militancy which has engulfed the Negro community must not lead us to distrust of all white people, for many of our white brothers, as evidenced by their presence here today, have come to realize that their destiny is tied up with our destiny and their freedom is inextricably bound to our freedom. We cannot walk alone...."

At last the rally ended and, on my own in that colossal gathering, suffering from my congenitally challenged sense of direction, I struggled, sick as I felt, to find the bus I'd come on, the vehicle that would take me home. Tucked in my handbag I found a scrap of paper I'd been given with a number printed on it. That number had been pointed out to us, written on a big card posted on its windshield. The bus itself, I remembered, had been chamois color trimmed with dark red. Somewhere in that seemingly endless expanse of vehicles I managed to find it. As I was waiting to climb on, another passenger recognized me. "Oh," she exclaimed, "oh! Dr. King, wasn't he wonderful?"

I agreed feebly, wishing I'd been able to concentrate on what he was saying, wondering most of all just how sick I was, wondering whether I'd have to vomit.

As soon as I found a seat, I doubled over holding my aching head in my hands. "Are you all right?" someone asked me.

"Not really, I think I've got heatstroke."

Some kind stranger handed me a canteen full of water and gently touched his hand to my forehead, checking my temperature.

Relieved, he said, "You'll be all right."

I just had heat exhaustion, not heatstroke which would have far more serious. I would have been burning up; instead my temperature was normal. This stranger on the bus was too tactful to contradict me. Instead he urged more water on me and started to lecture me about always wearing a hat in the sun and drinking lots of fluids. He'd been a Marine, he explained. His water helped a lot. Others on the bus helped me too. By the time I got back to New York I was fine.

Ever since that day in 1963, I've bragged that when Martin Luther King gave that famous speech, I was standing there in the audience. But what I remember most is coming into Washington past those radiant, grateful people sitting on their row house steps.

6

Berkeley in the Tumultuous Sixties

I WENT BACK TO WORKING AT my job in Oakland and volunteering at the peace center in Berkeley. Odd things were stirring in that distant place called Vietnam. Twelve thousand American military had recently been stationed there. Called advisers, their mission was to strengthen the army of South Vietnam's dictatorial and corrupt government because it was anti-communist. Dominated by a Catholic minority, it was unpopular with most of its own people. The great majority were Buddhists and they demonstrated against it. Buddhist monks immolated themselves in protest, they burned themselves to death in the streets. In response government forces attacked Buddhist pagodas.

In 1963, students on campus were still taking little notice of what was happening so far away but Pick, my mentor at the peace center, did. He invited Buddhist monks to come from Vietnam and explain what was happening in their homeland and some important people took notice. One day Joan Baez walked through the center with a tall, darkly good-looking young man who seemed to be her current boyfriend. Dr. Spock, peacenik author of what was then the bible for young parents on childcare, came by when he was in the area. It felt good to be an insider in Pick's campaign against the war.

Meanwhile, it was fun to be living in Berkeley. Life was free and easy. Rules were different here from the rest of the country which was pretty conventional in the early sixties. Here young people who weren't married might wear wedding bands; girls who were married often didn't wear rings. And people shared houses and apartments with whomever they liked. Guys and girls lived together, whether or not they were romantically involved.

In those days Telegraph Avenue, gateway to the campus, was an amiable street of tasteful restaurants, most of them inexpensive, plus a handy five-and-ten-cent store, a couple of banks, and a muted collage of understated shops that sold casual clothes and pretty things from far-off places. Against this serene backdrop, Berkeley's young adults—privileged and mannerly—quietly did as they damn well pleased.

If you were young in Berkeley, people assumed you were bright and knew how to behave so people gave "open parties." They invited their friends as party-givers always do but after 11 p.m. they opened their doors to whoever showed up. Crashing was accepted, crashing was good, cross-pollination among the select.

That fall I met Howard Wright at a Berkeley party. Five minutes after we met, I told him that my previous marriage had come apart amicably because I wanted to have a child and my husband didn't. Recently divorced, Howard was a zoologist who taught at St. Mary's, a small college east of Oakland. He had two small daughters he doted on. Given his modest salary, he felt burdened by his obligation to pay their mother alimony and child support; nonetheless he courted me. He started taking me to showings of old silent movies and folk music concerts on campus, and on hikes to beautiful beaches on the California coast.

He wasn't moody like Martinson. And if he wasn't as handsome and towering as Bob, still he was moderately tall and rangy and that was one of my addictions. He was helpful around the house, cheerful about washing dishes when I had him over for dinner. This new man in my life was easy and fun to be with and, though I still wasn't over my passion for Bob, as months went by in Howard's company I found myself falling in love with him.

That November, not long after Martinson's son, Michael, was born he sent me a gloomy letter.

"Things are not really going exactly right but they could be worse. Health-OK; Job-soso; Mike-fine. Me? I'm still in one piece and sociologizing criminology-wise.

"Hardly ever get to the Bay Area any more. I miss it and Berkeley generally.... Once in a while I get a word through from TTP but nothing has your name on it and I don't know if someone is ghosting for you [on the newsletter I still wrote for Turn Toward Peace.]

"This is a grey and sullen day. I need a haircut; I feel grimy as if I got off a freight and stepped into this grim office full of grim people. I'm just WORKING but not making any progress. Know what I mean?

"I hope you are fine."

Then he signed his name "Bob" with an elegant, arty flourish.

I didn't answer.

HOWARD WAS A WONDERFUL OUTDOORSMAN, THE only one I'd ever known. He'd grown up as the eldest boy of six children living on rented farms all over the Great Plains. He loved wilderness and it held no terrors for him. I was a strong hiker—though, alas, I had virtually no sense of direction. I trusted him to take care of me in wild places. Soon, generally with another experienced hiker or two, we went backpacking and camping in the California mountains. These were thrilling new experiences for me.

Back in Berkeley we moved into a little rental house. It was a pleasure for me to start spending time with Howard's two towheaded daughters. Every Tuesday night they had dinner with us, every Saturday we spent most of the day as a family. Eager as I was to have a child of my own, I cherished his daughters as I practiced being their surrogate parent.

Early in 1964 I got a letter from Martinson, forwarded from my old address. He said he'd left Rita. He didn't say he loved me but he did say he missed me and he wanted to see me the next time he came to town. On some level I wanted him to woo me back, to make some effort to win me away from the man I'd gotten involved with on the rebound from him. But the letter I wrote him was full of reproaches.

I told him quite a bit about my relationship with Howard. "We started living together a few weeks after we met so by now we know each other pretty well. I've often wished I'd had a chance to get to know you one half as well, to spend weeks or at least weekends with you. But even when that might have been feasible you shied away."

Still I said I would like to see him again. I gave him my work address and phone number so he could contact me and not alert Howard. But

Martinson didn't write and he didn't phone. I wouldn't hear his voice again until 1967.

MEANWHILE HOWARD AND I TACKLED A different challenge. Like lots of other men in town, Howard was ABD. A gifted student with an almost photographic memory, he'd attended the University of Kansas on a four-year scholarship that each year was awarded to only sixteen high school seniors in the state. At the University of California he'd finished all the coursework for his PhD but he'd never written a dissertation.

In my helpmate way I eased him toward earning a doctorate—something he needed if he was to go on teaching at the college level. Adding my modest income to his gave him a sense of security. And my matter-of-fact confidence that he would earn his degree seemed to give him a push he wanted and needed.

Howard was an animal behaviorist; he specialized in studying shore crabs. He'd go off to the coast, recording his observations carefully in ink in a special kind of notebook that he told me scientists used. It had a sewn binding so he couldn't tear out a page without leaving a mark.

By the spring of 1964, he'd finally decided what to work on for his dissertation. I'd told him that south of the border, the living was fun and cheap so he decided he'd study shore crabs just south of Mazatlán. As soon as Howard turned in his grades for spring semester at St. Mary's, he kissed me goodbye and started driving his ancient Chevy south to Mexico.

FREEDOM SUMMER CAME ON. STUDENTS FROM all over the country streamed down to join grassroots groups in a heroic effort to register Mississippi's long disenfranchised blacks to vote. Many of these plucky kids would be assaulted and brutalized there. At least three would be killed. Most would come back fiercely determined to change and improve the nation, using the tactics of militant nonviolence.

That summer, other issues disquieted Berkeley. For four days in mid-July, the Republican National Convention was held across the bay in San Francisco. On the Cal campus, moderate Republicans fumed that the convention was rigged to nominate Barry Goldwater, the most rightwing of the candidates—though he seemed to think that if people were poor they deserved to be and that legislating civil rights would be downright impolite. He also seemed more likely than his main opponent, Governor Scranton of Pennsylvania, to expand America's excursion into the jungles of Vietnam.

Campus Republicans set up a table just outside the university's Sather Gate to recruit students to go to the convention across the bay and demonstrate there for Scranton, the less warlike candidate. But not only was Goldwater's floor manager, former Senator Knowland, the publisher of the conservative daily newspaper in Berkeley's neighbor city—he was also a member of the university's board of regents. Knowland threw his weight around, Goldwater won the nomination. In response, activist students organized picket lines outside his *Oakland Tribune*. Twice I joined them, protesting its policies of racial discrimination.

Still mostly that summer, my heart was in Mexico with Howard. Like me, he was fiercely political. He'd been active in CORE (the Congress of Racial Equality) in Kansas in the late Forties before most people had ever heard of it. But that summer he was doing his research thing, 1,400 miles away. We'd agreed that if his research went well there, we'd get married when he returned—though I wouldn't dare get pregnant till he was sure he'd earned his PhD. That summer we corresponded almost every day. I located an agreeable Unitarian minister, then Howard and I set a date. But first I went down to Mexico to visit him.

Howard picked me up at the Mazatlán airport to drive me further south to San Blas, a village on the coast where he'd rented a small house. On the way down, he told me less than glowing stories of what it would be like. There was this iguana that lived on the ceiling, he said, and hordes of "American" roaches, far larger than the roaches, technically called "European," that people encountered routinely in New York. The iguana turned out to be entertaining. The living room ceiling was a huge sheet of canvas suspended from the roof. When the iguana wasn't out foraging, it lived on top of this cloth so I never actually saw it. All you could see when it was up there was the impression of its skinny-toed paws as it padded around. The roaches, however, were another matter.

They were huge, about two inches long and almost an inch wide, and they moved and waved their long antennae more slowly, almost meditatively than the New York variety. Howard had managed to banish most of them from the front of the house. But to use the bathroom at the rear took a special act of will. Clearly to these beasties, we were the interlopers. We were bigger than they were but they outnumbered us greatly. Eventually we'd leave, they knew, and they'd be in charge again.

Howard's undergraduate major had been entomology, the study of bugs—not all that far removed from the crabs he was studying now. In his academic wanderings he'd also picked up a master's in political science but then he'd returned to what you might call his first love. Far be it from me to judge how in his heart of hearts he felt about subjecting me to these creatures. Suffice it to say that, as our relationship matured, I would sense much that was passive-aggressive about him. Such insights however would come much later.

We stayed just a couple of days in shabby, muddy San Blas, Nayarit, on the Pacific. Then we started touristing about. Southeast we drove up into mountains, to Guadalajara, that beautiful old, provincial city. Then on to Pátzcuaro and its mile-high lake surrounded by volcanoes where the fishermen's graceful nets, bound to double hooped frames, looked like giant butterflies. Soon we were in Mexico City. There we visited wondrous museums and saw the artful Ballet Folklorico.

On our way back to San Blas we parked in yet another village and got out. Children, barefoot or wearing cheap huaraches surrounded us to beg. Then an old man came who was blind and he did a curious thing. He walked the length of the car slowly, touching it reverently. As he held out his hand for money he said in Spanish, "Please, please, you are rich. We are poor." And of course in a way he was right, though on American streets a car like ours advertised its owner's financial distress.

In those days, cars weren't manufactured in Mexico. To buy one, you had to pay an import duty of 100% so each cost twice what it did in the States and relatively few people owned any kind of vehicle. Now that's all changed. Mexico is full of cars, especially in the cities. And the sweet mountain air I remember in its capital is only too often gravely polluted.

ON SEPTEMBER 19TH, AFTER HOWARD DROVE back to Berkeley, we got married as we'd planned. My dark hair by then fell below my waist when

I didn't have it pulled back in a ponytail as I did that day; Howard had a beard. We got married on Carmel Highlands beach, not far from Monterey. "On the Saturday of the Jazz Festival," the local newpaper reported, someone sitting on the porch of his home near the shore saw a small wedding party making their way to the beach. "They were all slicked up in sheath dresses, dark suits, flowers in buttonholes and a few beards. They arrived at the beach, took off their shoes, and ankle deep in sand, the bride and groom were married on the spot."

From Carmel Highlands we drove to Nepenthe, the fabled restaurant first built as a private lodge by Orson Welles to be a hideaway for him to share with Rita Hayworth. A surpassing place, all redwood and glass, it sits high on a Big Sur cliff that commands a wide view of the ocean and looks south to lushly wooded headlands that reach westward into the surf. From there we drove inland to hike and camp in the Sierra Madre mountains near Santa Maria. Then we returned to Berkeley and growing turmoil there.

7

The Free Speech Movement and the VDC

AT FIRST IT WASN'T ABOUT THE Vietnam War. Civil rights was the issue that started the tumult in Berkeley, that and the fact that on September 14th the Dean of Students at the university banished all the tables set up by campaigners outside Sather Gate. That strip of pavement, she said, was actually part of campus and it was against university rules to recruit or raise money on campus for an off-campus cause. Suddenly groups like CORE and SNCC—the Student Nonviolent Coordinating Committee, usually referred to as "Snick"— were forbidden to table there, were forbidden to collect funds or volunteers to help in the battle for racial equality. But of course some young rebels disobeyed the rules.

On October first, Jack Weinberg, a former graduate student, was challenged for staffing a table for CORE. When he refused to show his ID to campus police, he was arrested and put into a Berkeley police car. If they'd driven off as expected, that would have been the end of it but there were lots of students nearby and some quick-thinking activist yelled, "Sit down!"

So began a historic sit-in that lasted for 32 hours and at one time involved an estimated 3,000 participants—and many more than that in all. The kids sitting on the ground could come and go freely. People wandered off, they ran around campus and the surrounding community urging more and more to join the protest. Some went and bought food, then came back to share bags of potato chips, cookies, pretzels,

7 • The Free Speech Movement and the VDC

whatever, with other demonstrators, some of whom came bearing sleeping bags. Meanwhile the cop car couldn't budge, the cops were the prisoners, forced to listen to a procession of speakers who climbed on top of their vehicle to further fire up the crowd. For the young people surrounding them it was a picnic, a party, a place to make new friends. Hey, suddenly politics could be fun, politics Berkeley style.

That's when the Free Speech Movement erupted. At first it was a coalition of political groups that ranged from the Campus Young Republicans chapter on the right through Democrats, Trotskyites and Maoists on the left. More vast sit-ins ensued, most famously inside the administration building. Thousands of neatly dressed, un-hippie-looking students got involved. Hundreds got arrested, but soon they were released. All over town, thousands of us wore buttons that said BAN THE BAN.

It was 1964—and the times really were a-changing. The New Left was muscling to the forefront of the news leaving old style liberals and radicals—people like my friends Bob Martinson and Bob Pickus—struggling to redefine themselves and find their place in the picture.

Whenever I strayed onto campus around lunchtime, students—often girls—were leafleting and some guy or other was making a speech. And always the media were conspicuously lurking. Tall, hefty men carrying heavy video cameras on their shoulders competed with one another, catching the action for the 6 o'clock news. Footage they shot was broadcast all over the country and because it was, more and more kids became activists and the organizers of the protests became more and more confident. To keep the nation's eyes on Berkeley, they grew ever more creative.

Alas, for the time being, Howard and I didn't get to play much of a part. That fall I started looking for a full-time job so I could make more money. That way my new husband could cut back on his teaching load and concentrate on writing his dissertation. When the Oakland Library offered me a position as a senior librarian, I quit my part-time job at the trade association and trained a new person to edit the peace center's newsletter. By winter, I'd quit working there.

Every month that passed, my old mentor at the center seemed less and less relevant. To most of the progressives we knew in town, his careful non-Communist line seemed like old fashioned red-baiting. In the past, like Pick, I might have worried about the role of the sprinkling of Communists—mostly "red diaper babies," the children of party faithful—who were openly participating in campus actions. I might have worried that their presence would discredit those actions or that they would successfully take the movement over, twisting its goals. But this New Left that was a-growing was decidedly something else. Why worry? Its wild and sassy young people had erected a gloriously big tent, a tent so big and inviting that it easily encompassed doctrinaire militants and blindly anti-establishment crazies and a rollicking mix of almost everything in between. Far away in Washington—and further away in Vietnam—events were conspiring to make their troop of adherents even bigger.

The previous August, Congress had passed the Gulf of Tonkin Resolution. On the basis of charges that North Vietnamese torpedo boats had attacked an American destroyer—charges that most historians now agree were trumped up—this congressional resolution empowered President Johnson to "take all necessary measures to repel an armed attack against the forces of the United States and to prevent further aggression." In the November presidential election, Johnson defeated Goldwater. But it soon became clear that he was as likely to expand the role of our military in Vietnam as Goldwater might have been. Marine and Air Force units were deployed to its shores; then Johnson authorized their use for offensive operations.

On April 1, 1965, a thousand students at the University of Wisconsin attended a 10-hour "teach-in" against the Vietnam War, the first of its kind. Not to be outdone, Free Speech Movement leaders organized a teach-in of their own. They called it Vietnam Day. It went on for 35 hours from May 21st through May 22nd and showcased nationally known anti-war speakers. At some point during those two days, at least 20,000 of us attended.

Howard was 34 and a veteran—he'd served Stateside in the army during the Korean War. As a result he had no fear of being drafted but all around us grad students, dropouts and other young ex-students did. (College undergraduates were exempt from the draft—but most of us found *that* offensively classist.) The fear and rage of the potential draftees around us was palpable. With that Vietnam Day teach-in, its organizers launched their sparkling new Vietnam Day Committee.

7 • The Free Speech Movement and the VDC

This is the group that launched those great, historic marches you still see on TV. And of course Howard and I joined in and so did all our friends and practically all our young neighbors and some older people too. Thousands more drove in from nearby places. Together we filled the streets with our homemade signs and our righteous anger. We marched burning with indignation and sensing strength in our multitude.

"Hey, hey, LBJ,

"How many kids did you kill today?"

Our chants rang out. They echoed up and down the avenues. Once, when the police arrested a leading activist, a thorn in their side, for jaywalking—jaywalking!—Howard and I chipped in more than we could afford to pay his bail. And when the cops tried to cut us all off or turn us around, we marchers chanted, "The whole world is watching, the whole world is watching." Because indeed that seemed to be true.

ONE NIGHT MY FATHER PHONED ME from New York. Usually he sent letters. Long distance phone calls cost a lot in those days but this time he splurged and phoned. "How come I'm always hearing about that pipsqueak town you live in?" he teased me. He still believed in his heart of hearts that New York was the center of the universe but he was thrilled that people in far-off Berkeley were speaking out against that god-awful war, old socialist and humanist that he was.

He was lonely, I guessed. My older brother and Bernice lived not many miles from him—still he missed my mother, no matter how turbulent their relationship had been.

When I saw her in the summer of 1962, she'd confided to me in a whisper, "Last winter some terrible things happened to me. Terrible things ..." She shuddered at recollections she wouldn't describe further. Was she talking about mini-strokes? "But I came through," she said, still trusting in Christian Science. Two years later, her lifelong disregard for her body's needs would catch up with her. She died three days after I married Howard.

SOON I STARTED WORKING FULL-TIME AT a branch of the Oakland Public Library. Once in a while, by way of nightlife, we drank beer or wine and danced at the Steppenwolf, the "in" tavern where Berkeley's young leftists congregated. (There a few years later, Mario Savio—the fabled orator of the Free Speech Movement and soon thereafter a Rhodes scholar—would tend bar after he returned from Oxford.) I'd just gone on "the pill." The high dosage of that new contraceptive made me clingy and a bit depressed. I had little time or energy for political action aside from joining the occasional peace march.

The next summer, Howard and I visited an older man I knew from work in his small, comfortably furnished house in Oakland. Claude was the library's maintenance man, a courtly, well-read brown-skinned person caught in the trap of being a "Negro." His menial job at the library paid reasonably well and offered benefits that at that time he probably couldn't have found elsewhere. Early that summer he and his wife, a clerical worker for the city, took a trip across the country. Soon after he returned to the library, he invited all of us on the staff to come and see his slides. I tell you this because this seemingly mundane event marked a remarkable transformation in America.

Two years before in his "I have a dream" speech, Dr. King had railed against the fact that blacks, "heavy with the fatigue of travel, [could not] gain lodging in the motels of the highways and the hotels of the cities." The Civil Rights Act passed in 1964 brought about an extraordinary sea change. This act outlawed Jim Crow laws in the South, racial segregation in schools, and discrimination in public accommodations like restaurants and hotels. Racists would circumvent some features of the law. But hoteliers and restaurant owners were delighted to comply with it, effortlessly increasing their clientele. That's why Claude and his wife decided to take their trip and afterwards proudly showed us their slides.

The times indeed were a-changing. But unfortunately the Vietnam War kept growing and growing. The Vietnam Day Committee organized protests and Howard and I kept marching in them but thrilling as they were, and cathartic too, for those of us who marched in them, how much good were they really doing? When would there be an end to the pointless slaughter and devastation that, in the name of preserving some indeterminate "American way of life," was bloodying and poisoning jungles faraway?

The VDC was governed by what they called participatory democracy. Whoever showed up for their evening meetings was welcome to

7 • The Free Speech Movement and the VDC

sit in. One night the two of us tried to take part but because already so much had happened, it was hard to follow the arguments. While theorizing and wrangling went on into the night I, a total morning person with a job to get up for the next day, left Howard behind so I could go and sleep in the car. Soon he joined me and drove us home.

EARLY THAT WINTER HOWARD FINISHED HIS dissertation. I edited it for him. He still had a few minor hoops to jump through at the university but at last he was confident that soon he'd get his PhD. Happily I went off the pill; finally we could try to get pregnant.

Howard applied for a prestigious post-doctoral fellowship offered by the Smithsonian Tropical Research Institute. If it came through, we would live in Panama for the next academic year so Howard could study tropical crabs on both coasts of the isthmus. Meanwhile, at the recommendation of his thesis adviser, he was offered a summer teaching position at the University of California, Santa Barbara. "The way it works," he told me, "if the department likes me, there's a pretty good chance they'll offer me a permanent job." That would be quite a plum. Everyone said it was a beautiful area in which to live and work. In mid-April we learned that he'd won the fellowship in Panama. Then I learned I was pregnant and due to give birth at Christmastime. I couldn't have been happier. I was riding high.

I quit my job to get ready for our move to Santa Barbara and hang out for a while. Now I had time to help out the VDC at its offices in an old frame house. A jauntily lettered sticker on the refrigerator said "Legalize Everything." The phone kept ringing, often with calls from the media. One day I folded fliers and stuffed envelopes for a huge mailing that asked for contributions. Another time, right before a march, I was one of three volunteers who painted signs. The guys who debated fine points of tactics set us loose to use their poster paint and brushes to paint any signs we wanted. A big sign propped against a wall gave me chills. I wondered about the suffering woman who had made it.

> **I AM A GOLD STAR MOTHER**
> **MY SON DIED IN VAIN**
> **BOYS REFUSE TO GO TO VIETNAM**
> **AND KILL CHILDREN**

One Sunday morning when Howard and I were driving with his kids near the headquarters of the Vietnam Day Committee, we saw a crowd gathering. Curious, we parked and got out. That's when we found out that someone had planted a bomb there and wrecked the place. Shards of shattered window glass glittered all over the sidewalk and over people's yards for hundreds of feet. Everywhere you looked, women with brooms were sweeping it away. Their windows, too, had been blown out. Tight lipped, they ignored the crowd around the VDC building. On its front steps stood a big cop, an inspector in civvies and a few VDC stalwarts. A sign that said VDC ACTIVISTS, then supplied a phone number, hung outside. Howard wandered off to talk to a friend, he left me with his daughters.

"Did anyone get hurt?" I asked spectators clustered nearby.

It was eerie to see the wreckage of that house where I'd volunteered.

"No," some stranger answered, "they blew it up when no one was around. But the bastards sure did a number on the place! Have you looked around back?"

The girls and I made our way through a crush of people, circling around to where most of the damage had been done. You couldn't get real close, the area was roped off and a policeman was standing guard, but mountains of litter seemed to fill it inside. A jumble of waste paper and splintered wood was all you could see beyond its shattered window frames. God, I thought, what's become of all their records? Their files, their lists of donors, their eccentrically organized clutter of letters and telegrams from supporters around the world? Outside lay crazily tilted piles of lumber that once must have been back steps or a back wall. Pipes were broken, sections flung askew.

"Ee-yooo, it's icky here," Roxy said, distaste wrinkling her cute little nose, "Do we have to stay here?"

"Yeah, it's icky here," her kid sister echoed. "Can't we just go to your place, Big Sylvia?"

"Later, kidlet," I tickled her under her armpits. She giggled.

"Anyhow, we're waiting for your dad," I said. "Remember those marches we've gone on against the war?"

Of course, they remembered. They were fun family expeditions for us all.

"Well, the group that organized them used to work in that house. Looks like some pretty bad people bombed it but, thank God, nobody got hurt."

"Did they catch the bad guys?"

I shrugged, "Don't think so. At least not yet."

Howard came back. As he started to greet us, a newcomer to the little patch of trampled yard where we were standing asked him, "You a vet?"

"Yeah."

"Me too," the stranger said, as if that made them buddies.

"Makes you sick, doesn't it, to hear them all whining and not a damn soul even injured. Jesus, when I was in Saigon, the gooks blew the officers' billets up. Bodies all over. These jerk-offs, they don't know shit."

Then taking note of me and the girls, he said, "Begging your pardon, ma'am."

Howard and I didn't answer him, this supporter of the war. The four of us left him behind before it could dawn on him which side we were on.

IN JUNE WE MOVED DOWN TO a new suburb of Santa Barbara. There we settled for the length of the summer session into a nicely furnished two-bedroom apartment in a lushly landscaped garden court with a pool. Howard's first wife had agreed to let his daughters stay with us there so we arranged for them to attend a nearby half-day program. As I started growing into my new wardrobe of budget maternity clothes, I looked forward to the four of us doing things together and enjoying being a family. But soon I sensed that something was wrong.

Howard acted distant or wasn't present at all. He spent lots of time at his office on campus—at least that's where he said he was. One day when he came home for dinner, he was wearing an expensive looking sport shirt I'd never seen before. When I asked him about it, he hesitated, then said, "Oh, you remember Sally, Phyllis's friend."

I nodded. I hardly knew the girl; she was a few years younger than I.

"Well, Sally has a new boyfriend," he explained, fumbling with change in his pants pocket, not looking at me. "She bought these two shirts for him but they didn't fit him so she thought I could use them."

"Really?" I asked a bit testily. "So there's another one too?"

"Yes, there's another one. She mailed them to me at the office."

The kids were listening. I shut up for the time being though the story sounded weird. Phyllis was an old friend of Howard's, one of a circle of people that we hung out with. Like me, Phyllis came from a Jewish background but she was a natural blonde and very tall, over six feet, taller than Howard. That's why I'd believed from the start that, as he insisted, he and Phyllis had never been lovers, just chums for years before we met. I knew and liked her current partner. As for Sally, I recalled her only as a good looking, quiet person I'd never been able to have a real conversation with. Like Phyllis she was tall and blonde but she was three or four inches shorter than Howard.

Later when the kids weren't around, I asked him, "So who's Sally's new boyfriend?" He shrugged as if he didn't know. "What difference does it make?" he said.

I took pride in not being a scold as my mother had been so I dropped the subject and put it out of my mind. Then one evening a week or so later, Howard did another disturbing thing. When the four of us were gathered in our living room, he switched on the tape recorder we'd been studying Spanish with, in preparation for our move to Panama. Suddenly, instead of the language lessons we usually heard from it, it was repeating a family conversation we'd had a few days before.

"Listen to yourself," he said to me in his most didactic, professorial manner. "You don't know how it bothers people to have to listen to you when you talk that way, screaming that way at us."

"Screaming?" I asked, once I'd finally figured out what he was talking about. "That's not screaming. I didn't raise my voice. Maybe I sounded a little pissed but I wasn't screaming. You don't know what screaming is."

"Oh yes I do," he asserted in his even, Midwestern tones, "like that time when we were hiking."

Immediately I knew what he was talking about—because I'd only truly screamed at him once in the two and a half years we'd been together. I'd tripped over a tree root and almost gone over the side of a mountain trail into a canyon. Shaken, I'd stumbled over to a big fallen log, taken off my pack, sat down and leaned back against it, resting. Before I'd quite caught my breath and regained the confidence to go on, Howard had come over to me and started clumsily trying to help me back into my pack. That's when I exploded, "Hey, for godsake, gimme another minute. Jesus Christ! Whew!"

He shrank away from me, backing up the trail. After a moment he said, "Don't you ever talk to me that way again," in that flat yet intense voice he sometimes used. "You don't know how it makes me feel when somebody yells at me that way."

I'd always known we came from different backgrounds with different norms. After that incident we made peace somehow. I never yelled at him again, it was easy. Almost all my adult life I'd worked at public service jobs—mostly in libraries, no less—where you didn't dare raise your voice or visibly lose your temper. I knew how to maintain the appearance of calm. But now he was raising the ante. No matter how furious I might be—and I reserved the right to get angry sometimes—like the Midwestern WASP he was and I would never be, I should never show anger in my voice.

It didn't seem to count to him that I was dealing with the mood swings of pregnancy and taking care of his kids, who had never lived with us before. I felt he was being unreasonable. Still after that evening, I tried hard to please him. I'd started thinking: Three strikes and you're out.

I was 33 years old and I'd been married three times. I'd known before I married Herb that I'd probably leave him. I'd loved Robert but I'd let my marriage to him slip away because I wanted a kid, he didn't, and I was enthralled by Berkeley, the peace center and Martinson. Now Howard's baby was growing inside me. And Howard was brilliant and politically progressive; during our first two years together he'd been a pleasure to live with. Now his career seemed to be taking off. I really wanted this marriage to last.

The summer session ended. Soon Howard's fellowship in Panama would begin. The problem, he told me, was that he had lab equipment he needed to take down. Now he was driving a newer car, a bright red Ford. He thought he could make it there in time driving thousands of miles southeast, diagonally across Mexico, then all the way through Central America down the Pan American Highway. We both knew it wouldn't be easy. Long stretches of that road weren't finished; parts of it were hardly roads at all. It was the kind of adventure he loved and I loved that spirit in him but by now I was over five months pregnant. Neither of us thought it was safe for me to make that wild trip with him.

So we agreed that he'd leave as soon as possible while I stayed on in our little rented house, packing up some of our things and arranging for most of them to go into storage. Late in August, I flew east to New York to briefly visit family and friends. Then early in September Howard met me at the airport in Panama. The airport was air-conditioned but outside, a smothering cloak of heat and humidity wrapped itself around me. They say that in the final months of pregnancy, you feel five or ten degrees warmer than you ordinarily would. That would be the least of my problems in Panama.

8

Panama: Introduction to the Third World

Howard took me to the attractive furnished apartment he'd rented for us in Panama City. On our side of a newly laid out street stood a row of boxy, modern looking houses, all white and three or four stories high. On the other side of the street lay an unpaved field with a few shacks clustered together two hundred feet away. Brown-skinned figures, dimly seen, lived in them.

Our place was one flight up in a handsome new building. It was inviting with terrazzo floors—pale marble chips laid in mastic and then polished to glistening smoothness. The simple furniture, locally made, was heavily varnished to protect the wood from mold and rot and whatever beasties might thrive in the tropics. The bedroom was air-conditioned and though the rest of the house was not, all its windows were fitted with horizontal slats of textured glass—translucent but not transparent—set in louvered frames to entice in every breeze. To top all this off, this apartment had a working phone, no small thing in Panama in those days long before cell phones.

Welcome to the Third World. For reasons of bureaucracy, corruption or lack of equipment—who knew?—it took a year to have a phone installed. Yes, a year or more. Best to rent a place that had a phone already. "It cost a little more," Howard said, "but seeing as how you're pregnant and might need to call me or call a cab, I figured it was kind of a necessity." Which was certainly true.

The next day, with a troubling lack of enthusiasm, he showed me around Old Panama, the picturesque part of town built by Spanish conquerors back in the sixteenth century. Obviously he'd seen it already. Then he started disappearing for much of the time, as he had in Santa Barbara, except that now he went off with a pair of binoculars slung around his neck, presumably to study crab behavior. Well, that was what he'd come to Panama to do. Soon he would have to write scholarly articles about his observations. The watchword for young professors like him was "publish or perish." Even when he came home for dinner, he seemed oddly distant.

Two of the top scientists from the Institute had us over to their homes. Their wives advised me about getting by and perhaps even thriving in Panama City. Soon we reciprocated and had them over for dinner. Their opinions of Howard were important, they were bound to affect his career.

I took classes in Spanish at the local Instituto Panameño Norteamericano, a low-profile arm of the U.S. Agency for International Development. The classes were unchallenging—our verbs never ventured beyond the present tense—but at least I picked up fluency with some elementary phrases. Armed with a pocket Spanish-English dictionary, I wandered around town on foot and by bus, exploring. Most of the city's workaday streets were lined with low frame buildings, each of them painted in two or three weather-beaten colors: orange and yellow alongside aqua and peach, mostly peeling and roofed with corrugated metal. Some of the older ones, like those in the French Quarter of New Orleans, had second story balconies trimmed with lacy ironwork; they perched precariously on spindly pillars.

On Avenida Central, the rundown-looking main drag, vendors sold incense or lottery numbers, lots of lottery numbers. People browsed from table to table where lottery slips lay side by side, searching for that special number that would bring them wealth. Almost nowhere did I run across inviting restaurants or shops but of course, I figured, I was still a stranger here. Eventually Howard and I were bound to find lots of fun places to go in Panama City.

THE OFFICES FOR THE INSTITUTE WERE in the Canal Zone. Its smooth roads were flanked by unrelentingly clipped green lawns that went on for

8 • Panama: Introduction to the Third World

miles. They were dotted with royal palms, all about the same size, posted beside the road at regular intervals. The bottom eight feet or so of their thick trunks were painted white; they stood perpetually at attention like sailors in summer uniform.

Every few days, Howard would drop me off at the commissary to go grocery shopping while he went on to the Institute to pick up our mail. (We weren't eligible to shop at the PX because Howard was a civilian. For buying American products at reasonable prices, the commissary was the next best thing.) One day, coming back with several mysterious letters for himself and just one for me, he pulled a bumper sticker from his back pocket. It read MAKE LOVE NOT WAR. It was the first time I'd ever seen the slogan. In October 1966 in this military outpost, it sounded confrontational and a bit risqué.

"Where'd you get *that?*" I asked him.

At first he didn't answer. Then he said, looking slantwise and down at the floor, "You remember Sally? Phyllis's friend? Sally sent it."

"You want to put it on the car? It'll make a lot of people mad," I said.

"It's the latest thing in Berkeley."

Howard stuffed the bumper sticker back in his pocket. "Let's go sit down," he said.

Not far from the commissary was a big cafeteria. Both were run by the Panama Canal Company. The PCC ran practically everything in the Zone that the Army didn't run. Whatever it ran was utilitarian, characterless and ugly—which pretty much sums up how this lunchroom looked.

We got coffee and pie. The crust of the pie was soggy and its fruit filling was surrounded by gelatinous glop.

"I've got something to tell you," Howard said, still averting his eyes from me. "I can't go on in this marriage, I really can't. At least I can't go on for long. Having the baby was *your* idea."

"For godsake, I told you I wanted to have a kid five minutes after we met."

I was struggling to follow what he was saying and somehow keep calm.

Howard swallowed, his Adam's apple wobbled, then he started again. "Having the baby was your idea. It's too late now for you to get rid of it but maybe you should think about giving it up for adoption. You'd be such a terrible mother, Phyllis and I are sure of that."

"My God. Phyllis said that? Since when does she know me that well and who gives her the right ...? And after all the time I've spent with your kids! All the time you've been *glad* to have me spend with your kids—but hey, this isn't about Phyllis—it's about Sally, isn't it?"

"Well, the fact is I'm in love with Sally and she loves me too."

Aha! So now the truth was out. He must be corresponding almost daily with her as he had with me when he was away in San Blas. Except that now he wanted to dump me for an all-American trophy blonde, now that he had his PhD in hand, the degree I'd helped him get. It was just another variation on a classic tale. We'd both seen loads of Berkeley marriages split up as soon as the husband got his degree after his wife put him through school. He'd let me stay on with him till summer, he said, till I was ready to move on with my infant child. The saddest part was that I was still in love with him and I was frantic to save our marriage.

Howard was incapable of full-fledged confrontation and I guess, alone with me here in Panama, he had no one else to turn to. Maybe he even loved me in his fashion. For the next few weeks he almost never mentioned that he wanted to end our marriage. We kept on doing things together, we seemed to be getting along. I cherished the hope that once our baby was born, he'd change his mind.

At Christmastime, I managed to find some greens in the commissary to decorate our living room along with ornaments I'd brought from the States. The neat, tile-roofed private homes in the fashionable part of town blazed with lights. Often an almost life-size image of Santa Claus smiled benevolently from the front door. Santa bundled up in his fur-trimmed costume looked surreal here in the tropics. But then lots of things were surreal about Panama. Out in the harbor, tankers, freighters, destroyers and ocean liners sat in a long row, motionless, waiting for their turns to go through the canal. Looking inland away from the ocean, you saw ships seeming to shear their way through the ground.

As my due date approached, we arranged for me to give birth in Gorgas Hospital. It was an immaculate facility in the Zone named for the American doctor who sixty years earlier had eradicated yellow fever and malaria in the area, enabling the completion of the Canal. Howard was slated to travel back to the States around the time I was due to give birth. Since UC Santa Barbara hadn't offered him to keep him on, he

8 • Panama: Introduction to the Third World

didn't have a teaching position lined up for next fall. He would have to attend a conference to find himself a job. This year, the Christmas meetings of what he called "the meat market" for zoologists were being held in Berkeley.

In mid-December we hired a maid, Victoria, to keep me company while he was away and to wash diapers once the baby was born. (Disposable diapers were not yet available in Panama.) We could have hired one much earlier if that had suited our style. Howard was paid $10,000 a year, half again as much as most post-docs received in the States. The going rate for servants was $30 a month. The people we met socially, all of whom had servants, urged us not to offer more money to the maid we hired, no matter how unfair the going rate sounded. "These poor country girls, they're grateful just to have free meals and a roof over their head."

The maid we hired wasn't desperate and we didn't hire her to live with us and be on call all the time. Victoria was a middle-aged, plump West Indian woman married to a man who worked in the Zone. Her kids were grown, she got bored just sitting home, and she loved babies. We hired Victoria to come in for a few hours daily on weekdays and do our wash.

I gave birth on December 24th. Howard visited me in the maternity ward and seemed pleased that I'd had a boy. We agreed to name him Rustin for Bayard Rustin and planned to call him Rusty while he was little. At that time our baby's namesake was a little known but influential black civil rights activist and pacifist credited with being the prime organizer of the 1963 March on Washington where Martin Luther King had made his famous speech. Years later he would be an elder statesman whom congressmen invited to address their committees.

The next day Howard flew to California for the meetings. Two days later I returned to my pretty apartment in Panama City and to Victoria. She was a warmhearted, reassuring presence who loved to cuddle Rusty and cluck over him. Much of the time she just sat and crocheted or read the local English language newspaper published by and for the West Indian minority. The meetings in Berkeley were supposed to end in a couple of days. Howard should be returning then.

I breastfed, healed and learned how to change diapers. Victoria cheerfully boiled water to wash them, then hung the clean ones up to dry on our balcony. Panamanian balconies were generally festooned with laundry, even outside elegant homes.

A long week passed and Howard didn't come home; he didn't phone. Then I got an unsettling call from the Institute. He hadn't picked up his monthly check, they said. What, they asked, should they do with it? Should they mail it to him at his address in Berkeley? I gulped, then asked them what that address was.

It was Sally's address. Now I knew he was staying with her. I had no idea if and when he'd return—still I asked them to hold his check for him. That's when I did what I'd never dreamt of doing before; I drove our red Ford to his office in Balboa and started going through his desk. I found no evidence that he was working on a scholarly paper. Instead, stuffed in his desk's big bottom drawer were dozens of letters from Sally.

That afternoon the office that he shared was empty except for me. One of the things my upbringing had taught me was that it is never honorable to read someone else's letters. But this time, I thought, what choice did I have? I needed to know what Howard was thinking and what he'd been doing behind my back.

The most astonishing thing I learned was that Sally had ridden down to Panama with him. He hadn't needed to carry down lab equipment. He'd just brought along his latest love to make that wild journey with him down the Pan American Highway. She'd stayed on with him in Panama City for a couple of days; they'd toured around together. No wonder that when he showed me around Old Panama, he seemed remote and preoccupied.

A few days later, Howard showed up.

"So you came back," I said, feeling more wary than relieved.

"Of course, I came back. This is my home," he said as if nothing was wrong. "How's Rusty?"

"He's fine. Go, see for yourself."

I nodded toward our bedroom where our son lay sleeping in his bassinet.

"I thought you'd never come back," I said, struggling to keep my voice steady. "I know where you've been. I know you've been staying with Sally."

8 • Panama: Introduction to the Third World

For a couple of minutes he stood beside his son, gently stroking his hair and his fingers and whispering. Then he went to the kitchen, fixed himself a sandwich, and poured himself a glass of orange juice. That's when I told him that I'd gone to his office and read his mail.

"So where's that article you said you were working on?" I asked. "Remember, it's publish or perish."

"That's none of your business," he said between bites.

"God, what a fool I was to believe you when you said you had to bring lab equipment down. Lab equipment—what a joke!—you just wanted to joyride on down with your latest passion."

"I never said I was traveling alone."

"Oh, for godsake," I blurted. "The truth means nothing to you."

I turned my back on him and went back to the bedroom. There I stood, watching my son's tiny chest move up and down, fearful that something might go wrong with him—hoping I could manage to keep him alive and well. When at last I went back to the living room, I asked Howard a question I'd been brooding about for days.

"So, if everything's so peachy between you and Sally, why don't you just pitch me and your latest kid out on the street now and have her come down here right away so the two of you can play house?"

"Don't you think it's better for you to take a little time till summer, so you can get used to taking care of Rusty and make some plans?"

"Oh, you're so considerate. Thanks a lot! What's the problem? Does she want to finish working on her master's?"

He didn't answer me but I figured I was right. Who knows, I thought, maybe by summer she'll change her mind about this great romance of hers.

HOWARD PICKED UP HIS CHECK AT the Institute office. He told me he wasn't sure if he'd landed a job for the fall; he'd have to wait and see. We resumed our life together but now that life was radically changed. Sometime soon, I—the youngest in my family, who knew virtually nothing about childcare—would probably have to start again somewhere else as a single parent. Meanwhile I was thousands of miles away from my natural support systems, from networks of friends in Berkeley and friends and family in New York.

I wrote mournful letters to people I trusted. They wrote back, trying to help, sometimes giving advice—none of which helped much. I who was trying to breastfeed could barely eat. When Rusty was six weeks old, the nurse at the well-baby clinic told me he wasn't gaining weight quickly enough. Formula wasn't available in Panama to supplement his diet so, taking her advice, I filled bottles for him with canned evaporated milk diluted down and went on nursing him as best I could. It worked for him, he thrived but I stayed skinny.

Howard seemed to cherish this new child of his. He played with him and recited nursery rhymes to him as he held him on his lap—but he still insisted that, come summer, we'd split up. My 74-year-old father who had only ridden in a plane once before, when he was in the Navy during World War I, flew down and tried to talk sense to my husband. The two talked past each other until my dad acknowledged Howard's intransigence and gave up trying.

Instead my sturdy, balding old dad, not very tall, who spoke scarcely a word of Spanish but was gregarious to a fault, crossed the street from our apartment house to the field with a cluster of shacks. Man of the people that my father was, he reached out to the folks who lived there. He came back saying that each of those shacks boasted a single weak light bulb and the folks he'd talked to—God knows how—were pretty fed up with their government.

When it was time for him to leave, he studied me somberly in the airport and said, "You don't look so good."

"I know."

"Well, remember, you can always come home."

"I know," I said. Then he was gone.

LIFE WENT ON. I SHOPPED FOR food. Though I couldn't eat much, I still did all the cooking at home. Sometimes I bought fresh vegetables and fruit and other good things at the city's big covered market where, near tables heaped with newly caught fish stacked with ice, giant live sea turtles lay helpless on their backs waiting to be bought and slaughtered. Off to one side, hard-faced men offered colorful birds and fidgety, frightened looking monkeys for sale.

Once when I was shopping in the only American style supermarket I knew of, a stately Panamanian woman named Felicia struck up a conversation with me in educated English. We became friends and I visited her often.

8 • Panama: Introduction to the Third World

Felicia was an older woman who came from one of Panama's top twenty families. This didn't mean she was rich but she was well connected. She taught me about the oligarchy; those twenty families ran the show. That was the way things worked in much of Latin America, she told me. The oligarchs owned most of the land, they owned and ran important businesses, they held important posts in the government. Once, when she accompanied me to a doctor's office, she made a point of telling him about her family connections. But though Felicia still owned land, she had fallen out of favor with her relatives long ago because of what they judged to be her scandalous behavior. Maybe that was why her finances seemed shaky though she worked to keep up appearances. Often, at her request, I bought products for her at the commissary that she couldn't find in town.

As a girl Felicia had studied voice. (I too had studied voice; sometimes I would play her piano and sing. Music was an interest we shared, a big part of our friendship.) After her marriage to the right sort of husband, she'd fallen in love with the conductor of the symphony. In those days—during World War II—a lot more Americans were stationed in the Zone; many of them were fine musicians. So Ricardo, this man she loved, put together an orchestra that played classical music. Those were their glory days, as she recalled them, except that her husband wouldn't give her a divorce—even after she gave birth to Ricardo's daughter.

Many years later her husband died. At last she could marry her lifelong love—but by then he was suffering from emphysema. When he was younger, he must have been unusually tall. Now Ricardo was a stooped man with a racking cough. His genes had done an odd disservice to his daughter: she was almost as tall as he, too tall for most Panamanian men except for the blacks—and they were considered beneath her. Like her mother, she spoke good educated English. Unmarried and ungainly, with a sullen look, she worked as an international telephone operator. That, Felicia assured me, was a very good job in Panama.

To help keep myself sane—or as sane as I could manage—I located the Peace Corps office in town and volunteered to organize their chaotic pamphlet collection. Now I had a tribe of young free spirits to hang out with, like the crowd I'd known at the peace center. They were a motley crew with a variety of jobs.

Steve and his buddy Nat had backgrounds in theater; they put on bargain basement educational productions around the city, using Indonesian shadow puppets—large, ornate, flat metal figures—that had been shipped to Panama from faraway. Marge, a consummate craftswoman, could build and repair almost anything. She lived in an impoverished *barriata* on a big hill outside of town where she'd fashioned a tiny house for herself; there she served as an all purpose resource and advocate for her neighbors. Some volunteers just turned up in the office now and then. They worked far out in the *campo* or on the San Blas Islands where the Kuna Indians lived. One young woman was developing a co-op to market the molas[1]—unique sewn and embroidered folk art—that those Indian women made.

I started inviting Peace Corps staff to join Howard and me for dinner. He enjoyed their company as much as I did. Our guests, for their part, seemed grateful for a chance to relax in our place and enjoy middle class comforts for a change. We laughed when they griped to us about the *botellas*—literally "bottles" but more like clueless empty "suits"—they had to deal with in the Panamanian bureaucracy.

Soon, at the Peace Corps office, I confided in some of our regulars that, sunny as my relationship with my husband might seem in public, our marriage was coming apart. Steve and Nat prescribed marijuana to raise my spirits. They introduced me to Panama Red, we turned on together. For a modest sum they entrusted me with a small supply to smoke at home. Soon Victoria, worried about me, came up with the same suggestion. She offered to supply me with *ganja* at minimal cost. Here the situation turned farcical; Victoria's stash was stronger and cost less than what Steve and Nat were paying so now she became their supplier. Meanwhile I, who had grown almost immune to the effects of herb, had virtually no desire to turn on.

One day when I ran into Marge at the office, she took me aside.

"You doing okay? You look like you could use a change in your routine."

"Sure," I said wryly. "That's not all I could use."

"Why don't you come out with me someday soon to where I live? I'd love to show you my house. Whenever you want to go back to your place, I can just put you on the bus."

8 • Panama: Introduction to the Third World

The next day I left Rusty with Victoria and traveled out to Marge's home site with her. Her *barriata* was set on a hillside. We hiked up a rugged path past small shacks set four or five yards apart. A tot maybe two years old toddled by. He was barefoot and dressed in just a torn, dirty tee shirt, his bare bottom showing. Marge greeted his mother by name with a smile. The two of us climbed higher.

Near the top of the hill we came on her miniature house. Unlike the hovels around it, her place was a thing of beauty. It had an A-frame roof with wide overhangs and from shoulder height up, its walls were made of sturdy lattice so breezes could come through night and day. We sat facing each other on benches she'd built with storage cupboards fitted underneath, and drank a delicious concoction she'd put together from guanabana and passion fruit mixed with water that she'd purified specially for me. (Peace Corps staff were required to get used to drinking the local water.) Marge told me about the harsh conditions the people here faced. I told her more than she already knew about my deteriorating relationship with Howard.

"You could live here with me," she offered out of the blue.

It was a startling idea. It scared me. Almost immediately I turned her down. I'd suspected for some time that she was a lesbian. Marge assured me—indirectly, tactfully—that she'd never pressure me that way. Yeah, sure, I thought, but oh, the stress of dealing with her latent desires—that would be more than I could manage.

Space needn't be an issue, she assured me. She could build a tiny addition and in the tropics the poor spent most of the time outdoors. The main thing, I responded, fumbling for excuses, was how hard it would be to live here. She'd just finished telling me how people here had to fetch less than reliable water from a faucet down below which only supplied it a few hours a day. Besides, it was easy to see that when it rained, the trail down the hill would be muddy and precarious. If something went wrong with Rusty, how would I get him to a doctor right away?

"But people here get by," she said.

Of course she was right but I couldn't take a risk like that with my precious only child. Marge put me on the bus. Afterwards we would always feel uncomfortable with each other. I wished I felt secure enough to move in with Marge. Whenever I tried to rebuild my self-respect at home, Howard found some quiet way to put me down. Sometimes he even said anti-Semitic things that didn't fit the person he used to be. Howard had always had Jewish friends.

He still didn't have a position for the fall, mostly because he'd frittered away his chance to write articles on the local crabs. The senior scientists at the Institute made it clear they wouldn't recommend him and his major professor back in Berkeley had cooled on him as well. That month, hard pressed, he flew to Chicago for a professional conference there and managed to land a job in Texas. In June he announced that we'd be moving into a bigger apartment. We needed a bigger apartment, he said, because after school let out in Berkeley his daughters would come down to stay with us. Then in mid-July, as soon as I flew back to the States, Sally would take my place.

One day, right after we moved into a larger apartment in the Zone, I stopped to eat at a place not far from the Peace Corps office. It was called Don Samy's and it was little more than an outdoor food stand covered by a wide canopy designed to fend off rain. There were still very few foods that I could get down and they were an odd assortment. One of them was the custard pie they served in the Zone cafeteria. Don Samy's served another: chicken tamales wrapped in banana leaves. The cooked *masa*—cornmeal treated with lime—that made up the bulk of the tamales seemed to soothe my sensitive innards and made the chicken, olives and other goodies it contained taste all the better. Here at Don Samy's, while sitting at the counter on a high stool next to mine, a well-dressed Panamanian struck up a conversation with me.

Ramon was a pleasant looking man in his thirties who had gone to school in California and, like Felicia, spoke excellent English. We chatted for a few minutes about our experiences in California. Then he told me that he was an impresario. Thanks to his efforts, in another two weeks a Russian ballet troupe would be performing in Panama City. Starved for culture, I could scarcely wait to see them. Just now, he said, he was bringing a circus to town but for the moment the animals were in quarantine; he was on his way to check on them. Would I like to ride along? Then he would drive me home.

He didn't seem to be making a pass at me. In Panama City in those days, educated Americans seemed to be viewed as welcome novelties by the bored local elite so after a moment's thought I said, "Sure, okay, sounds good to me."

A cowed looking aide of Ramon's sat waiting in the back seat of his car. Ramon had scarcely started driving off with the two of us, when a member of the Guardia Nacional—which at this time served as the local police as well as Panama's military force—blocked our way demanding to know how come he was driving around without license plates on his vehicle? He demanded to see Ramon's driver's license. But he wasn't carrying a license either. His main defense was that he was a member of one of the country's top families.

Apparently, just as Felicia had told me, Panama's top twenty families ran the show and considered themselves above the law. The cop could barely contain his resentment. He hauled us into a fenced-in compound. Good lord, I thought, am I being arrested? Ramon was led in one direction, I in another. Ramon's aide was quickly released. Then a member of the Guardia started questioning me in Spanish. He seemed to be asking what I was doing with this man. A tricky question in this socially conservative, male chauvinist country. I figured I'd better improvise.

Ramon, I explained, was *"un amigo de mi marido."* Surely it would be all right for me to accept a lift from a friend of my husband. Of course I had no clue how Ramon would explain my presence to his questioner but for the moment, my story seemed to work. Until some poor clerk tried to write down the details.

First, I couldn't remember my exact address because I'd moved to this new apartment in the Zone so recently. As for my husband's name, "Howard Wright," it was hard for me to spell the letters out clearly in Spanish and nobody suggested that I write it down. Instead, since "H" and "W" are practically unknown in the language and half of the letters in "Wright" are silent, the poor clerk trying to note facts down in a ledger grew visibly confused and distressed. The next thing I knew, I was being released—saved by the improbable spelling of my native tongue—and an officer was assigned to gallantly drive me home. The next day Ramon phoned to check on me and say that he, too, had been released.

I saw him once again. We shared a sedate lunch in the Panama Hilton, the only place I knew in town where you could find copies of the Miami papers and *Time* magazine, though both were at least a week out of date. Soon I bought tickets for Howard and me to attend the ballet on the second night of its two-day engagement but we never got to use them. After the troupe's first performance they took off in a huff, complaining that the stage in the Teatro Nacional where they were booked was unsafe to dance on.

When school let out for the summer in Berkeley, Howard's daughters flew down to visit us. Roxy, now 12, and Little Sylvia, 8, were loving kids, patient and adaptable, who quietly put up with their father's penchant for changing his female partners. They made a big fuss over their new baby brother. It was a bittersweet pleasure for me to watch them play with him, knowing that soon they'd be living far apart.

And where should I go now? I was tempted to return to beautiful, exciting Berkeley, there I still had a network of friends. But to live there I'd have to buy a car—a daunting prospect for me since I knew nothing about choosing or maintaining one. In New York I wouldn't need a car and I had many relatives as well as friends. I'd probably be able to choose among a wider range of jobs and make more money—important now that I'd have to arrange for childcare in order to hold a job at all.

Should I just walk out on my faithless husband? That would be a grand gesture. But then he could claim I'd deserted him and I'd forfeit my right to child support. Both of us took it for granted that Howard, a man in a man's profession, would make more than I, a woman in a woman's profession. I'd never believed in alimony but surely, I thought, he should help support our child. Howard agreed. We talked about the details, we asked around for a lawyer. I went on nursing as best I could but still I could barely eat.

Down at the Peace Corps office Steve, sometime actor that he was, told me with a bit of swagger that in a few days he'd be starring in a locally produced telenovela, cast as an American baseball player who falls in love with a Panamanian girl whom he meets when they're seated side by side on a plane. At the appointed hour, the four of us watched television together. Steve's usually unkempt mop of hair was freshly trimmed and styled. As he flirted in Spanish with his actress ladylove, his profile looked matinee idol perfect.

"Oh, he's so *cute*," my older stepdaughter exclaimed. "He looks just like George Harrison, *doesn't* he? *Doesn't* he?"

Her kid sister agreed.

Their father fantasized about how maybe after Steve got out of the Corps, he'd come to the university where Howard would soon be teaching and might study zoology under him. The two had played with that idea one evening when several Peace Corps volunteers came over for dinner. *Many years later I'd learn that Stephen Treacy really did go on to become a zoologist. He moved north—far north—and became a noted expert on polar bears.*

NEITHER HOWARD NOR I COULD FILE for divorce since we weren't legally resident anywhere. Instead we arranged for a legal separation. On July 17th, 1967, I flew to New York with two large suitcases, a folding crib and my not quite seven-month-old son, wondering how I'd rebuild my life and provide a decent home for him.

9

Getting Back on My Feet

I WAS EMOTIONALLY EXHAUSTED. MY FATHER met me at the airport. He was a dear man in many ways but soon after I moved in with him I realized I'd have to find somewhere else to live. He didn't own an iron or an ironing board. His shower and his stove needed fixing. He was a befuddled widower living in a begrimed apartment, badly in need of someone to take care of *him*.

Ten days later I moved in with Bernice. Her kindness and equanimity were a balm to me. I set up housekeeping with Rusty in the large living room of her pleasant four-room apartment in Queens. She had a job, a husband and a teenage son still at home, yet she made me feel safe and comfortable. My father came back from a vacation in the Catskills saying he'd just met the woman he was going to marry. She turned out to be an agreeable, take charge sort of person, sixteen years younger than he was, perfectly suited to taking care of my father.

By September I'd found an inexpensive three-room apartment in Upper Manhattan, in Washington Heights. I bought a daybed I could use as a couch. My soon-to-be stepmother lent me a card table and some pots and blankets to tide me over until my share of the furnishings Howard and I had stored in Berkeley arrived in New York. Then I hired a live-in babysitter—a kindly, intelligent West Indian woman, younger and brighter than Victoria but just as loving to Rusty.

I gave her the bedroom. My son's crib sat in the foyer and I slept on the daybed in the living room. I'd lost so much weight during my

9 • Getting Back on My Feet

breakup with Howard that my pre-pregnancy clothes hung on me but since I couldn't afford to replace them, I started taking some old birth control pills left over from two years before just to gain six pounds. Then I put a Positions Wanted ad in *The New York Times.* Several offers came through and soon I had a salary coming in.

Nonetheless, each weekday morning I'd wake up in a panic. Before I went to work, to keep myself from yielding to the feelings of humiliation and despair that the end of my marriage had left me with, I'd rush to turn on the radio. News, the time, the weather, a little chatter. Reliable noise from strangers hooked me into that world outside and pulled me out of the darker regions of my mind. Gradually my sense of desperation lessened. With inexpensive touches I fixed up my new apartment till it started feeling more like home, my babysitter came to seem more like a welcome presence, and my anxiety started to wane away.

Howard called from Texas where he was now teaching, to let me know my child support check would be a little late. "By the way," he said, "your old friend Martinson is living in New York now. I hear he's split with his wife."[1] It was good of him to tell me this, he knew about my affair with Bob. I checked the Manhattan phone book. Sure enough, a Robert Martinson was living on West 76th Street. But I didn't call him right away. I waited until I was a bit more solidly on my feet.

By Thanksgiving I'd settled into a job with a subscription agency, a company that supplied long lists of magazines to libraries and other institutions. They didn't exactly need me but the company's president thought other librarians would like to hear that one of their own worked for his company, especially someone named Sylvia Wright. He thought it was a pretty name. He kept me busy preparing indexes and bibliographies that might, he figured, impress other librarians. The work was deadly dull but it paid fairly well and now I had a babysitter to pay on top of my other expenses. As soon as I felt stronger, I thought, I'd look for something more suitable.

At last I felt confident enough to call the man listed in the phone book.

"Is this the Bob Martinson who used to live in Berkeley?"

"Sure is," he chuckled. "Sylvia?"

He'd recognized my voice and sounded pleased—and hearing *his* voice again gave me goose bumps.

Reconnecting with Martinson did wonders for me. His affection for me and the pleasure he clearly took in sharing with me what he was reading and thinking about soothed my wounded ego. We started seeing each other every week or ten days.

The preceding year, Bob had moved to Manhattan to be one of three primary investigators on a study commissioned by the State of New York. It was a giant project designed to pull together all the significant research on rehabilitating criminals and so determine how best to lessen recidivism, the rate at which convicts return to prison after they've been released. Bob suggested that I moonlight on this project. His boss, a pleasant young man named Douglas Lipton, signed me on as their bibliographer. Now I could pay my dad back the $700 he'd lent me and save a few bucks to tide me over whenever I decided to leave my dreary grind at the subscription agency.

During the early Sixties, Martinson had evaluated programs designed to rehabilitate alcoholics. Then the vagaries of the job market turned him into a criminologist, studying the efforts of the state's penal system to transform institutions for delinquent boys into "therapeutic communities." As part of his job, he had written all but one chapter of a book that concluded that those efforts, complex and costly, had met with little if any success. Now it was Martinson's task, in cooperation with Lipton and another criminologist, to evaluate how the whole nation's criminal justice system treated those in its charge.

A couple of evenings a week, after my regular job across the bridge in New Jersey, I worked at their downtown Manhattan office. Dr. Lipton, who had hired me on Bob's recommendation, was a career state employee—unlike Bob and his colleague Judith Wilks. Though these two were paid generously, they were paid by the hour as consultants. Neither of them had doctorates. Judith, a former probation officer who had taught criminology at N.Y.U., looked like a prison guard in a B movie from the thirties about women behind bars. She was big and stolid with no figure to speak of and seemed vaguely butch. No competition there for Bob's affections, I thought.

It was my job to sort through hundreds of items the project's researchers had amassed and pull them together into a bibliography. At night in the project's unremarkable office with its Steelcase furniture and Naugahyde chairs on casters, its electric typewriters and cork bulletin

9 • Getting Back on My Feet

boards, I shuffled through books and journals and mimeographed reports piled helter-skelter on a table. For each source, I copied onto an index card its author, title, publication date and other dry facts. Worst of all were the scraps of paper with incomplete notes that researchers had scribbled before they mislaid the items themselves. Once I'd completed each citation as best I could, I filed the cards alphabetically.

Working as a team, Martinson and his colleagues had to read all these items and figure out what if anything they proved. There were many kinds of "correctional" programs to be weighed. Job training, traditional schooling, individual counseling, group therapy, programs for the addicted.

"We've had to set aside more than half of these studies," he told me. "Couldn't use 'em. Poor methodology, not enough data, that sort of thing."

"And the others?"

"It ain't easy," he made a face. "Trouble is even when a treatment works in one place it might not work in another."

"Like for instance?"

"Like maybe one psychiatric social worker is really doing a great job. When her patients are released, they don't come back into the system, at least not to the same degree. But other social workers with the same credentials, you can't rely on them to do any good at all."

"But at least that one person is helping, isn't that right?"

He shook his head, "Not in the big picture. How can an administrator justify a program if he can't predict how it'll turn out?"

His answer puzzled me but I was in awe of him. Anyhow, what did I know about penology? No way could I have guessed that he'd just sketched out a theory that in time would send shock waves through the entire criminal justice system. That would send him up and then crashing down again on an out-of-control roller coaster ride.

He yearned, I knew, to have a positive impact on the world. He admired his father, a man who with little education had made a big difference in his community. His dad had been one of five founding members of a consumer co-op that had grown into a huge presence all over the Bay Area. As for his mother, Martinson almost never mentioned her to me. The only exception: He recalled that once when she was venting her anger at one of his younger brothers—Bob was the eldest of four—she'd broken the hairbrush she was spanking him with. "She broke the hairbrush. *Broke* the *hairbrush!*" He laughed about that. I didn't think it was funny. The home I came from had often echoed with verbal abuse but otherwise we were all pretty nonviolent. Clearly he had no warm and fuzzy memories of his mother. It was a wonder, I thought, that he didn't still suck his thumb, this oversized, sometimes overwhelming man.

THE BEST PART OF WORKING ON that research study was being in Bob's presence even if he was only in the next room. The hardest part was being away from my son during those extra hours that I worked downtown. At less than a year old Rusty had figured out that his mom came home after work at night; if he wanted to see me, he'd better be awake then. So during the day he slept even more than other little kids his age but after I got home—usually around 6:30—he'd stay wide awake until ten or eleven. That's when I got to cuddle him and talk to him and play with him.

In March when I'd completed the bibliography, the researchers gave me another assignment. They asked me to type it up so they could add it to their final report. But in those days there was no such thing as word processing, let alone photo-reducing it cleanly. One evening, a guy from the office delivered a special typewriter to my apartment. It had unusually small type, like print in the index of an academic book. Fortunately my eyes were pretty good and remained so even as I struggled at that machine for hours. My tiny son grew jealous of that typewriter. Whenever I sat down at it, he'd cry or sulk. We were both relieved when at last I finished that job.

The State of New York sent me my last paycheck. Not a moment too soon. The subscription agency I'd been working for was a subsidiary of some corporate giant. Unseen powers on high ordered cutbacks. Then one by one, all around me mid-level employees that our eccentric boss had hired for no convincing reason were called to the office of a usually genial man who was stuck with the task of firing them. When my turn came, he looked like he wanted to flee and hide. Poor man, he must have felt guilty about tossing this hard-working, presumably desperate single mother into the street. It was almost fun to tell him I had some money saved because I'd been moonlighting and I'd been planning to give notice soon because I'd lined up something else.

I'd been promised a position as a librarian in a New York junior high school, to start that fall. A gracious, harried looking woman put me on her payroll for the rest of the spring term as a consultant for a special project at the headquarters of the city's Board of Education. Thanks to one of President Johnson's Great Society programs, school libraries, public and parochial, around the city had been granted extra money to buy books and magazine subscriptions for their collections. Working just six hours a day, I advised their librarians, helping them choose their purchases wisely.

That spring of 1968, life was pretty good. My son was learning to toddle and talk and I was still dating Martinson. Not swamped by job and childcare responsibilities, I went shopping for new clothes and did things to make his life easier and more pleasant, like buying tickets to Broadway shows. He reimbursed me amiably. Meanwhile, he worked compulsively six days a week, paid by the hour but also driven by the opportunity the Governor's Special Committee on Criminal Offenders was giving him to have a major impact on its landmark study.

One day he phoned me, sounding frantic. He was sick—I think he was having a panic attack—would I please come over right away? I eased my fifteen-month-old son into my baby carrier and, with Rusty on my back, rushed down to Martinson's place. When I got there, a doctor who made house calls had arrived already. After he left, Bob told me the doctor had told him he was working too hard.

"How hard?" I asked.

He shrugged, "Mmm, sixty-five, seventy hours a week."

He was doing work that required immense concentration, still he had no intention of cutting back. He was thrilled to have a job that made full use of his talents.

One weekend when I was walking with him in Greenwich Village, we passed the Lion's Head bar. He nodded at it cheerfully. "I go there sometimes," he said. That was one way he ticked down after work. Three steps down on Christopher Street, the Lion's Head was a fashionable hangout for writers and reporters, politicians and actors. With his gift for witty, knowledgeable conversation and his manly good looks, Bob Martinson could more than hold his own and make connections. I envied him, free to play the man about town—but felt grateful that he still took the time to see me.

On April 4, 1968, we had tickets to see *Man of La Mancha,* a musical about Don Quixote, on Broadway. We'd arranged to meet before the show at a restaurant on the Upper West Side. I got there first. But as his rangy figure passed by the restaurant window, I knew right away that something was wrong.

He was dressed more formally than usual, wearing a dark suit over a shirt and tie, but his leonine head, which he usually held high, was tipped forward and his shoulders were hunched. As he came through the restaurant's inner door, I saw from the twist of his lips and the thrust of his jaw that he was struggling with bitterness and rage. As soon as he spotted me, his face relaxed into gentle, vulnerable sadness. He'd barely reached my table when he said, "They shot King. They shot him dead."

"Dr. King? My god. You're sure?"

People seated nearby chimed in. A woman at the next table had heard reports already. A circle of us—all white Upper West Side liberals—shared details and lamentations.

"We all knew it might happen."

"Yeah, it's just like with President Kennedy and Malcolm X."

"Jesus, it's scary. I bet there'll be riots."

"Shit," Bob said. "There's so much wrong with this country. So many things need changing. Then someone like King comes along and you start seeing progress and then some redneck bastard blows him away." He shook his head and ran a long fingered hand through his thick, prematurely gray hair. "We're living in parlous times, *parlous* times," he repeated, savoring the word, "and there's so much work to do."

Shaken though I was by his terrible news, I looked at him with deep affection, trusting him to figure things out and advocate policies I could believe in. Bob was a visionary, driven to work for a better world. That was one of the reasons I loved him.

A waiter came by. Sheepishly we ordered dinner and managed to eat it. We did, after all, have theater tickets but we wondered if they'd cancel the performance. We took the subway down to Times Square and found the customary gaggle of people outside the Martin Beck Theatre.

Apparently all these folks thought the show would go on. And indeed the doors beyond the box office were open.

We found our seats amid the rustling excitement of an audience waiting for the show to start, then the house lights dimmed and someone stepped outside the curtain to make an announcement. They'd thought of canceling that night's performance, the man said, out of respect for Martin Luther King. Instead they would dedicate this performance of a show about Don Quixote who had dreamed an impossible dream to Dr. King who'd also had a dream and had worked so brilliantly to make it come true. Bob reached his arm around me as the curtain opened on the scene of a common room in a sixteenth century prison. There Cervantes, entertaining a ragtag circle of his fellow prisoners, set them to acting out his story of Don Quixote.

Bob squeezed my shoulder. "Back to the slammer," he said.

I chuckled. "Yeah, can't get away from it no matter where we go."

SUMMER CAME AND MARTINSON'S CONSULTANT GIG ended. He took off for California but said he'd be back in the fall. Early in July an old acquaintance of mine from Berkeley came by to visit. His name was Bill Meade and we'd worked together at the peace center there. Before I quit writing the Turn Toward Peace newsletter in 1964, I'd trained him to take over that unpaid job. He was a little guy a few years younger than I with the look of an overage Boy Scout and an enthusiastic manner. Now he was a VISTA volunteer—Volunteers In Service To America was one of Johnson's Great Society programs—and he was living in Brooklyn, in what was then a poor black ghetto.

Bill had dinner with Rusty and me. Then as we strolled in the park nearby that overlooked the Hudson River, he bubbled, "Hey, there's a job you ought to apply for. There's this new program you'd be great for that's looking for a librarian."

Bill had only been in town a few months but already he knew loads of people and was hip to lots of things that were going on. There was this pre-college anti-poverty program, he said, that was just getting off the ground. In the center of Manhattan, easy to get to, and they were expanding and hiring new staff.

"But I've got a job lined up."

"*You* boxed up in a junior high! Is that really what you want to do with your life?"

"Well, the hours are short, long vacations, *you* know. It could be secure...."

"Look," he insisted, "you oughta at least give it a try."

The University Center SEEK Program[2] was housed on two floors of the Alamac, a big old hotel on West 71st Street that had once been imposing but more recently was noted for its Puerto Rican hookers. It was that kind of neighborhood, a cockeyed mix of elegance and crime and decay. A couple of blocks north, the Ansonia loomed over Broadway. It was an ornate, 18-story white confection built early in the century to be New York's grandest residential hotel. It had housed Toscanini, Stravinsky and Lily Pons, Jack Dempsey and Babe Ruth, in spacious apartments but these had since been broken up. Now talented, arty folk, many of them musicians, populated its one bedrooms and studios.

Closer to the Alamac, a monumental bank looked imperiously down on a series of traffic islands, planted with a few feeble trees and occasional benches, that filled in where Amsterdam Avenue crossed Broadway. This area was popularly referred to as Needle Park for the flotsam of white heroin addicts, sick looking and disheveled, who passed away their time there between fixes. A short stroll to the southwest, Lincoln Center's theaters, faced in matching travertine, glistened. To the north lay Zabar's deli, jammed with pricey gourmet treats, and the fashionable Dakota Apartments where John Lennon lived and a dozen years later would be shot to death.

That July I sat down with the director of the SEEK Program in his office. Dr. Branman looked to be in his early forties. He was a medium sized, energetic man dressed in a professorial summer weight jacket and gray pants.

"Our students come from the poorest neighborhoods," he said. "We choose them by census tracts, not race, but mostly they're black or Puerto Rican and they're all high school graduates—they're not dropouts—but ordinarily they wouldn't have a prayer of getting into college."

He glanced at my resume, then he leaned forward, "You went to a public high school in New York?"

I nodded.

"Then you know about tracking."

"Sure. They always put *me* in the academic track, college prep, but I bet most of these kids were tracked to get general diplomas. Or maybe vocational. So they never studied a foreign language or much science. And what they *did* study was watered down. And the teachers they had probably couldn't focus enough on teaching because much of the time, some kids in their classes were raising hell."

Dr. Branman looked pleased that I knew the score.

"We give them stipends," he said. "There's federal money for that so they can concentrate on going to school, not working all the time. Though, of course, most of them still have part-time jobs just to keep themselves afloat. And we have counselors too, to help them deal with problems. Family, health, housing, all kinds of things. And most of our instructors are young. They're in grad school themselves and they do their best to hold our students' interest."

I asked what the curriculum was.

"Well, there's basic skills and there's beginning college courses when the student's ready. These courses, the way we're set up they cover serious academic subjects but they're introduced more slowly, so these young people won't be overwhelmed at the start."

Basic skills, he explained, meant teaching them how to take notes and write papers and give short talks. "So now we need a library, nothing huge, but a place where they can find reliable sources for the reports they have to make."

"And I bet the subjects better sound relevant to them," I said. In those days when so much of the old and conventional was being questioned, "relevant" was the latest catchword.

Dr. Branman took a deep breath. He seemed to be choosing his next words.

"We could use you here. You say you have a job already for the fall."

This program of his tempted me but anti-poverty programs tended to come and go. I didn't think I could afford to forego the job I'd lined up for September with the public schools. Still I told him I'd be happy to work there as a consultant for the summer, just to get the library started.

"There's money," Branman said. "We started out with 125 students last year but this fall we'll be expanding to 500. That's what we're funded for."

Activist Odyssey

We worked out a deal where I'd start working there the next week and continue at the Center through the month of August.

IT'S NOT EASY TO START A library from scratch. Another librarian already had come and gone. All she'd left behind in the improvised space the collection was supposed to occupy—two hotel rooms with the walls between them knocked out—were some steel industrial shelves, a handful of books and an order for a still undelivered set of the Random House Modern Library of classics.

Before I moved west, I'd worked for five years for the New York Public Library. I'd never stopped being impressed by its dedication to community service and the vast range of information it supplied in its 82 neighborhood branches and its colossal central research collection. So I went steaming on down to its Reader's Advisor's Office and told the experts on duty about the SEEK Program and what I'd been hired to do. They loaned me a volume compiled by the American Library Association that described a core collection of books appropriate for a new two-year community college. This guide was organized by subject; it was easy to pass over areas the program didn't cover and just order books that suited its curriculum.

Libraries didn't have computerized databases in those days so I started ordering the catalog cards we'd need and tracked down sources for library supplies. Then I sent a notice to faculty inviting them to recommend books and magazines. I was still planning to move on but as the fall term approached and our young instructors started drifting in, and then students too—black, brown and white but all optimistic and excited—came in to meet with their counselors, the program started coming to life. Teachers sparked up their offices with irreverent cartoons and radical posters. Che Guevara lounged in some wild, wooded place in military fatigues above a caption that proclaimed CHE LIVES. Huey Newton, the West Coast Black Panther leader, stared insolently down from a great wicker chair, his head haloed by the curve of its back. He held a rifle in one hand and a spear in the other.

Branman's secretary kept a pot of coffee going for the staff. At relaxed moments during the day we gathered around her coffee pot talking and laughing. Soon I knew I didn't want to move on. I'd found a place where I could make a difference, where I could work for positive social change. So when Dr. Branman asked me if I'd reconsider and sign on for the fall, it was hard for me not to sound too eager, so he'd offer me a high enough salary to pay my bills. That was when I learned for the first time that this program was run by the City University of New York. It offered fine benefits and relative stability. This might be the start of a new career.

Martinson got back to New York. I met him for dinner. Almost as soon as we sat down together, I exulted to him about my new job. He listened politely. But like most of the men I'd known, this man I was hopelessly smitten with much preferred to talk about himself. He too had something new to brag about. He'd landed a position teaching sociology that fall at the City College of New York.

"You're looking at *Professor* Martinson," he said. He seemed surprised at his good luck. At forty he was finally starting up the academic ladder that less brilliant men with whom he'd gone to graduate school had been climbing for years.

"They hired you without a PhD?"

"Lady, you're not going to believe this. I'm not sure *I* believe this but the good gray eminences in the sociology department in Berkeley finally took pity on me. The thing is, for my last job before I came east, I wrote a book[3]—a goddam book!—so they dreamed up a way to give me a PhD on the basis of that."

Everyone in Bob's field in Berkeley knew he was brilliant; they knew he thought clearly and wrote easily and quickly. He even had a talent for dealing with statistics; his bachelor's degree had been in engineering. But like legions of ABDs he couldn't seem to plan and complete a massive task like a book without someone prodding him along. In the fall of 1968, CCNY hired Bob as an instructor. In December his doctorate came through officially. The next semester City College would promote him to assistant professor.

AFTER I STARTED TO WORK AT the SEEK Program, things between Martinson and me started to sour.[4] He started telling me about Broadway shows he was seeing without me. Sometime actor that Martinson was, he loved theater but he was usually too obsessed with his work to plan outings to plays. I guessed that now someone else was buying tickets for him. Meanwhile I was unrelentingly busy, a single mother with a tiny son. Engrossed as I was by my new responsibilities at that groundbreaking program at the Alamac Hotel, I couldn't focus on Bob as I had last spring. Besides, now that I had a child to soak up much of my affection, I no longer worshiped Bob as I had before—and that was probably what bothered him most. I sensed that if I treated him like an equal instead of idolizing him, he'd drop me—but I figured I had to take that chance.

I was high on the challenge and rewards of my new job. I'd always enjoyed dealing with teenagers in libraries. Their rebellious energy had never scared me, it sparked my own. At the SEEK Center, our students were 18 to 25 and they were even more fun to deal with, hopeful and enthusiastic if you gave them half a chance.

A few of the fellows in our student body wore what looked like a uniform. They dressed in black: black leather jacket, black pants and black boots, all topped by a felt beret with a thin band of glossy leather that rimmed the wearer's brow. They called themselves Black Panthers, copycatting the band of militants who'd flared into the news in Oakland. Since legally they couldn't pack guns in New York, as the California Panthers did, each wore around his neck a giant cartridge on a thong. Sometimes they strutted a bit, but to me they still looked like kids.

One day Yusef, one of our Panthers, came in to confront me. He was medium height and muscular with a resolute air about him. Yusef wasn't the name that had come to us on his high school records. Those records called him Joseph McDaniel but all the New York Panthers had ditched what they called their "slave names" and had taken others that sounded African or Muslim. That was fine with me; I figured it was something they needed to do, something that bolstered their shaky self-images. Just now Yusef looked especially determined. *Soul on Ice* had just come out.

"I been looking for that book," he said. "How come you ain't got no copy?"

"Oh my God," I said, "*Soul on Ice* by Eldridge Cleaver. You are so right. I've gotta get it. Hey, sit down," I urged him, "sit down."

Yusef looked confused but he grabbed the flimsy plastic chair beside my desk, flipped it around and straddled it, his brown hands clutching its back. Here was my big chance to recruit him to my side. I waved at the mostly empty shelves around us.

9 • Getting Back on My Feet

"Most of the books I've ordered haven't come in yet but *Soul on Ice*, it's so new, I don't think it was on any of my lists so I'm really glad you reminded me. I'll see what I can do. Do you want me to hold the first copy I get for you?"

He hesitated, "Well the brothers, they got their rights too. I ain't looking for no favors. But okay, if you want to."

He got up and slipped out of the room, looking like he was in a hurry to get out of my sight so he could figure me out and decide what his next move should be. Guess I hadn't acted like the timid, prejudiced white lady librarian he'd steeled himself to bully—but my life style had never been all that ladylike, had it? And I liked to think I wasn't all that timid or prejudiced either. I could scarcely wait for my coffee break so I could run out to the nearest bookstore and, with money from my petty cash fund, buy two copies of that runaway bestseller by a notorious Oakland Panther who was an ambusher of cops and self-confessed rapist who'd spent 14 years in the criminal justice system.

Because, dammit, it was obvious to me that for this program to work we had to acknowledge the world as our students saw it. We had to lure them in with books and magazines they'd be hungry to read. Throughout the public schooling they'd managed to endure, they'd felt left out; in those days, school texts barely mentioned minorities. To change our students' minds about their chance to succeed, we had to recognize the perilous nature of life as they knew it.

Here at this experimental anti-poverty program we were funded in a flexible way that let me set up an account with a local bookstore—and later with one in Harlem as well—and subscribe to magazines on no one's approved list. Soon Yusef was recommending books to me and so was our radical faculty. And sometimes what they asked me to buy surprised me, like when Yusef urged me to buy copies of *The Prophet* by Kahlil Gibran because he and his brothers in black were passing that gentle, inspiring book from hand to hand just as multitudes of other college students had been doing for scores of years. Except that for him and his buddies it mattered that Gibran was from Lebanon and Lebanon was in the Middle East so they figured he wasn't exactly white and probably he was an Arab.

That fall, one of the women I worked with told me about attractive housing that I could afford not far from the SEEK Center, built as part of a New York State program to keep the middle class in the city. I filed an application and settled down to wait, returning by subway each evening from work to my small, dark apartment five miles away near the northern tip of Manhattan. Now and then Bob visited me there, sometimes I went to his place, but in December he stopped calling me and when I called him, he cut me off abruptly saying, "This is a bad time. I'll get back to you." Except that he didn't.

Finally, the week before Christmas, Bob phoned and his voice sounded different; he sounded like a hard-nosed boss giving orders.

"I've got something to tell you," he said, pausing dramatically for a moment. Then he added sternly, "I don't want to see you anymore."

I think he expected me to break down or beg but I wasn't about to give him that satisfaction.

"Is that right?" I said. "I kind of thought that was coming. Well okay, my friend, I wish you well. If you change your mind, you know where you can find me."

Of course, I still loved him, I couldn't imagine not loving him. But whatever was going on in that handsome, complicated head of his was more than I could fathom. If I had to choose between keeping my dignity and keeping Bob in my life, I figured I'd just have to do without him again.

10

Jordan and My Favorite Black Panther

I<small>N THE SPRING OF</small> 1968, <small>MANY</small> campuses had erupted with protests against the Vietnam War. Soon the frenzy spread to City College, our sister institution in the City University. CCNY was a proud place noted for its high academic standards. "Harvard on the subway" was its cherished nickname. For over sixty years it had sat on the edge of Harlem yet its student body was almost completely white. That fall, black activists who said it should be "Harlem University" overran it. They battled with students and burned one of its old stone buildings to a sooty shell. Meanwhile at SEEK four miles to the south, we enjoyed a blissful sense of unity. In the spring of 1969 that unity shattered.

The issue, the insurgents said, was neocolonialism. In a program where most of the students were black or Hispanic the director, Dr. Branman, was white and Jewish. (Though many of the young faculty members who were leading the rebellion were white and Jewish too.)

Classes were cancelled. School-wide protest meetings were called—which many students avoided. One weekend Branman's office was trashed. Phones were knocked out when someone stuffed a garbage can with greasy cardboard, set it next to the master circuit box and set fire to it. Some teachers got threatening phone calls at home. Others had valuables stolen from their offices. Our whole building seethed with anger and fear until a student-faculty coalition ousted Branman and replaced him with, of all things, a Pakistani poet.

Aijaz Ahmad[1] was an articulate, thoughtful fellow, conveniently viewed as neither white, black nor Hispanic. For a week or two things at the SEEK Center settled down. But then our Latin-American teachers and students accused Ahmad of being too closely aligned with the blacks; they said we needed to have a Hispanic co-director. More cancelled classes, more frantic meetings, more reasons for our students not to show up. The only time all our young people swarmed back into the building was when it was time for them to pick up their stipend checks.

Each day, tense and apprehensive, I showed up at my library wondering whether I'd be a target next. But I guess that was pretty unlikely. By this time I'd hired a black woman, a Howard graduate with a master's in psychology, as my assistant librarian and a tall, handsome Puerto Rican as my part-time clerk. My staff and my collection were as integrated as they could get. At last the spring semester ran out. Ran out without final exams. With mid-term marks pegged in as final grades. With no college credits granted for courses taken that term. I felt drained and disappointed—but at least now I had the summer off.

In July I got a welcome call. An agency I'd applied to months before, offered me one of the apartments they managed: a spacious and affordable two-bedroom apartment with a balcony on the fourteenth floor of a new building on the Upper West Side.

Joyfully I moved in with my son. By now I'd lost my live-in babysitter; once more I had to arrange for Rusty's childcare. But at least now, with a second bedroom, I could act on a plan I'd had in mind since I moved to New York. I bought room dividers with translucent panels and set them up in the larger bedroom so my son could occupy one half and a live-in roommate could have the other. Then I advertised for a young woman to live rent free in exchange for twelve hours of babysitting a week, mostly evenings and weekends, and I scoured the neighborhood for childcare during regular working hours. Finally I found an intelligent, responsible woman who took care of little kids in her garden apartment not far from me. Then it was time to return to the SEEK Center for the fall semester.

When I came back, much had changed. The mighty hand of the City University had come down hard on the leaders of the rebellion. All the white radicals had been fired, the minority teachers and counselors had been kept on, and an African-American woman professor from City

College was our new director. Those faculty members who remained were put under the supervision of matching departments at City College; now I was nominally a member of the staff of the City College Library. Though many of the students had been promoted to CUNY's four-year colleges, some familiar faces remained, roaming our corridors along with newcomers. The old enthusiasm had drained away but our valuable mission remained: preparing needy young people to venture on to higher education.

That year a man named Jordan Smith started taking an interest in me. He ran a dormitory upstairs in the Alamac for especially needy students. I'd seen him around before but we rarely spoke when he dropped into my library, looking for a student or counselor he needed to talk to. Now he started finding occasion to talk to me.

Jordan was a tall, husky man in his mid-thirties with small, pretty features much like Muhammad Ali's. Unlike the heavyweight boxer, he wore a neatly trimmed black beard that, in our improvised college setting, gave him a vaguely academic look. Still our Black Panthers seemed to gravitate to him. Often I'd spot one of them talking earnestly to him, hovering gratefully in his presence. They seemed to seek him out as a mentor.

The speech of most of our minority faculty was as polished as that of their white colleagues. Unlike them, Jordan spoke a Manhattan version of the dialect that was beginning to be called Black English. But his mind was lightning quick and his will was strong. He was grounded, a total realist—at a time when only too many at the Center were drunk on fashionable revolutionary theories or intimidated by the passions of others. Nothing deluded or intimidated Jordan. He worked within the system. But only because he was totally committed to improving conditions for those he called "my people." As I got to know him, I grew to respect him and look forward to seeing him around the Center.

One afternoon he asked me what my sign was. (In those days, this astrological question was a popular opening gambit for a conversation.)

"Aquarius," I answered.

"Like in the Age of Aquarius?"

"Yeah, guess I'm stuck with that. Actually they tell me I'm a four-way Aquarian, got three planets in Aquarius—though I don't know exactly what that means."

"So what does it mean to be an Aquarian?"

"Oh, Aquarians live in the future, they're comfortable at the cutting edge, they're comfortable with all kinds of people. And they don't root deep, people that have close relationships with them sometimes complain about that. It's not too hard for people like me to move on."

"So it's no big deal for you that you been married twice?"

"Now where the hell did you hear about that?"

I wasn't angry, just curious and teasing. He shrugged and didn't answer. His figures weren't accurate but they were close enough to make me uncomfortable.

"So what's *your* sign?" I asked him.

"Leo."

I laughed because it sounded so appropriate. "Born to run the show."

Again he shrugged. "I do what I gotta do."

"Our signs aren't supposed to be compatible," I said, "if you believe in that sort of thing."

"If you believe in tha' sort of thing," he repeated skeptically, shaking his head.

AROUND THIS TIME, FRIENDS OF MINE asked me to join the Socialist Party which had shrunk to a small band of mostly academic Old Left radicals. They wanted me to vote in a coming party election, supporting Michael Harrington's faction. Harrington was one of my heroes; he'd written an amazingly influential book. In *The Other America,* his description of the plight of the poor and his suggestions for realistic ways to remedy their situation had inspired first John F. Kennedy's New Frontier and then Lyndon Johnson's War on Poverty. I probably owed my new job to him.

In time he would be credited with the creation of Medicaid and Medicare and several other programs like food stamps. But my image of him had an earthier side. For Harrington, like Martinson, had been a Schachtmanite—a member of a tiny, fiercely anti-Soviet offshoot of the Trotskyites—and when I was attending library school, my roommate was a Schachtmanite too. Mike Harrington used to drop by our place once in a while. That's how I first met him.

The apartment I shared with Judi had just one bedroom. I slept on a daybed in the living room and sometimes, dare I say, she had a gentleman caller who stayed the night. Because the two of us came and went on different schedules, there was no guarantee I'd know if someone was staying with Judi, so we worked out a simple visual code. When Judi had company and didn't want me to barge in, she'd put her visitor's shoes outside her bedroom door. One night Mike Harrington's shoes stood guard outside Judi's door.

One evening not long after I moved to the Upper West Side, I got a call from someone asking if they could use my apartment for a party, "a Socialist Party party" a giggly young female voice explained. After she promised that they'd clean up afterwards, I said yes. In the back of my mind I was wondering if Martinson would show up. He didn't. But curiously enough, about six months later he moved into an apartment in a big older building a block and a half away from me.

Did reports about that party reassure Bob that this was a suitable neighborhood for him? I have no idea. But now I never knew when I'd see Bob Martinson in the street or run into him in the little grocery across from where he lived. One day Martinson showed up at the SEEK Center to meet with a sociology instructor there. I invited him to take a look at my innovative little library but he cruised on by as if it couldn't possibly matter to him. Nonetheless it had started attracting attention.

The library association of the City University asked me to give a talk about it at one of their meetings. In the audience that day was John Berry, the editor of *Library Journal*, must reading for librarians across the country. Berry liked my talk. He asked me if I could submit something in writing and it just so happened that, on top of the script I'd used that day, I'd been drafting an article. I sent Berry copies of both my papers. Weeks passed. I didn't hear from *Library Journal* but I did get a call from one of my new colleagues at City College asking if he and another librarian could take me out to lunch.

My visitors were a trim older woman and a young man, clearly gay. They accepted without comment the less than formal clothes I was wearing: a miniskirt with a sweater, a couple of strings of beads, and black pantyhose—the kind of comfortable hippie outfit that helped me relate to our student body. This odd couple looked over my little collection and said nice things, then they told me something I should have been told before. Unless I went back to school and got a second master's degree, I wouldn't be able to keep my job at City College. All fulltime librarians at the City University were required to have a master's in an academic subject as well as their degree in librarianship—that was how they qualified for faculty status.

So here was one more hoop for me to jump through if I was going to go on supporting myself and my son. I signed up to work toward a master's in sociology at N.Y.U. which offered lots of courses at night. It sounded like a dreary slog, still I made plans to start taking classes there soon.

AT LAST I RECEIVED A LETTER from *Library Journal* that set me to running around my apartment whooping for joy. They wanted to print my article. Soon their photographer arrived to take pictures of my library and its happily multi-racial staff. One shot featured our magazine collection shelved in pamphlet boxes with the slightly sloppy labels I'd printed by hand. The caption read, "A periodical potpourri of 'Ramparts,' 'Reader's Digest,' and 'The Realist.' " *Ramparts* was combatively New Left, though not without the occasional touch of wit. One of its more startling covers showed a large and shaggy brown gorilla rushing off with, slung over his shoulder, a curvy and expectantly smiling blonde. As for *The Realist,* its politics were New Left too, its satire was clever and biting, but it was also pretty consistently raunchy and scatological. Both featured excellent, provocative writing and appealed to the educated *avant garde.* Why, I figured, shouldn't our students enjoy these too?

My article, "A Pre-College Program for the Disadvantaged,"[2] went far beyond these pictures. It sketched out the day-to-day challenges our young people faced. It listed books and magazines that worked well in meeting their needs. Then at a time when, unfortunately, many conventional librarians were likely to treat minority kids with fear or condescension, I offered hints on how to gauge each patron's abilities without preconceptions.

THAT FALL, I STARTED TAKING GRADUATE classes two nights a week. Girlfriends who wanted to gab with me had to come over to my place other evenings. After I'd put my son to bed and read him a story, they could keep me company while I folded laundry or sewed bright patches, fashionable in those days, on his small jeans. Otherwise almost all my "free" time was booked for attending classes, studying, and writing papers. I was overextended. I felt the need for the kind of intense diversion that wouldn't take long. Pretty soon I let myself yield to subtle advances from Jordan Smith.

In a way I was belatedly paying my dues. I'd known other white girls who'd gone to bed with black men. In those days it was the thing to do for women on the left—but usually their affairs were fleeting, little more than symbolic. I'd had chances to do the same before but I'd shared few interests with the guys who came on to me and they'd acted too respectful and wheedling to suit my taste. It was different with Jordan—I could learn from him. I wasn't streetwise, I didn't understand his world. He made it pretty clear he thought he was doing me a favor when he opened my eyes to some of the things he knew.

That dormitory he ran—when first he took it over from a well meaning but less perceptive white man, one of the girls was turning tricks there and two of the guys were dealing drugs. He'd come down hard on them, he'd set ground rules and enforced them strictly. "Ain't no place in a college dorm for tha kind of messin around."

Jordan rarely used four letter words—at least not in my presence. He was also at least as overworked as I. He didn't just run the dormitory. He also ran a separate youth program on the weekends. Its office on the Upper West Side was where we usually went to be alone on weekday nights if he didn't decide to rent a hotel room. (I wasn't about to confuse my increasingly observant son by letting him catch me having sex with Jordan.)

Often he drove me to the program's office in his black Mercedes. "It's important," he said, "for kids to know a black man can make a decent living without courtin trouble with the law."

Jordan would glance out his car window, spot a couple of "brothers" hanging out in an entryway and say bitterly, "Don't you jus know they doin drugs." He'd grown up in the heart of Harlem, one of five kids living in a basement apartment, the son of the building superintendent.

One night as he sat half-dressed on the bed where we'd just had sex, he phoned a member of the State Senate about some program for single young mothers that was losing its funding. He urged him to get the Black Caucus in Albany to take action to restore state support. Another time, he dropped by my library during the day to unburden himself of how he felt about some corporate offices he'd just visited, trying to raise funds for another anti-poverty program. "Desses and desses" he kept saying to me, "desses and desses." At first I didn't understand, then I figured it out. "Desks and desks." Jordan was dismayed to see so many corporate slaveys laboring away in one vast room. (Funny, I thought, the sympathy he felt for these workers, most of whom were probably white.)

Once he borrowed $200 from me to help pay a lawyer for some teenage boy who'd gotten arrested "for being in the wrong place at the wrong time" when a buddy of his was caught trying to fence stolen goods. Jordan promised to pay me back but he never did. It didn't really matter. I was making good money and Howard sent me child support besides. It was just charity I couldn't deduct on my taxes. Hell, I thought, it was exciting and fulfilling to be having an affair with this man whose past and present world was totally different from my own. I really liked Jordan Smith, I learned a lot from him, but I had no intention of falling in love with him, let alone looking on him as a marriage prospect. How could a man like that relate to my son without resenting my innocent blue-eyed little kid on some level for his white skin and the privilege it was bound to buy him for the rest of his life?

My affair with Jordan probably had a positive effect on my relationship with the Panthers. I'm sure he kissed and told; this made me an honorary soul sister to them. But in fact I was already on good terms with these strutting young men in black, especially with Yusef who early in my first semester there, had recommended *Soul on Ice* to me.

One day during that first semester, when one of our students came into the library holding her five-year-old son by the hand and told me she needed to go to a job interview nearby but had no place to leave him, I offered to babysit him for an hour. I knew this was unconventional but it was the right thing to do; besides, it would counter student stereotypes. I liked to mess with their heads in a positive way.

The kid was stringing paperclips into necklaces when Yusef came by. My favorite Black Panther made a fatherly fuss over this little boy. He mock boxed with him and invited him to touch the giant cartridge that New York Panthers wore then. It dangled from a thong, low on his chest.

10 • Jordan and My Favorite Black Panther

"Bullet like that," he exulted, "could tear up an armored car! Hey, you gonna grow up to be a soldier for your people?"

Then on his way out he told the kid to behave himself with me. "Ms. Wright, she's a good lady. She got *white* soul."

Another time Yusef came in and, full of enthusiasm, tried to recruit me into a class in self defense for women that he was going to be teaching. I declined, saying it really wasn't my thing but I took that opportunity to thank the Panthers for organizing a chess club—yes, that was one of the things they did—and for campaigning for lockers for students.

They were doing their best, as they understood their options, to counter the pathology of their poor black community. They started putting up posters in the halls of the Center and elsewhere in the sepia parts of town blasting drug dealers for making fortunes by destroying lives. But pretty soon they stopped wearing those black uniforms of theirs, they stopped wearing those giant cartridges dangling, because the cops had started seriously harassing them. The cops were after them because in California, faraway, Black Panthers had dared to challenge the police. And would they dare to do the same here? Had they already done so? Now and then a few of them still wore their berets.

11

Bill's Pet Panther

ONE AFTERNOON LATE IN AUGUST 1969, my friend from Berkeley who had told me about the program at the Alamac came over for dinner as he did fairly often. This time Bill called in advance to ask if he could bring a new friend over. The Oakland A's were playing the Yankees. Would I mind if they watched the game on my TV?

No problem, I told him. His friend turned out to go by an African name, Aminifu. He said it meant "loyal" in Swahili. He was a slightly built young man with a neatly trimmed afro and an intelligent expression on his narrow, brown face. Bill introduced him to Rusty who by now was two and a half. Aminifu glanced my way. He gestured toward my kid sitting on the floor and asked me, "Do you mind if I...?"

"No problem. Go for it," I said.

Kneeling beside Rusty he bantered with him gently about his foot-long, brightly painted, toy wooden truck; the two of them pushed it back and forth making fanciful truck noises. Then my son grew bored. He abandoned the truck and took off for the bedroom he shared with his new part-time babysitter.

While Bill caught me up on his latest news from Bedford-Stuyvesant where he was working as a VISTA with community groups, Aminifu rambled appreciatively around the spacious living room of the

11 • Bill's Pet Panther

apartment I'd just moved into. He studied the books on my bookshelves and the pictures on my walls, then relaxed into my pillow backed sofa.

After a few minutes, Bill invited him out onto the terrace to check out the view. When Aminifu got up, he did a curious thing. He picked up the pillow he'd been leaning back on and slapped its sides gently to fluff it up as if it were stuffed with down—a luxury I didn't permit myself. Had his mother trained him to do that? Was that the kind of home he came from?

I joined the other two outside. Aminifu shifted around to get his bearings, "We're facing east, right?" then he looked north toward Harlem. "I see the brothers have been spreading the word," he said, more to Bill than to me.

He'd spotted a slogan painted on the wall of a handball court eight or ten blocks uptown. In giant block letters it said OFF THE PIG. I'd never consciously noticed it before. It meant nothing to me except that I knew "pig" was the latest and angriest epithet for a cop.

"What does it mean?" I asked Bill.

Aminifu looked wary.

"You know what 'pig' means, don't you?" Bill said. "Well, 'off,' that's like 'knock off.'"

"Kill?"

Neither of them answered me. I took that as a yes. It sounded creepy.

We went inside, I turned on my TV for them, the baseball game was beginning. While Aminifu watched it, Bill joined me in the kitchen where I was working on dinner. The afternoon was warm. I was roasting half a smoked pork shoulder—hearty and inexpensive—with yams in a small electric oven that wouldn't heat the house up much. I basted the roast with the juices in the pan, then put some green beans on to steam.

"You know," Bill confided in me excitedly, "Aminifu? He's a Panther—you'd never guess it, would you? And he's from Oakland."

Bill had always struck me as kind of asexual. Now he seemed to be cozying up to this new friend of his with puppy-dog admiration.

"Really? Did the Panthers there send him to organize in Brooklyn?"

Oakland was where the Black Panthers had started. As far as I knew it was still their strongest chapter.

"No, no, it wasn't like that," Bill explained. "He'd been drifting around after he got out of prison...."

"He was in prison?"

"Yeah, he did five years in jail, poor guy, gave up five years of his life. It's sickening, just sickening, but you know how it is. Some bastards said he killed a guy but it was just self-defense. This other guy had a knife—Aminifu was just protecting himself but the courts, they just steamed ahead and railroaded him. The whole shitty system was rigged against him."

Aminifu was barely fifteen feet away, watching the baseball game on the other side of a short wall that separated my contemporary alley of a kitchen from the living room. I ducked back a few steps to glance at him briefly. I was trying to get my head around the idea that this soft-spoken, polite young man had killed someone. It didn't feel good to have a killer in my house.

"So how did he wind up in Brooklyn?" I asked.

"Well, he was drifting around, like I said, he was doing a lot of reading and thinking and he figured he could make a fresh start on the East Coast. The Brooklyn Panthers, they're lucky to have him, he's a sharp guy."

For three years I'd worked in Oakland. I wondered if by some weird chance I'd heard about his case.

"You don't happen to know what his slave name was, do you?"

My friend Bill hesitated. "Gee, I haven't a clue."

I started making a salad. I put out flatware for Bill to set the table while I hauled Rusty back from his room and lifted him into his highchair. After dinner, Aminifu volunteered to carry dishes into the kitchen for me; he seemed startled to see that I didn't have a dishwasher. After we ate dessert—apple pie and ice cream from the supermarket—Aminifu again helped me clear the dishes. When he returned to the sofa, once more he went through his ritual of fluffing the pillow.

"Please don't bother," I said, "it's just foam. We're not that fancy around here."

His ritual with the pillow and his assumption that I'd have a dishwasher seemed very Black Bourgeoisie to me.

"Well, thanks for having me over," he said. "It's nice to get out of Bed-Stuy for a change."

11 • Bill's Pet Panther

Bedford-Stuyvesant was a dangerous black ghetto at that time.

"Hey," I responded as casually as I could manage. "Bill tells me that you're from Oakland. You know, I worked there for years while I was living in Berkeley. I was wondering if maybe when I was working there I might've maybe heard of your case."

He hesitated, then said, "It wasn't that big a deal for anyone but me. I don't think it ever made the papers."

"Yeah, but I was just wondering. What was your slave name?"

"Oh, that," he replied easily. "Pete, Pete Corelli. My dad's part Italian."

I was beginning to get goosebumps—this was too much of a coincidence—but I tried to act relaxed.

"Any relation to Sergeant Corelli of the Oakland Police?"

"Yeah, he's my dad," Aminifu said with obvious pride.

I got up and wiped dabs of pie and ice cream off Rusty's face. I carried him back to his bedroom and asked my roommate if she would please watch him for a while. I was stalling for time because the Panther's answer was a little more than I could deal with.

I'd heard of Sergeant Corelli. He was the highest ranking black man in the Oakland force and activists in the East Bay detested him. Most of the Oakland cops were Southern whites; they were notoriously brutal to people of color.[1] Corelli was their "show nigger." The force would trot him out whenever they'd done something outrageous and they needed to make a show of being impartial and fair. Corelli would say whatever they wanted him to say, and say it deftly enough.

According to Aminifu's story, he'd been railroaded into prison, the system had worked against him. That might have made sense if he was on the outs with his father. But Aminifu was proud of his father and Sergeant Corelli was a valued member of the system. His dad had clout. He could have protected his son, whether or not he was guilty.

It didn't compute, it didn't compute. I couldn't believe his story that he'd done time in prison. But who better could the F.B.I. recruit to infiltrate the Brooklyn Panthers than the son of a proven Uncle Tom from the other side of the continent? Did he feel that because I was white and middle class he could let down his guard with me?

For days and nights that stretched into weeks, I agonized over whether I should tell the Panthers at SEEK about him. I phoned Bill and told him I thought this new friend of his might be an FBI plant. He didn't take me seriously. "Hell, no," he said. "He's a great guy. He wouldn't do a thing like that."

Still the admiring puppy dog, I thought. Or even worse, could Bill be some kind of double agent?

One of the girls in our program at the Alamac was married to a Panther who was being tried as one of the Panther 11, charged with conspiring to plan a string of bizarre bombings which the New York cops conceded had never taken place. Everyone at the Center felt sorry for her as, tense and distracted, she dragged herself from class to class.

"They was probably set up," Jordan said about the young men on trial, one day when he dropped by my library.

"By an agent provocateur?"

"Wouldn't be the first time. Some dude on the FBI payroll talks them into planning some crazy, badass stunts, promises to teach them how to make bombs, then he blows the whistle on them."

I could tell Jordan about my suspicions. Unlike Bill, he'd pay attention. But then what would happen? He'd tell the Panthers—they'd take it from there. Except that I kept picturing Aminifu in a basement somewhere tied to a chair, being questioned, beaten, tortured, maybe even killed. Could I do this? Could I have his murder on my conscience? From what the media said, there was no telling what the Panthers might do.

But how could I trust the media? Yusef was the only Panther I really knew and I didn't know him all that well. Still I sensed his idealism, I sensed that he had a good heart. Still what might even Yusef do if he felt the movement he was willing to give his life for was in danger?

Weeks passed, months passed. I did nothing and my inaction shamed me. Then something happened that pushed me over the edge.

At 4:40 a.m. on December 4, 1969, a team of fourteen Chicago police, supposedly looking to confiscate illegal weapons, raided a three-bedroom apartment in a shabby building near Black Panther headquarters. It was being rented by Fred Hampton,[2] the creative and charismatic 21-year-old leader of the Chicago Panthers. Other Panthers and a couple of their girlfriends were sleeping there too. According to the first accounts released by the police, they had a search warrant but the occupants refused to let them in. One of them shouted, "Shoot it out!" Soon two young men lay dead: Fred Hampton and Mark Clark, 22, a Panther leader from Peoria. Four more young people had been wounded, two of them girls, none of them more than 19 years old. Everyone in the apartment was charged with attempted murder—though police injuries were remarkably light.

One officer had suffered glancing gunshot wounds, another had been cut by flying glass. Yet the cops claimed the Panthers had quantities of firearms and the shootout had lasted ten to fifteen minutes.

The next day community leaders, black and white, demanded an independent investigation. Panthers led tours through the apartment to prove that no shootout had occurred. Film clips on TV showed no bullet holes near the door where the police had entered, no sign that anyone but cops had fired a shot. Just inside the apartment, however, by the front door, was a two-foot wide pool of blood. It indicated, said the president of Chicago's league of black policemen, that "whoever opened the door to let them in got his then and there."

Doctors came forward to swear that Hampton, drugged with barbiturates, had died in his sleep. And others said that a spy must have leaked the layout of the apartment so the cops could eradicate their enemies with impunity. But their enemies were not my enemies. The Chicago Panthers, like their models in Oakland, had taken it upon themselves to challenge police brutality. They'd armed themselves and demanded radical change. Now I grieved for the dead and the wounded while I burned with anger at their murderers.

I set out to find Yusef. As soon as I spotted him in the hall at the Center I asked him gently but urgently to please come into my office. Then I whispered to him what I knew about Aminifu and what I suspected. Yusef didn't have his usual swagger that day; he was grieving too. And he was probably scared, with reason.

"I'll see what I can do," he said. "He's with the Brooklyn Panthers, you say?"

Yusef lived in Manhattan.

"Uh-huh. Don't you guys keep track of each other?"

He made a face. "I'll check him out," he said.

I waited anxiously to hear what happened next. A few days later he came by. I ushered him into my office, then closed my office door.

"I checked him out, this cat Aminifu," Yusef said, leaning his head close to mine. "The brothers in Brooklyn, they thought he was really together—didn't think he was no spy. He's been teaching them things." He bit his lip, dark and purplish. "Like about making bombs. He says he can get supplies …"

"But of course he'd say that," I interrupted him, my voice rising. "Of course he's got connections—but it's all a trap. He's setting them up."

Yusef's face was as composed as an African mask. "Tha's what I said too," he told me, "so we made this plan. One of the brothers—he works for the phone company—he's gonna tap this dude's phone and some of us from the Manhattan chapter, guys he don't know, we'll tail 'im. If he makes one false move …"

He turned his thumb down. It was a chilling gesture—straight from the days of gladiators in ancient Rome when spectators used it to sentence men to death. I wondered if that was what the brothers had in mind for that devious young man from Oakland. I could barely sleep until, after almost a week, Yusef came by to see me again.

"He split," Yusef told me. "He musta caught wise. First he borrowed a lot of money offa community people—the pig—then he took off. Now the brothers in Brooklyn, they pretty sure you was right. Like he musta planted stolen property on these other two members of the chapter that was pulled in for armed robbery but he was so slick, this dude, he turned the brothers against them."

"I shoulda told you about him sooner."

"Well … you did a lot more than most people woulda done."

The Center closed for Christmas break. The next semester, Yusef transferred out to another campus of the City University. I wouldn't see him again for almost a year but before I did, I had an odd contact with another Panther.

By then it was Thanksgiving weekend, 1970. I was strolling down a street in my middle-class interracial neighborhood, when I noticed a car with a U-Haul hitched to it parking at the other end of the block. One of the two young African-Americans in the car got out and climbed onto the trailer, unloading something. His partner remained in the driver's seat, nervously tapping rhythms on the steering wheel. As I passed by, I recognized him. He'd been a Panther, that first year at the Center, though now he was dressed in ordinary clothes. The name he'd used then was Sababa.

11 • Bill's Pet Panther

I crossed the street and turned around to watch for a minute. The U-Haul was stacked with flimsy looking cartons which brightly advertised that they held Johnny Lightning sets. That fall TV was full of ads for Johnny Lightning toys: tiny, futuristic cars and assemblies of thin plastic track on which to race them. The boxes I could see were maybe two feet long by six inches high and wide. Sababa's partner eased two of them off a pile and climbed down with them carefully, heading for the door of an apartment house.

I ducked into a store. When I emerged, the U-Haul was still parked across the street and Sababa had gotten out of the car to help his partner carry a larger Johnny Lightning carton, about twice as bulky as the others had been. As I waited for the light to change, they carried it into the house together, each holding one end of the carton. Something about their manner seemed strange to me but for the moment I couldn't place what it was.

A couple of weeks later I ran into Yusef, waiting for the elevator in the lobby of the Alamac though he wasn't a student there anymore.

"Whatcha doin here?" I asked him cordially.

"Oh, just visiting some friends upstairs in the dorm."

"Playing Santa Claus?" I kidded him because he was carrying two shopping bags, one in each hand.

"Somethin like that," he said with half a smile and a devilish glint in his eyes.

We got on the elevator together; I had to get off first. But before I did, I glanced down and saw that each of his bags was double—a bag within a bag as if it contained something very heavy—but each contained just one Johnny Lightning carton. Strange, very strange. It was a puzzlement to me. I thought about it for a moment, then put it out of my mind.

School closed down for the holidays. Soon after it reopened in January, Yusef turned up in my library. "I got something to show you," he said, looking around with what seemed to be caution.

"You want to come in my office?"

He followed me in and closed the door quietly behind him. As soon as I sat down, he flipped a straight chair around so he could sit on it backwards. He pulled something out of his jacket pocket and set it down on my desk. It seemed to be just a small model car.

"I put it together myself," he said, bragging.

It seemed like a childish thing to be bragging about.

"You get this kit that has all the parts that go in a car and then you put it together."

I touched the model car lightly and looked back at him confused.

"And I been working in a garage," he continued. "Only I ain't just been fixing other people's cars. I been learning how to fix cars so they fast, real fast, faster even than pig cars."

I was beginning to get his drift. It made my heart beat faster to have him telling me this. He was revealing a back alley, hidden part of his life I never would have dared to ask him about.

Yusef waited a moment, to let this statement of his sink in. Then he went on in the same cool, portentous tone. "I winged me a cop this fall."

"You did? You ... shot a cop?"

Now fear started tearing through me—fear for this radiant young man. I didn't want to believe him.

"Yeah, it was easy," he said.

"Nobody knew?"

My voice sounded odd to me, I was hoarse with concern.

"Well, some of the brothers knew, some of the brothers and sisters. I just winged me a cop. He was bad news in the community. It was easy. No problem if the brothers know."

"But you didn't kill him?"

"No. I coulda killed him if I wanted to. He wasn't that bad."

The media always said the Panthers wanted to slaughter cops. It had never occurred to me that—like Mafia moneylenders and the Irish Republican Army which sometimes "kneecapped" its enemies to cripple them—they might take measured, non-lethal revenge. Still I wondered, had he made this whole story up to impress me? His braggadocio, if that was what it was, terrified me. This wasn't the sort of news he should be spreading around. Of course I wouldn't rat on him but what if someone else did? What if someone he bragged to told somebody else who sold him out to the police?

"I wish you hadn't told me," I whispered. "I'd rather I didn't know. For your sake."

He was saying something about a trial but I couldn't make out if he was being tried or the cop had been tried or some trial was set to take

11 • Bill's Pet Panther

place in the future. Then it seemed to me that Yusef had started mumbling and contradicting himself. But my mind was in such turmoil that I wasn't sure of anything. Finally he got up and set his chair back in its original place.

"Take it easy," he said. "Catch you later."

I nodded weakly. "Take care," I said.

DAY AND NIGHT QUESTIONS POUNDED AT me. Why had Yusef confided in me? Why had he taken such a foolish chance? Then I thought again about those Johnny Lightning boxes and the whole bizarre sequence of events started to make sense.

Those boxes I'd seen Panthers delivering—they hadn't contained toys, they were too heavy for that. Johnny Lightning assemblies were flimsy and insubstantial. They were made to thrill kids on Christmas Day but soon they would surely fall to glossy plastic scraps. Yet Sababa and his partner together had carried one large box carefully, precariously, as if the box was fragile but its contents, probably enclosed in sturdier wrappings inside it, were very heavy.

So what had they been delivering? Guns, grenades, ammunition? Whatever they could get to protect themselves from raids by cops like the ones in Chicago, to strike fear in their enemies and move on with their agenda? They'd delivered them to students in the dorm two floors above where I worked each day. They'd delivered them to people in my neighborhood, maybe people I knew, respectable middle-class people who could store them and maybe even provide a safe house for a fugitive if push came to shove. When Yusef came by my office was he hoping to recruit me to do the same? Or did he have even bolder plans for me?

It was 1971. Despite the best efforts of the nonviolent peace movement I'd worked for in Berkeley and still supported with all my heart, the Vietnam War kept grinding on. My country's war machine kept despoiling the Vietnamese countryside with napalm and Agent Orange, killing and maiming men, women and children in their homeland half a world away. Meanwhile, over 45,000 American troops had been killed there to date, not to mention the multitude wounded in body or mind.

For years now, homegrown white militants had been blowing up American buildings and robbing banks in their struggle against that endless, bloody war. The poor and powerless in our own country were still being drafted to fight in Vietnam's jungles. But if campus rebels and ghetto rebels and returned Vietnam vets could merge into one guerilla army, I thought, maybe real change could come.

Ah, the romance of it, the glamour of it! Stories I'd heard of luminaries who'd dared and survived challenged me to take a chance; my reckless streak made me discount the dangers. For the next few days I drifted like a sleepwalker, dreaming about what little I knew of other people's adventures. George Orwell and Howard Fast fighting with the Loyalists in the Spanish Civil War, Jean-Paul Sartre in the French underground during World War II. Celia Sánchez shouldering a rifle in the Sierra Maestra alongside Fidel Castro. And those ululating women in the Algerian Revolution who carried bombs in their market baskets.

For sometimes impossible causes did succeed. Afterwards the winning side glorified its heroes—so why not help the Panthers? At least I could store something for them. If conflict was inevitable, maybe I should take a stand.

Yusef had said, "Catch you later," but weeks passed and he didn't show up. I had no idea how to reach him—but I could talk to Jordan. He hadn't called or dropped by the library for at least a week. The next time I spotted him at the Center, I stopped him in the hall and told him, "Say, I really need to talk to you. Not here. Could we maybe go out on a coffee break together?"

His expression turned very reserved, he seemed to be sizing me up. Had he guessed why I wanted to talk to him? And if so, why was he looking at me so coldly? Still he agreed to pick me up at the library in an hour. We stopped by a café, bought two coffees and a couple of pastries to go, then started walking over to Riverside Park.

"Yusef came over to see me, did you know about that?" I asked him as we found ourselves a bench far from anyone else.

He shrugged. "Why would he tell me if he did?"

We sat down together and started sipping our coffee; it had cooled to lukewarm in the chill winter air. Jordan ate his pastry in leisurely fashion, I broke off a piece of mine and nibbled at it nervously.

"It's what he said that got me. He told me he winged a cop. Really! God, I was so scared for him. I couldn't figure out why he would come and tell me a thing like that but then—oh, God, it took me weeks—but then I started getting this idea."

I told Jordan I'd seen Sababa and Yusef with Johnny Lightning boxes. I told him what I suspected they contained. I told him I'd be willing to store something for them in my place. It might not be easy. There was my roommate to consider and my kid might get snoopy, still I was sure I could manage. It went without saying that I thought my white skin and my lady librarian image would protect me.

My black lover sipped his coffee. He crumpled the wrapper his pastry had come in and tossed it on the ground. I picked it up and stashed it in the paper bag the café had given us, so I could throw it away properly later. That gesture of mine made him look mildly amused in a sour sort of way.

He wouldn't confirm or deny that the Panthers were distributing weapons. "What makes you think I'd know about a thing like that?" he said. "Got enough on my plate jus takin care of business."

"But then why do you think Yusef came to see me?"

He crumpled his empty coffee cup and handed it to me so I could put it in the bag, then he pulled back and looked down at me coldly. His coal-black eyes bored into me.

"When Yusef told you what he did, it didn't make you feel good, did it?"

"No, it scared me to death, I told you that."

"So don't you worry about it none. Ain't nothin but a jive tale. Someone better tell him to stop jivin that way."

I didn't believe him, I felt sure he was blowing me off. At first I was mad. But once I simmered down and thought about it, I decided he was probably doing the cagiest thing.

He'd always told me I wasn't streetwise. And considering how I'd reacted when Yusef told me his story, I clearly wasn't hot for battle and bloodshed. I didn't suffer as his people did, I had responsibilities of my own I could barely cope with. Jordan must have figured all this out long before I did, Jordan was pretty sharp about practical things. Whatever role the Panthers had fancied I might play, Jordan must have told them they couldn't take a chance on me.

I NEVER SAW YUSEF AGAIN. My affair with Jordan faded into memory. At the end of the spring semester, the City University shut the Center down. The powers that be transferred me to the library at City College; I would start working there after my summer vacation. I had mixed feelings about that. By now my dear old friend Bob Martinson, who'd dropped me with a thud a year and a half earlier, was a professor in the sociology department there.

12

The Man Who Changed the Criminal Justice System

THAT FALL WHEN I JOINED THE staff at the main City College library, Martinson was not only ensconced in the sociology department, his colleagues had chosen him to serve as its chairman. Most of them had more publications and academic experience but, ah, what a point man he made when minority students came demanding changes in the curriculum. Martinson had been a Freedom Rider, he'd married a black girl. Besides, experienced debater that he was, Bob didn't mind sparring with the latest crop of radicals. Though his own political position had been changing—was he even a radical anymore?

We'd met in a peace center. I assumed that, like me, he still opposed the Vietnam War. But much later I'd learn that, soon after I joined the Socialist Party to vote for Michael Harrington, that party splintered into three factions. Harrington's center group, opposed to the war, eased into the leftwing of the Democratic Party. Pacifists further to the left surfaced as the Socialist Party USA. But Martinson, following his old political mentor, Max Schachtman, swung right to—of all things— support Nixon and the war.

Schachtman's theory[1] was that Soviet-style totalitarianism was so all-inclusive and monolithic that once established anywhere it could not be successfully fought from within; it had to be attacked from outside its borders. Martinson's master's thesis on the Spanish Civil War, submitted in 1953, had reached the same conclusion. History would disprove this theory when the U.S.S.R., after years of unrest in its satellite states, self destructed in 1991. Nonetheless, strange as it seems, out of this obscure little band of academic Schachtmanites would come the neoconservatives who eventually shaped one disastrous policy after another during the George W. Bush administration. Most of Bob's old socialist friends took to shunning him for this bizarre shift of his. Insecure as he was deep in his core, he missed his old support system desperately. But I didn't know this at the time. We were barely speaking and my tenuous ties to the Socialist Party had melted away. Still sometimes I saw Bob Martinson on campus.

One day when I was sitting in the faculty dining room, he strode in with a couple of male colleagues. He spotted me, then called out to me twenty feet away, with what sounded like confused incredulity, "You wrote an article about that library of yours?"

"Yeah," I shot back accusingly, "but when I invited you to see it, you couldn't be bothered." That little article of mine was the only publication that had won national notice for the now defunct SEEK Program at the Alamac.

Martinson didn't leave his colleagues to say another word to me. Instead he slumped away beside them, looking as deflated as a good little boy who'd accidentally broken his mother's favorite vase. Well, I thought, at least he felt guilty.

Heads turned. I felt hurt that he couldn't spare me another minute—still given the tone of our interchange it was obvious that once upon a time our relationship had been closer than professional. I took perverse pleasure in that. If some of those stodgy academics in the dining room guessed this, I figured, so much the better.

I never found out how Bob learned of my article and he never referred to it again. He was busy with weightier things. He was following up on that huge overview study where I'd moonlighted as a bibliographer, the study that asked: What kinds of rehabilitation keep offenders from coming back into the criminal justice system after they've been released? Early in 1972, the *New Republic* published a series of articles[2] in which Martinson outlined what he called the paradox of prison reform. Drawing on the findings of the study we'd both worked on, he called for major policy changes.

12 • The Man Who Changed the Criminal Justice System

Crime in the streets was a major issue then. Expanded drug use had spawned an epidemic of muggings by addicts desperate for the price of their next fix. What was society to do with them? And how should society deal with others found guilty of victimless crimes like possession of narcotics, "deviant" sex acts and prostitution?

In the prisons of the Sixties and Seventies, humanitarian reformers had created an assortment of treatment programs. They were confident that a mix of basic education, vocational training, group and individual therapy, reinforced by rehabilitation for substance abusers would convert offenders to well-behaved sorts ready to be released back into society. In California, where Martinson had worked, faith in these programs spawned unexpected consequences. Officials sentenced offenders to flexible sentences, sometimes as vague as "one year to life." Then they left it up to untrained parole boards—typically political appointees—to determine how ready each applicant was for release.

Inmates detested indeterminate sentences, Martinson reported. They much preferred fixed sentences with a chance at time off for good behavior. Even parole looked like a trap; most of the information prisoners had about it came from losers tossed back into prison because they hadn't met its often arbitrary standards. (To this day, a parolee can be thrown back in prison for years for a trivial violation like missing an appointment with a parole officer, failing to notify the post office of a change of address, or possessing a "weapon" as minimal as a pocket knife or a badly-behaved dog. Outside the context of parole these are not crimes at all.)

The median time served in California rose sharply. Between 1944 and 1965 it went from 24 to 36 months, the longest in the country, and the percentage of people imprisoned more than doubled.[3] It didn't look to Martinson like the system was working. He argued that the longer the sentence, the more harm incarceration was likely to do—not merely to inmates but to society. The longer convicts were barred from the normal sequence of experiences and achievements—going to high school or college, first job, bank account, marriage, maybe parenthood—the harder it became for them to live in the outside world by society's rules. No wonder they were likely to land back in the joint in the next three years or so.

It was time to focus on the victim when designing public policy. The goal should be "to protect the public and to inhibit public vengefulness by compensating the victim for the failure of the state to provide protection." One of the primary functions of law, he said, was to express society's morality. But no matter how severe society made its laws, the sad fact was that only a tiny percentage of violent crime (2%) and property crime (less than 1%) actually ended in anyone's conviction and imprisonment. Meanwhile imprisonment by its very nature tended to turn convicts into career criminals.

For this reason, he urged that victimless crimes be decriminalized and police work be improved—made better informed, efficient and coordinated. Whenever possible, perpetrators should be kept in the community but they should be strictly monitored. He saw value in programs like work release and weekend jail lockup, as well as the old standbys, probation and parole. Buckets of money could be saved in the process. Supervision in the community, he pointed out, costs just one-tenth as much as locking bad guys away.

All these recommendations flowed, he said, from the findings of New York State's giant overview study for which he'd been one of three primary researchers—and for which I'd served as bibliographer. This study, he said, would be published later that year (1972) "if all goes well." All did not go well. It would not be made public for another three years.

AT CITY COLLEGE AROUND THIS TIME there was a maverick professor who cut a striking if irritating figure on campus. Like Martinson he was tall but he was also a loudmouth and an oddball and his appearance completed his image. He had a bushy full beard and lots of long hair like the Old Man of the Mountains and, alas, he was smelly. Martinson was never smelly, he'd always been clean and neat. Nonetheless now he seemed to take this oddball as his physical model. Soon his sharp, even features were framed by a full beard and his by now mostly white hair fell to his shoulders.

Meanwhile my personal life was going through changes. Soon after I moved to the Upper West Side, I'd started attending a local Unitarian-Universalist Church with my small son. My religious background—Jewish and Christian Scientist with a dash of Catholic

12 • The Man Who Changed the Criminal Justice System

influence—was dizzyingly ecumenical. To add to the potpourri, Rusty's father was the son of Methodists who'd dabbled in Asian religions. I couldn't wish this kind of muddle on him. So I gravitated to this small U-U congregation, most of whose members had been raised as something else. They were an arty, casual, intellectual lot who made me feel welcome. That church became my home away from home, much as the Berkeley peace center had been.

That's where I met Paul Fletcher, a barrel-chested, gregarious man with a wild and witty sense of humor. Paul was a transplanted Tennessean with more than a dash of Cherokee blood; he had striking Native American cheekbones that set off his kindly hazel eyes. Cosmopolitan to a fault—he'd lived one year in London and five years in Paris and spoke fluent French—he could always make me laugh, even when I was in my most introverted and somber moods. Though he was a recovering alcoholic, he'd been dry for many years.

We spent hours together in Central Park, watching Rusty gambol up and down its lawns and boulders while we did the Sunday Times crossword and acrostic together, but only when I stopped carrying a torch for Martinson did Paul and I start to date. In the fall of 1972, he moved in with Rusty and me. Soon he demanded to marry me, not out of propriety but because he wanted to be able to say he was my son's stepfather, not just his mother's boyfriend. He was wonderful with my son, loving and cheerful yet far better than I was at setting limits. In March 1973 we got married.

By this time, I'd finished almost all the course work for my master's in sociology. I picked a thesis topic and started doing research, comparing use patterns in my old SEEK Program library with those in a couple of public libraries in Queens. I scheduled a systematic random sample of visits to these two contrasting collections. Then, while Paul babysat my six year-old son, I spent hours observing these libraries in action.

One day the three of us set out together from our apartment to the corner on Broadway where I had to catch the subway for my trip out to Queens. We were all holding hands, with me in the middle, but then I pulled free so I could take the train. I tucked Rusty's hand into Paul's. As I did so, I felt eyes on me. Turning I saw Martinson standing across the street staring at us with the saddest expression on his face. Because he was single now and wasn't raising his own son? I wondered. Or might some of his regrets have to do with me?

By this time, Martinson's son would later tell me, the tiny brunette he'd dropped me for and thought was the love of his life had left him behind, so on that day in 1973 he was alone again.

In 1974, I received my degree in sociology. Early the next year the library association of City University published my thesis.[4] Most library schools bought it. Briefly in that obscure circle, I was a minor celebrity. Soon Bob Martinson would dazzlingly outshine me. One evening when Paul was off at a meeting, I turned on *Sixty Minutes* and there was Bob in all his glory.

At last, at 48, the Berkeley drifter I'd known for a dozen years was making it big. Mike Wallace interviewed him for a segment they called, "It Doesn't Work." He was the first sociologist ever to do a comprehensive study of prison programs to rehabilitate inmates, Wallace said. Dr. Martinson's findings had just been published two months earlier. There on the screen was Bob asserting that correctional treatment didn't work. Some programs made inmates easier to control but they had no effect on recidivism. Wallace, backing him up, asserted that two out of three ex-prisoners ended up behind bars again.

The camera panned over hardcore inmates seated in the bleachers of a modern prison's baseball field. Rehabilitation programs would never make a dent, they said, so long as prison cut them off from the workaday world and then, when they got out, people refused to hire them for an honest job. Wallace summed it up, "Cons insist the biggest barrier of all is society's attitude toward the ex-convict."

The best way to lower the recidivism rate would be to break down the barriers that faced offenders when they were released: obstacles to getting licenses, to getting bonded, to voting, to entering many professions. Though perversely, the great majority of criminals never went to jail at all. What was needed was a system that effectively tracked offenders down, tried them quickly, sent them away for a flat prison term and then, "Just pay your debt, and out!"

I left my son in the living room and phoned Bob from my bedroom to congratulate him. Thank God, I thought, Paul was out that evening

12 • The Man Who Changed the Criminal Justice System

so he'd never guess how much this man on the tube still mattered to me, this man who lived just a block and a half away.

"Hey, guess I didn't look too bad," Bob said, sounding exuberant. "Never thought I'd be a star, did ya? Well, you know, there you have it, there's my fifteen minutes of fame."

I laughed, "You'll always be a star to me, baby. For better or worse."

"Say, you've gotta see the book," he said. "So how should we do this?"

I could meet him at the grocery across from his place, I suggested, but I could only stay a few minutes because my husband was out and I'd have to leave my eight-year-old son alone. By the time I got there he was waiting for me, looking triumphant, holding a big black tome, over 700 pages long, *The Effectiveness of Correctional Treatment*.[5]

"That report I worked on for the Governor's Committee downtown? It should have come out years ago but they sat on it. It's been one helluva drama." He bounced the book lightly in his long-fingered hands, "This copy's for you."

He flipped to the page where my bibliography began. I thought of all the dreary hours I'd labored over it. Good lord, it was 92 pages long! Then he inscribed the inside front cover, "To Sylvia—an old and very dear friend."

"After we turned it in, the state refused to release it to the public. Judith and I ..." Bob hesitated for a second, "Judith really pushed. Finally she got a lawyer to subpoena it. Anyhow, I'd already spilled the beans in an article so they really didn't have much choice."

"What Works? Questions and Answers about Prison Reform"[6] appeared in 1974, the year before the book did. It was published in a leading neoconservative journal. And that, in itself, was startling. For now Bob was writing for the neocons. As of this writing, it's been cited about 4,000 times in publications around the world. And lately that number has been rising fast.

In it, Martinson asked what could be done inside "correctional institutions" to rehabilitate offenders, to make it less likely that once they were released they didn't end up back in prison. In 28 authoritatively reasoned pages, Bob argued that virtually nothing worked. "This is not to say," he noted, "that we found no instances of success or partial success [but] these instances have been isolated, producing no clear pattern to indicate the efficacy of any particular method of treatment."

Soon after its publication, this article became required reading for criminologists and policy wonks around the world. They focused on his indictment of what he viewed as ineffectual efforts to "treat" convicted offenders and turn them around. Nobody seems to have read his closing paragraph.

In it he called for "something that does not so much reform convicted offenders as prevent criminal behavior in the first place" and calls for "a new family of studies ... [that may help policy makers] judge to what degree the prison has become an anachronism and can be replaced by more effective means of social control." My guess is that he was hinting at the kind of welfare state policies—long followed in Scandinavia and other Western European democracies—that would lessen the gaps between rich and poor, privileged and underprivileged, and that would provide some kind of dole for the structurally unemployed, people for whom no jobs were available. Research has shown that policies like these would almost certainly lower the crime rate.

THESE IDEOLOGICAL BOMB BLASTS, "WHAT WORKS" and *The Effectiveness of Correctional Treatment,* made Martinson the celebrity he'd always longed to be. Soon after that *Sixty Minutes* interview, he was invited to speak at conferences all over the country and written up in *People* magazine[7]. In *People* he argued that the Charles Mansons of the world, the dangerous sociopaths, were less than 10% of criminal offenders. "Lock 'em up and weld the door shut," he said. But don't spend a fortune on building new prisons for less dangerous criminals. What was needed instead, he argued, was more suspended sentences bolstered by effective monitoring of lesser wrongdoers who remained in the community. This would cut the crime rate while costing a fraction of what incarceration did.

Something of the sort already had been tried in Texas, employing an ever-shifting mix of the culprit's neighbors—ex-offenders, unemployed teenagers, stay-at-home moms and others. Nowadays similar strategies are commonplace. Those of us who watch cop shows have seen endless close-ups of snitches ratting in dark doorways to the police. In less lurid fashion, electronic monitoring bracelets locked around the ankles of minor criminals efficiently perform much the same function.

After "What Works?"[7] appeared, the response in the field was what one researcher called "Martinson-shock." Then pushback erupted on many fronts. His belittling appraisal of correctional treatment garnered him battalions of enemies among the teachers, therapists, and prison guards who made their living behind bars. Meanwhile his old criminologist colleagues blitzed him with sarcastic attacks. The data, they said, did not support his generalizations.

In 1976, the National Council on Crime and Delinquency set out to document both sides of this controversy, since "the name Robert Martinson invariably arises in any assessment of rehabilitation." It issued a small book[8] which reprinted "What Works?," two critiques of it, and Martinson's responses to these critiques. He took to this fray with savage joy—burning behind him his bridges to the establishment.

"The history of corrections," he began, "is a graveyard of abandoned fads." Responding to the criticisms of a former co-worker[9] in California, he ridiculed the man's papers, saying that he himself and his colleagues had spent months "struggling ... to translate the footnotes, appendices, cross references and tables from the original Egyptian.... To review one of Palmer's research reports is ... something like translating the Moscow telephone book into Swahili."

Responding to Palmer's argument that Martinson's own data showed that certain types of convicts could be effectively turned around by specific forms of rehabilitation, Bob changed the focus from treatment of offenders to looking at what led them to offend in the first place. "'Criminals' are human beings engaged in 'illegitimate' activities who will cease to do so if they are given 'legitimate' ones to engage in. This can be accomplished ...[by making sure crime doesn't pay for them while] making the legitimate, full-time world of work more attractive."

AS MENTIONED BEFORE, MOST OF BOB'S old Socialist friends shunned him after he started supporting the Vietnam War. One rare exception was a colorful figure named Bogdan Denitch who, on and off for over twenty years, was a close friend of Martinson. The author of many scholarly books about the politics of Eastern Europe, Bogdan was an ethnic Croatian who immigrated to the United States in the 1950s. He and Martinson first met in Berkeley.

It was through Bogdan that Bob first met Rita Carter, the girl who would become his second wife. (Years before he'd been married briefly to a redheaded Jewish artist.) Rita struck up an acquaintance with Denitch in 1960 when, barely seventeen, she joined a picket line outside the Democratic National Convention in L.A. and attached herself to the Berkeley socialists. Bogdan, then the youth organizer for the Socialist Party in Berkeley, let her stay with him and his wife in their home. No sexual innocent, Rita soon hooked up with Martinson, almost twice her age. The next summer, Bob and Rita traveled south together as Freedom Riders. Fortunately for them, by the time their bus reached Mississippi from California, violent opposition to the Riders had ceased. They went almost directly into local jails.

Over the years that followed, Denitch shuttled between Europe and the States, often doing research in Yugoslavia. He moved from Berkeley to join the faculty of the City University of New York. He and Bob managed to remain friends by studiously avoiding controversy. "We got on, the friendship was more and more personal. He used to come to my house. We'd play chess. I got the impression he was terribly lonely because he really had no friends in the faction he went with. He backed them ideologically but he couldn't stand them personally."

Despite opposition from the left, Martinson and Wilks were riding a magic carpet of rightwing support. Gerald Ford was president. "Tough on crime" advocates were delighted to interpret Martinson's findings as proving that softhearted programs were a boondoggle and that for most criminals, long mandatory sentences were the way to go. Though neither of these conclusions had been endorsed by Martinson and Wilks. Funded by a federal grant, they set up an office on Manhattan's fashionable Upper East Side and called it the Center for Knowledge in Criminal Justice Planning. My first inkling of these developments came late in 1975 when once again I met him in the neighborhood. He was working on a new overview study, he told me, he had his own think tank. Hey, he asked, how would I like to work with him again as their bibliographer?

He offered me what he seemed to think was a generous rate of pay. For several years I'd been climbing the salary ladder at CUNY so in fact what he offered was quite a bit lower than what I was making on my regular job. I didn't bargain, I accepted it anyway. Some nostalgic urge impelled me to inhabit an office with him again for whatever hours I could shoehorn into my schedule.

I told Paul as little as possible about my new commitment. My husband of less than two years was a sensitive man who never felt I loved him as much as he loved me. I just told him that I'd worked with Martinson before and it would look good on my vita at CUNY to report I was a consultant at his center.

A few weeks later, my bosses at City College put me in charge of the library for the School of Architecture and Environmental Studies. They did this not because I was an expert on architecture—I wasn't—but because there was a citywide hiring freeze. They couldn't hire anyone new, no one else was available on the staff who knew much about architecture, and since I'd already run the SEEK Program library successfully, they figured I probably wouldn't botch this one up too badly.

Over the next three months I didn't show up much at Martinson's think tank. My other responsibilities kept me busy. Besides, writing up citations was tedious and boring.

I wanted to know more about what Bob and his small staff were aiming to accomplish—not just the titles of hundreds of reports. There were a couple of other assistants; they were pleasant enough but I had almost no occasion to speak to them. At a desk near mine, a young woman pored over papers and filled in worksheets; when I asked her what she was working on, she was unresponsive. She seemed afraid to interrupt what she was doing to talk to me.

Half the time Bob wasn't there. Sometimes, when he wasn't scheduled to teach or go to meetings in the city, people would say he was "upstate." But where upstate they wouldn't say. In fact, he was probably at the Hudson Institute which, unbeknownst to me at the time, was administering his federal grant. This institute, cordially hated by progressives, was headed by Herman Kahn, best known as the model for Dr. Strangelove.

When Martinson was in the office, I was only too aware of him, puffing cigarette after cigarette and drinking black coffee. But he almost never stopped by my desk to touch base with me. Of course, Bob was almost incapable of small talk; he had never been one to sociably pass the time of day. On the other hand, in the past he had confided in me the most personal of revelations. When I agreed to work on this bibliography, I'd imagined that sometimes we'd go out to lunch together but nothing of the sort materialized.

Judith Wilks was associate director. She seemed always to sit, silent and somber, stiffly erect behind her desk in drab shapeless clothes. Was her sternly observant presence what made that young woman who sat nearby unwilling to chat with me? One day Bob came and sat beside my desk. Out of the blue he told me the most improbable thing. He tipped his head back toward Judith and, in a voice that was only slightly muted told me cheerfully, "I'm making it with her now."

My response was non-verbal. Too shocked to say a word, the face I made and the startled way my body reacted must have spoken volumes.

"She's not *that* bad, is she?" he asked.

I was not the sort to say something insulting or catty. Instead I said, "Whatever. Whatever works for you."

This striking man, newly famous and successful, didn't answer me. He just wandered off and poured himself another cup of coffee.

Another time, when Judith wasn't in the office, Bob livened up and focused his attention on me. He danced around waving his long arms, telling me that nowadays the powers that be in the world of criminology had him flying all over, here and abroad, to give talks at conferences. In retrospect I suspect he was carefully avoiding telling me about his new rightwing connections. He must have dreaded alienating me, a rare vestige of his old circle of friends from Berkeley.

"I use all these actor's tricks," he said, "they eat it up." And with nothing in his hands, he proceeded skillfully to mime rolling a joint, carefully lighting it, taking a deep drag. Then coughing. I laughed and so did he.

"Sometimes I do the same sort of thing in class. The students love it."

He made it sound like life for him these days was one long party. I was glad for him but it was becoming clear that I'd better move on. A couple of weeks later, I broke my decision to him as gently as I could. "I'm sorry I have to do this," I told him, "but I just don't have the time and I don't need the money. And now that I have this new assignment at the college, I have a helluva lot to learn at the architecture library, really I do."

I trained the woman he hired to take over from me, then billed the Center for what they owed me. He sent me an odd letter, enclosing a

12 • The Man Who Changed the Criminal Justice System

check and mentioning that I'd only been hired as a consultant to set things up—though that had never been the case at all. A couple of weeks later, I realized I still had the high-tech key to the Center that he'd given me so I could let myself in at night or on weekends. I bought a cheery greeting card, wrote a friendly note, taped the key inside and mailed it off. I didn't give it another thought until a few months thereafter when I came up for promotion to assistant professor at the college. Now I had to collect letters of reference from people off campus who were familiar with my work.

Well, I'd done the bibliography, all 92 pages of it, for his magnum opus. He'd invited me to be his bibliographer again. And not all that long before, he'd referred to me in writing as his "old and very dear friend." I tried to phone him on campus and at the Center. When I couldn't reach him directly and he didn't return my calls, I popped into his think tank and managed to find him in. Except that when he glanced up at me from his desk, he had the craziest look in his eyes as if I were the Wicked Witch of the West swooping down on him.

I took a deep breath. Expect good and everything will turn out fine. That's what Christian Scientists believe, that's one thing I'd picked up from my mom. So I sat down calmly across from him, flipped open the portfolio I was carrying, pulled out a form to give him, and started trying to explain.

"Oh, I know why you're here," he said, "pretty cheeky after what you said to me..."

"Said to you when?"

"When you sent me that card."

"With the key?"

That look in his eyes seemed to be saying I've figured you out. I'm really smart so I've figured you out. You're just like the others, you're all against me.

God only knows what he'd made of the innocent words I'd written on that greeting card. Well, I thought, we're back to square one. I'd always known that sometimes he struggled with mental illness. He was marooned on some barren island of his own creation.

I got the recommendations I needed from other people. One day I ran into an elderly English professor I knew, an avuncular sort who served on some campus committee with Bob. As soon as I could slip the question in casually, I asked if he knew how Dr. Martinson was doing.

He shook his head and leaned toward me confidentially. "Lately he's not the easiest person to deal with, you know. Hard to get through to, doesn't seem to hear what you say. Beset by his own demons, by the look of it."

After that, whenever I saw Bob on campus or in the neighborhood, I steered clear of him. I didn't want to get assaulted again by his anger.

The 19-year-old girl on the right, posing with a girlfriend in 1915, would one day become my mother. Then Ruth Meyers, she was admired for her beauty. I would be her second child, born when she was 36.

During the Depression, my family didn't have a car so my much older cousin Herbie Williams took us for rides in his roadster with a rumble seat. I'm the little girl being fussed over by my mother, now much heavier, perched on the car's running board. In the foreground are my brother Hiram and Bernice, my orphaned cousin, raised as my sister.

Me in my late teens in Ithaca, New York, where I went to Cornell University. My tuition was covered by two scholarships I'd won at sixteen by scoring very high in a statewide competitive exam.

A picture taken the day I graduated from college. From left: my mother Ruth Hart, my fiancé Herbert Goldstone, me, my brother Hiram Hart, and my father Max Hart.

My second husband, Robert Nadler (on the left, smoking a pipe) in early 1961 outside UN headquarters in New York, demonstrating against the Bay of Pigs invasion of Cuba which had been aided by the CIA. I demonstrated with him and took this picture. Later the same year, he accepted a job in the San Francisco Bay Area so we moved to Berkeley.

With Howard Wright whom I met in Berkeley. After getting an amicable divorce from Robert Nadler who had decided to leave Berkeley and move back east, I married Howard in 1964. In this photo, we're sunburned from backpacking in the California mountains.

In 1959, Robert Martinson ran for mayor of Berkeley as the Socialist Party candidate and received 18% of the vote. The next year he traveled to Mississippi as a Freedom Rider. I met him in 1962 when we were both volunteering many hours a week at the Berkeley peace center. For two years, I edited its newsletter. For a long time thereafter, Martinson played an important role in my life.

Robert Martinson in the early 1970s with his son, Michael.

Here I am in an innovative library I created and ran, 1968-1971, in New York for a pioneering anti-poverty program. It helped prepare disadvantaged high school graduates to attend college.

Me with my son, Rustin, at around age 7, and Paul Fletcher, my new husband.

Paul Fletcher under a deluge of little boys. The blondes are brothers from a neighbor family, the Mantons; the brunette is my son.

Rustin Wright and my father, Max Hart, play-boxing. In his youth, my dad had competed as an amateur boxer and wrestler.

My brother Hiram and I in my Manhattan apartment sometime in the late 1970s.

In Manhattan around 1984, with the Hudson River and New Jersey behind me.

In Nicaragua in the summer of 1990 with a delegation led by Witness for Peace. I'm the woman in the white hat laying brick to help build a schoolhouse to replace one destroyed by the Contras during the Contra War there, 1981-1990.

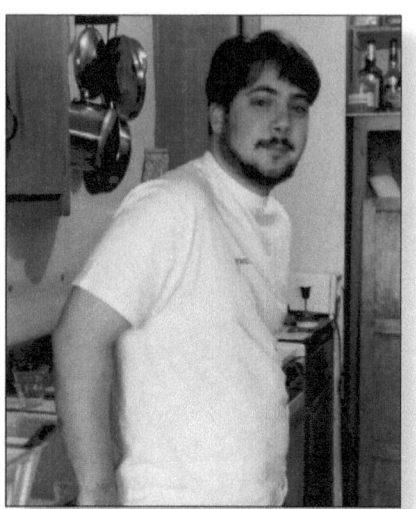

Rustin as a young man

In 1991 I moved to Eugene, Oregon, from New York. In 1993 I made the front page of the local newspaper when I demonstrated against U.S. Senator Bob Packwood. He'd been accused of sexual harassment and abuse, primarily directed at women on his staff. I'm the dark-haired woman shown directly behind the man in the foreground pushing on a door.

With Charles Gray, a longtime peace activist committed to simple living, in an undated photo. He's wearing a shirt he embroidered himself. Embroidery was one of his inexpensive pastimes.

With Charles at our wedding in 1997. At the conclusion of our Quaker ceremony, I threw my hat in the air.

Three weeks after our wedding, I traveled to Africa to tour briefly with a member of the Peace Corps there. Here I'm standing on a platform, about ten feet high, feeding "giraffe chow" to a member of an endangered species at the Giraffe Center, Nairobi, Kenya.

At the Masai Mara Game Reserve in Kenya, with three Masai tribesmen, members of the staff at the company with which I traveled on a photo safari.

With my hostess, Mary Henya, and one of Mrs. Henya's five children. For several days, I stayed on the Henyas' small farm in Kenya.

With Charles Gray in the Yosemite Valley where we backpacked and camped with another couple in 1999. Its famous rock formation, Half Dome, is in the background.

In 2000, Charles and I were active in organizing the Eugene chapter of Alliance for Democracy. Charles built this display panel.

In 2001, Charles and I traveled as international observers on a weeks-long Zapatista caravan through Mexico, offering protective accompaniment to their unarmed leaders who were threatened by paramilitaries. Here I'm standing beside a colorful banner in support of the Zapatista rebels and their goals.

In 2009, I again made the front page of the Eugene Register-Guard. *I'm holding the sign, HEALTH CARE CAN'T WAIT, at a political event held by Congressman Peter de Fazio.*

In 2016 I spoke at a memorial service, a celebration of the life of my activist comrade, Margaret "Peg" Morton.

13

Rumblings about Abortion

I DIDN'T FRET MUCH ABOUT BOB'S rejection of me. My son was doing well in a good and relatively inexpensive private school. Paul insisted on paying Rusty's fees there while I paid our rent and many of our other expenses.

(For philosophical reasons as well as financial, we'd tried to send my son to public school but in first grade he discovered that when he answered all the questions in a workbook correctly, the teacher paid no attention to him—so he started deliberately making mistakes. Disappointed and frustrated, we transferred him to a private school.)

Paul didn't seem to mind that I made more money than he did. He was unfailingly unselfish and kind. He just tried to do what he judged was honorable and right for my son and me. More than once, improbable as it seemed, he gave evidence of being psychic. Not long after we married, Paul confided to me that he "smelled death"; he sensed that people important to him would pass on in the coming year. Sure enough, two men who'd been close to him in Alcoholics Anonymous—men with no recent history of serious health problems—died within a few weeks of each other, just as he'd foreseen. "Never two without three," he said. A few months later, another good friend of his died after a brief illness.

Then there was the afternoon when we were chatting in our apartment and suddenly Paul announced, "Gotta go," and raced out the door.

13 • Rumblings About Abortion

He took the elevator down from our fourteenth floor apartment and broke up a fight in which Rusty was being attacked by two neighbor boys outside our building. He couldn't have heard the noise of their conflict—none of our windows faced the street—still somehow he knew his stepson was being bullied and he rushed to help.

The three of us went on far-flung vacations together. When Rusty was away visiting his father or off at camp, Paul and I traveled some more. Sometimes we stayed with his in-laws from his first marriage, to a young Frenchwoman. They lived in the heart of Paris, across the street from the Madeleine, a grand neoclassical temple built by Napoleon. Twice we brought Rusty along with us.

When Paul first moved in with my son and me in 1973, it was a relief after five years as a single parent to have a cultivated adult to talk to at dinnertime, not just my son, dearly though I loved him. By the mid-1970s, Rusty didn't just listen to our conversations, he participated and held his own. Paul was a punster. I followed suit from the beginning, and Rusty soon learned to do the same. Often a flurry of preposterous puns and wordplay sparked around our dinner table. Once when we were eating frozen yogurt topped with ripe peaches I'd stewed, Paul observed to Rusty, "Our ma's a peach, isn't she?"

"Sure is, without her we'd be in a jam."

"Or nutty as a fruitcake."

"Oh, go on," I demurred, "life is just a bowl of cherries."

"Or it's the pits," quickly countered our son.

"Hey, don't get crusty on me!" said Paul.

Whereupon the two of them moved on to lines about mom and apple pie and "the apple doesn't fall far from the tree."

The three of us had fun together. And I enjoyed my new job as chief of the college's architecture library. It was housed within the architecture school, far from my supervisors in the Library Department, so I had a lot of freedom to improvise. My small unit was under-funded and understaffed, still I supervised another librarian, a clerk, and an ever-changing roster of student aides who had to be trained and scheduled. When I got home, it was restful for me to prepare dinner and then sit down with my little family, confident that afterwards Paul and Rusty would clean up. Later I'd skim through the mail I received at home.

When, in the fall of 1976, the National Abortion Rights Action League sent me a significant letter, I responded to it without much thought.

I'd long been an active member of NARAL. Once, when it organized a lobbying expedition to urge fewer restrictions on abortion clinics, it first distributed postcards aimed at state legislators for its supporters to sign. I got dozens of people at my church to sign them. Then I traveled with busloads of like-minded folks to the state capital. There we tramped from one representative's office to another, delivering to each the cards signed by people in their district. Now NARAL was planning to put an ad in *The New York Times*.

Three years earlier, the Supreme Court had legalized abortion with their groundbreaking decision, *Roe v. Wade,* but soon opponents in Congress started chipping away at this. In 1976 they passed the Hyde Amendment; it banned federal funding for the procedure. The ad that NARAL planned to put in the paper, framed as a petition, would assert that "American Women Demand That Abortion Remain Legal." I signed on and agreed to have my name listed.

It was easy. I skimmed through the cover letter, checked off a couple of boxes on a sheet they enclosed, and signed it. Where it asked about my job title, I was happy at last to be able to fill in "assistant professor." Due to the unconventional way I'd been hired at the SEEK program plus the university's financial difficulties during the early Seventies, my rise to professorial status had been delayed. Finally the powers that be at CCNY had recommended my promotion to take effect on January 1st. Without much thought, I mailed the sheet back to NARAL.

A couple of weeks later, I received an irritating memo. Due to a bureaucratic glitch, my promotion wouldn't be final until September. Oh well, I thought, what the hell—waiting a few more months wouldn't much affect my salary or my life. But on January 23rd, that ad appeared in *The New York Times*. (Eventually it would appear also in *The Washington Post* and I would get a letter from Howard Wright's mother, who'd had six children and now was living in the capital, thanking me for signing onto it.)

This ad explained something I hadn't known before. All the women NARAL had asked to sign had been listed in either *Who's Who in America* or *Who's Who of American Women.* (I'd always wondered how I made the cut for the latter. I guessed that the editors of reference books like these, which sold primarily to libraries, were eager to find librarians to include.) NARAL had printed just a partial list of those who'd signed onto the petition. The names of 137 women, along with brief identifying details, appeared in the ad. Fifty-nine of us, myself included, acknowledged that we'd had an abortion.

I wasn't ashamed to admit this. I'd never once regretted the choice I'd made when I was 23 and single, ten years before I had the child I cherished. What worried me was that there in *The New York Times,* for all to see, I was listed as an assistant professor—but in fact on January 23rd, that wasn't strictly true and it made me nervous. Looking for support from my church community, I made copies of a form at the bottom of the ad that invited people to support this cause. The next Sunday, I brought them to the Universalist Church in its landmark Gothic building on Central Park West where I'd first met Paul. Stepping forward when the minister called for people to share their "joys and concerns," I explained what had happened and asked folks who supported abortion rights to pick up a form from me after the service.

Members flocked to pick up copies. Then one of our dignified elders, the retired headmistress of one of the city's top private schools, came up to me with a determined look on her craggy face. She had in tow a man I didn't know. Introducing him to me, she explained that he was the director of an abortion clinic.

"You two should get together," she announced. "You'd do us all a service if you'd write up a resolution for our congregation to send on to the General Assembly."

So that's what happened. We composed a resolution urging full abortion rights for all women, with government funding for the needy among them; then we presented it to a meeting of delegates from U-U churches in the New York metropolitan area. A committee tweaked it and sent it on to a higher level. I don't know how much impact statements from small religious denominations ever have, still it gave me a thrill when many months later the Unitarian-Universalists at their annual national meeting, approved an expanded version of the text we'd drafted as a General Resolution. This was a happy and unexpected consequence of a melodrama I'd lived through 21 years before.

At the time I was twenty-three and living with my prudish parents while I tried to recover from a miserable marriage where every sexual contact with my husband felt like a joyless obligation. I was in no hurry to remarry, I just wanted to feel again, as I had with my first boyfriend, that a man's touch could give me pleasure. Besides, I sensed that having sex now and then would help me stay cheerful and relaxed while I juggled a hectic schedule of graduate school and work.

I'd taken a job as a clerk in a branch of the New York Public Library. My supervisor gently talked me into signing on as a trainee. As soon as I got admitted to library school, she told me, I'd become a Trainee A and get a raise. Once I earned six credits I'd get another raise and be a Trainee B. And so on till I got my degree and was a full-fledged librarian. What a deal! So I enrolled in a master's program at Columbia, switched from full time to part time on my job, and one weekend that summer a girlfriend and I went to Fire Island to sunbathe and party.

That's where I met Gene. He wasn't the love of my life. I wasn't ready for the love of my life. I just wanted somebody simpatico to play with and, for better or worse, that's all he wanted from me. I'd meet him at his apartment in Brooklyn Heights and sometimes we'd go out for dinner, more often we'd fix dinner together at his place, but always we'd end up in bed together because that was what our relationship was really all about. I sure didn't want to get pregnant by him—or anyone else. I didn't feel ready to be anybody's mom. In those days, using a diaphragm and jelly was the way to go, 98% safe the experts told us. Nothing available was 100% safe. I was one of the unlucky 2%.

I got pregnant. To find out for sure, in those days before you could buy a pregnancy test in any drugstore, I didn't go to my regular doctor; I didn't dare let my new and threatening condition show up on my medical record. Instead I went to some fancy Park Avenue gynecologist a girlfriend recommended. He said yes, I was pregnant all right—then he started asking me questions. Where had I gone to school? Cornell. What kind of man was the father? A stock analyst on Wall Street. I'd lied about our names but it soon became clear that this doctor wasn't going to report us to anyone. He was angling to get me to have the baby so he could pass it on for a handsome fee to some wealthy childless couple with high intellectual standards.

I said no thank you and went on my way. I definitely *didn't* want to have a baby. I wasn't ready to take care of one and I couldn't bear the thought of messing up my ostensibly respectable life to accommodate

13 • Rumblings About Abortion

strangers. Worse yet, the thought of having a baby and then turning over my own flesh and blood to someone else revolted me. But that left me still "in trouble" as the saying went.

Gene started treating me with barely veiled suspicion. He seemed to wonder whether I'd gotten pregnant on purpose or just been a careless slob. He let slip that, all the time he'd been having sex with me, he'd been engaged to someone else. Now I *definitely* didn't want to have his kid. But at least he quickly came up with a solution. It wasn't simple: I'd have to leave the country.

By this time I'd just missed two periods. Theoretically I could have waited longer, hoping that I'd miscarry. (One-fifth of all pregnancies end that way.) Instead, because the winter holidays were coming up and it seemed discreet to pretend I was taking a jolly old vacation, I took a week off from my job and the day after Christmas, 1956, I flew to Cuba.

I'd never been out of the country before. Of course I was scared—but I was a lot more scared of having my belly grow bigger and bigger and totally screwing up my future. I'd never learned Spanish but I'd studied French and Latin in school. In Miami where I had to change planes, I bought a tiny Berlitz book from which I learned some basic phrases. As soon as I arrived in the Havana airport I headed for a public phone. The only guidance I'd been given for this expedition was a phone number. "You call this number," Gene told me, "and ask for Coco." So that's what I did.

Coco told me where to wait for him in the airport. He turned out to be a slight, swarthy man, a few years older than I. Don't worry about the operation, he told me. "Is like when a *dentista* take a tooth." A couple months before, he said, he'd met a well-known movie star at the airport, coming to see the doctor just like me. He told me her name. Everybody knew her name. "She come out fine," he said. "You come out fine too."

Coco was right. I got first-rate care from a gynecologist assisted by an anesthesiologist. I was barely pregnant, six weeks and two days as best I could figure. The embryo inside me then, too young to be called a fetus, would have been the size of a peanut and barely mammalian, with a rudimentary tail and with slits across the front of its face where eventually its mouth and nose might have developed. When I came to, the gynecologist told me in educated English that everything had gone well but in a week or so I'd have a very heavy period. He'd just loosened the embryo from the wall of my uterus so I'd have a miscarriage back in the States.

Because I was middle class and Gene had connections, my experience with abortion wasn't all that bad. In time I would hear stories of hairier experiences. When my girlfriend Vicky got pregnant at seventeen, her parents convinced their doctor to give her a kitchen table abortion—but the doctor refused to use an anesthetic because he thought she should suffer for her sins. Her parents held her down on the table. She writhed with pain while he scraped around inside her. The curette he should have been using, if indeed that's what he used, must have slipped. He cut her. She ended up damaged, with urinary problems that wouldn't go away.

Even in those days when abortion was illegal, dilation and curettages (usually called D and Cs) were done fairly often all over the country—but usually they were done to save a woman's life when she was in danger of bleeding to death. Too many victims to count—often already mothers of more kids than they could care for—poked themselves frantically with a knitting needle or a wire hanger or went to some half-trained, back alley person. The lucky ones were those who, when things went badly wrong, managed to get to a hospital where doctors patched them up. The year after abortion became legal in New York, the death toll for abortion related deaths in the city dropped to 15 from 24.

AT LAST MY PROMOTION TO ASSISTANT professor came through. But a harrowing new problem arose at home. Paul had had diabetes for over twenty years. Not long after we got married, his doctor discovered danger signs in his eyes, tiny blood vessels that might rupture if they weren't treated, signs of diabetic retinopathy, a common cause of blindness. Paul got laser treatments to cauterize the threatening spots. Two years later, he suddenly lost all vision in one of his eyes—but he could still see very well with the other.

He still looked the same. He went on teaching French at Stuyvesant, a remarkable public high school where admission was by competitive exam and a multicultural mix of New York's brightest kids felt privileged to attend. I went on cheerfully, totally in denial, thinking he'd get by fine with his one good eye. Until, one day in November of 1977, he phoned me from his doctor's office and asked me to come and get him. He'd had a hemorrhage in his "good eye" and could barely see.

Blood and vitreous fluid were blocking out the light in the center of that eye; only a little blurry vision remained in its outer edges. There was nothing to do but wait until this muck was gradually absorbed by his body. Months went by. Paul couldn't teach anymore. He bought a good Gibson guitar secondhand and started relearning chords he'd used when he played in a quartet as a kid. As the hemorrhage cleared somewhat, he discovered he could read again if he had enough light. He bought a floor lamp that held four bulbs that could give off a total of 330 watts; we called it Paul's lamp. My son and I never turned on more than one or two of those bulbs but Paul read under that lamp, fully lit, for hours.

Often he ventured out with his blind man's cane and, helped by strangers along the way, took the bus down to the Universalist Church where we'd met. There he worked as a volunteer assisting Clive, the church's business manager, by answering the phone and fielding questions from people who dropped by. (Much of the income that supported the church came not from its small congregation but from rentals by groups which used its facilities.) Clive, a part-time artist, and Gulabchad, a Hindu trained as an engineer who managed the physical plant, became good friends of his.

After I came home from work, Paul and I would go out for a walk together, often in Central Park or on the path alongside it. He'd hold my upper arm with one hand, his cane in the other. My Tennessee Frenchman—that was one of my nicknames for him—had always been able to make me laugh and now, more than ever, he seemed to save up all his good humor, all the funny anecdotes he'd garnered from phone calls he'd made or received that day, things he'd read, radio programs he'd heard, to entertain me while we walked.

Much of his vision returned. I lived in hope that his good eye would clear completely. We traveled to Boston so he could be treated by a specialist at Massachusetts General. The treatment helped—but eleven months after the first hemorrhage, his good eye bled again.

14

The Harder They Fall

On New Year's Day, 1979, I was standing in a crowded subway car heading home from downtown when I saw my sometime friend Bob Martinson standing ten feet away. He was wearing a meticulously tailored overcoat that looked warm and expensive. I averted my gaze, afraid he'd snub me if I acted like I knew him. But then, sensing eyes on me I turned and saw that he was weaving closer through a tangle of straphangers and looking at me intently. Our eyes met and he smiled with relief.

"Happy New Year!" he proclaimed with great ceremony. He took off a fur-lined leather glove to shake my hand. People stared as we exchanged excited greetings. Then he invited me to come to his place.

"Okay," I smiled, "why not?"

I knew the building where he lived but I'd never been in his apartment. The elevator took us to the twelfth floor. His place was dimly lit as he stepped into the kitchen and started rummaging around for a bottle.

"Would you like a drink?"

"No thanks, I don't think so."

If Paul smelled booze on my breath, he'd ask questions I didn't feel like answering. As soon as I spoke, a male voice called out from somewhere in the apartment, "Hi, Shana."

"It's not Shana, it's Sylvia," Bob called back. "Come out and say hello."

14 • The Harder They Fall

A boy emerged from a shadowy hall. At sixteen Michael was well over six feet, slightly shorter than his father. As his mother's son too, he had tawny skin and extraordinary eyes, their irises dark-centered but ringed with blue.

"The first time I met you," I told him, "you were three and a half years old. Your father told me your whole name, I remember: Michael Stephen-Constantine Martinson."

(When Howard and I were living in Berkeley, we'd dropped in on old friends of his and there in their living room had been Bob and his little son. Our hostess would tell me later that when we walked in, she sensed the air crackle between Bob and me.)

Michael seemed unimpressed by what I'd remembered. He headed back into the inner recesses of the apartment, leaving his father and me standing in the kitchen. Bob told me his son was terribly bright and what he'd been doing. He was sipping a couple of fingers of gin from a water glass. Bob drank martinis when someone else mixed them but otherwise he drank gin straight. He put down the glass and stepped closer to me. He stooped, put his arms around me and kissed me.

He didn't kiss me like an old friend. He kissed me like a lover—or an actor portraying a lover. (Sometimes with Bob it was hard to tell the difference at first until his fear of intimacy yielded to trust and desire.) I stood on my toes, embraced him and kissed him back. I stroked his beautiful bearded face that looked so much more worn than when first I'd known him. I stroked his broad forehead, his long thick hair. But then I pulled away.

I'd never been the most chaste of women and no man had ever moved me more than this one but where could all this be going, with his son in the apartment and Rusty and Paul a block and a half away, waiting for me to come home and make dinner and warm myself in the glow of their affection? Paul was very sensitive to me, arguably psychic, and now I lived in fear that any misstep of mine might set off another hemorrhage in his eyes. That was the worst of it.

"I've gotta go," I said, "I'm sorry. Look, we ought to get together. We ought to talk. I'll call you on campus. We could have lunch at least, for starters." What I was saying sounded hopelessly banal but it was the best I could do at the moment. After this sudden change in his attitude toward me, I needed to catch my breath and think.

As soon as the new semester started after winter break, I phoned him on campus and left a message on his machine. I wanted to have lunch with him. It felt good to be his friend again, not walled off from him by some inscrutable delusion. I wanted to be his confidante as I had been years before. I sensed he needed someone to talk to, someone without an ax to grind, someone who just wanted to help him.

But he didn't call back. I felt shy about reaching out again to him. I was afraid he'd rebuff me as he had before so I never called him a second time. A couple of months later, I ran into him in the street near his house. Maybe he'd lost weight. He certainly looked haggard. The weirdest thing about him was the way he was dressed. Bob Martinson loved to wear nice things, but now he was wearing pants that belonged on a clown in the circus. Strange polyester pants in a gaudy, blotchy plaid, pants that hung on him absurdly.

I didn't know what to say so I just said, "I called you."

I was wondering if he'd ever picked up my message.

"Yes, you *called* me," he said looking pleased, as if I'd granted him some special boon. Except, of course, that he hadn't bothered to call back. This time he said vaguely, yes, we ought to get together but as I went on my way I was pretty sure I wouldn't hear from him.

AROUND THIS TIME, PAUL'S "GOOD EYE" hemorrhaged once more. He started taking classes in "cane travel" and other survival skills at the Lighthouse for the Blind. He helped out at the Universalist Church. After I came home from work we still took walks. He could still make me laugh. We both worked hard to convince each other that things were going just fine. But I lived in constant dread of what might happen next to him.

One evening late in 1979, Paul, Rusty and I went out to dinner as we customarily did one night each week. A young couple was sitting at the next table. The woman looked familiar but I couldn't place her. She turned toward me and said pleasantly, "You're Sylvia, aren't you? You used to work at the Center on 85th Street?"

"Right, right." She'd been one of the assistants there. Then she said, "You know the Center's closed."

I shook my head. I hadn't heard.

"Did you know he died?"

14 • The Harder They Fall

"Who died?"

"Bob died, that was months ago." She paused for a moment, leaned closer and lowered her voice, "Actually he killed himself."

What was there to say except "Oh, my God," and ask how it happened.

"He jumped out a window."

She didn't seem to know why but she mentioned that Judith Wilks had had a breakdown sometime before. That was all this young woman seemed willing or able to tell us.

The three of us finished dinner, the three of us went home. By then, Paul couldn't make out the expression on my face but it really didn't matter. He was so sensitive to me that he must've known I felt stricken.

My son went to his room and left Paul and me alone together. I realized with relief that at last I could tell him the truth about Bob—that this man who was our neighbor and my colleague had, in the distant past, been my lover. Because Bob was no longer a threat to our marriage and I'd never betrayed Paul with him. And then this good man did the kindest thing.

I was in misery, wondering what had really happened.

"We could go round and ask the super there," he said. "Not tonight, it's too late, but maybe tomorrow. We'll go together."

So the next day we went and the super told us that in the middle of a muggy August night, a tenant looked out a window that faced an interior courtyard, saw someone sprawled there and called the police. When the police arrived they woke the super and asked him if he could identify the body. He let them into Bob's apartment and there was Michael fast asleep.

"The boy moved away, couple of months ago," he told us. "Had family out west, I think."

"Did Dr. Martinson leave a note?" I asked.

The man shrugged, "I don't think so. But he'd been acting a little strange. He paid an extra month's rent in advance. He'd never done that before."

Now I know more than I knew then. Soon after I stopped working at his think tank, Martinson changed sides. He started battling the forces that his article, "What Works?" had set in motion.

Hardliners determined to keep convicts locked up as long as possible had started attacking the use of parole to release prisoners before the end of their sentences. An article by Martinson and Wilks[1] challenged this. "Effective parole supervision insures that fewer offenders will be rearrested, convicted, and returned to prison." But never thereafter would Martinson write with Wilks for publication. He seems to have turned against her—probably for pushing him and guiding his work in the disastrous way it had gone. And Bob could be slashing and vitriolic, as he'd been when he derided the work of criminologists who questioned his findings. As he'd been in Berkeley, old acquaintances remembered, when he debated political foes there.

So what became of Judith Wilks who had taught at N.Y.U. and co-authored a book and articles with Bob? She had a breakdown, a really bad breakdown. Years later, people would see her living as a bag lady in Manhattan, then dishing out food in a mental hospital.

In 1978, Bob started lashing out by himself. Responding to an article[2] which called him a "strong advocate ... of the sure-fire punitive approach," he said that he favored *shorter* sentences accompanied by "increases in the *certainty* of punishment.... What the hell is wrong with a short, fixed and certain sentence?" At a conference workshop,[3] he unleashed "a blistering critique of his own book." In it, he said, he and his co-authors "threw out the baby but clung rigorously to the bath water." They overlooked significant studies because they didn't meet arbitrary standards of methodology. In his next article he asserted that "contrary to my previous position, some treatment programs *do* have an appreciable effect on recidivism. Some programs are indeed beneficial."

One professional publication reported that when a professor in a seminar, dismayed by Martinson's about-face, asked him, "What will I now tell my students?" Bob replied, "Tell them I was full of crap."[4]

Most telling of all to me was how he responded[5] when *Contemporary Authors*, a major research service, invited him to submit biographical information. He listed the books his writings had appeared in but with regard to magazines, he said he'd contributed "articles and reviews to professional journals and to *Liberation, Anvil, Nation, New America, Liberal Democrat, New Republic,* and *Dissent*"—all publications on the left. Conspicuous by its absence was *The Public Interest,* the prime publication of the neoconservatives, where "What Works?"—the article that made him famous and only too influential—first appeared.

14 • The Harder They Fall

During Martinson's final years, his son has told me, Bob was terribly depressed and under psychiatric care. That spring Bob's therapist sent him to a specialist. He thought this doctor would make him sign himself into an institution so he gave Michael three checks: enough for two months' rent and his airfare back to his mother and grandparents in Southern California. But when he saw this second doctor, the man just prescribed an even stronger anti-depressant, one which turned out to have the nasty side effect of not letting him sleep. Probably that's one reason why he looked so haggard, that day when I saw him wearing circus clown pants.

Still Bob had always been a fighter. I asked anyone I thought might know: what depressed him enough to make him take his own life? One day at a City College luncheon I happened to sit next to a former colleague of his from the sociology department. I asked him about Martinson and he didn't give me much of an answer. So I told him I'd known Bob in Berkeley, years before, and I'd always felt there was a hollow space inside him where confidence and stability should reside. His mother was only sixteen when he was born, hardly ready to take proper care of him. In his sleep, I said, he used to make suckling noises because he hadn't had enough love as a child. I knew this was a bold, unladylike thing to say but what the hell—I had to break through. His colleague turned and looked at me differently. He pondered for a moment before he replied.

"Well, first when he said nothing works, he became the darling of the hard-line conservatives and all his old friends on the left started shunning him. That was okay as long as he was riding high and he thought he had truth by the tail but then he started having second thoughts. He started writing articles and letters to journals saying people were misreading what he'd said earlier and anyhow he should've looked at additional studies. And the next thing, he didn't have friends on the right *or* the left."

And Martinson had to have friends, that man with a hollow center. The frightened child inside that towering man always roused my need to be needed, my longing to soothe him and make him feel whole.

Now change is afoot in the American criminal justice system. Ever since the Great Recession, politicians have been looking for ways to save money on it. Instead of building new prisons, states have begun releasing more non-violent convicts into the community. Leaders are debating ways to be *smart* on crime, rather than just *tough* on crime. And Martinson's findings are being reexamined.[6]

Still not enough money is spent on prevention or on the treatment of addicts. Sentences are too long, far longer than in countries with much lower crime rates. Unlike all other nations, we spend less money on policing than on incarceration. Meanwhile, most offenses—including assaults, break-ins, rapes, even murders—go unpunished, no matter what the TV dramas say.

15

A Book, Some Insights, and a Giant March

IN JANUARY 1976, I'D BEEN PUT in charge of the library of CCNY's architecture school. That was fine—except that I had no background in architecture. In those days before computerized databases, librarians often used reference books to answer questions. My library was well supplied with them. The problem was that none of them quickly answered many questions my students bombarded me with.

Architecture students heard the name of an important building and wanted to learn more about it. Or they had to design a certain kind of project—a hotel or a hospital, a fire station or a convention center—and they wanted to see the best examples of that kind of structure. The problem was that the prime reference set in the field, the *Avery Index to Architectural Periodicals,* seventeen tall and hefty green volumes, was arranged almost completely by the name of the architect or architectural firm. If you didn't know the architect's name you were out of luck.

It dawned on me that someone should put together a different kind of guide, a guide to the most notable contemporary American buildings, that facilitated that kind of research. Maybe that someone should be me. From earliest childhood, I'd been told I was very bright. But for most of my adult life, I'd been treated by my family like an under-achiever, someone too busy having fun and adventures to ever get anything worthwhile done. I tried to look nonchalant but guilt was my almost constant companion, guilt and an aching sense of failure. I felt driven to accomplish something—though just *what* I should accomplish was another question.

I certainly hadn't succeeded in writing the Great American Novel but at least I'd created guides before. For that subscription agency I worked for, I'd prepared widely-used pamphlets that listed magazines recommended for special audiences. But all I knew about architecture I was learning on the job. How could I systematically select the architectural projects to include?

I asked around in the architecture school but none of the profs seemed to have a clue. So I called the American Institute of Architects and asked for their advice. They invited me to come down to their headquarters in Washington, DC; then they'd see what they could do for me. By the time I could visit them it was winter. The capital had just had its worst snowfall in years. I slogged into the AIA's sleek offices wrapped from head to toe in my warmest socially acceptable clothes, from a stylish sheepskin cloche I'd bought at a crafts fair to black leather boots, with a fleecy plaid wool scarf swaying in between. For a minute the young woman I talked to looked puzzled. Then she made a couple of phone calls and suddenly my project took a great leap forward. There was this man I should talk to, she said. He knew everything, *everything* about this sort of thing. His name was John Fondersmith, he edited *American Urban Guidenotes,* and he'd agreed to see me.

That evening I took a cab which labored through the snow and deposited me a couple of drifts away from Fondersmith's doorstep. He was younger than I was and at least as nervous but he sat me down in his book-lined living room and offered me a beer. A beer! Blessed relief! I'd loved beer ever since I was a 16-year-old coed at Cornell, drinking with dates at student hangouts. (Thanks, I guess, to unwritten rules in that college town, I was never carded.) Good beer contains relaxing B vitamins as well as a modest ration of alcohol. For the next two hours, the glass after glass we sipped lubricated our intellectual efforts.

Fondersmith wasn't just encyclopedic, he was a problem solver. He educated me about awards given by the AIA and the leading magazines[1] in the field, and told me when they were announced each year. He pulled book after book from his shelves and glanced through them to find and recommend a select few works that authoritatively discussed the most influential—or most controversial—projects of the past few

15 • A Book, Some Insights, and a Giant March

decades. I listened gratefully and leafed through the journals and volumes he handed me. I took lots of notes. By the time I made my way back through snowdrifts to the cab he'd called for me, I was well on my way to making an informed selection of buildings to include.

I applied for a year's sabbatical which my department granted. Starting in September, I'd be a free woman with money coming in. That summer, the American Library Association was slated to hold its annual conference in Manhattan. Early that June, I put together a sample section of the guide that covered just sixteen buildings, plus samples of the indexes I planned to include—indexes that would make it easy for researchers to look projects up by building type, building name or location. I'd heard that sometimes you could find a publisher by checking with the folks who exhibited at professional meetings so that's what I did.

I walked up and down long aisles of tables at the Coliseum, off Columbus Circle, looking for the booths of publishers who sold to libraries. Two middle-aged men in business suits were staffing the table for Scarecrow Press. I'd heard of Scarecrow Press, it was nothing fancy, just a respectable house that put out good gray reference works that librarians bought. I showed them what I had; they looked moderately interested. They took my name and address and the sample pages I offered them. I assumed that, if they liked them, they'd pass them on to their bosses.

It turned out that *they* were the bosses: the president of the firm and the head of sales. One of them wrote me a letter asking me for more details about my background and my credentials. I agonized, then wrote him back. I'd barely caught my breath when I received another letter asking questions about my project. Somehow I managed to send back an answer. This process went on for one more exchange. I guess these guys were testing me. Publishers need to know if their authors can meet deadlines. Pretty soon I had a contract and I realized that, wonder of wonders, it had taken me less than an hour of legwork—and beginner's luck—to find a house to publish my book.

Meanwhile Paul's "good eye" kept hemorrhaging. Each time it cleared somewhat, murky fluid leaked into it again. These episodes came on ever more often and each of them blocked more light from his retina.

Late in 1980, Paul went for an operation to improve his vision. Instead it failed miserably. Now my husband was totally blind.

I did my best to keep him living what looked like a normal life but this involved odd expedients. When he had a check to cash,[2] I went with him to the bank. There I sorted out for him the different denominations of paper money he'd received and he systematically folded all $5 bills one way, tens another, and twenties still a third way as he'd been taught to do at the Lighthouse for the Blind.

As he struggled to keep up his spirits in total darkness, the sphere in which he could function grew ever smaller and more confining. For years a good friend of his from the Universalist Church, who also happened to be from his hometown, had phoned him each morning. They would razz each other and joke around; the call started Paul's day off pleasantly. Now this buddy moved faraway and stopped calling.

There were other blows, each small in itself but terrible taken together. When the three of us went to restaurants, waiters would foolishly raise their voices when they spoke to Paul as if he were hard of hearing, or they wouldn't speak to him at all. They'd ask me what they should bring him to eat, as if he weren't capable of making a choice. Paul had always been very gregarious. He loved to start conversations with neighbors in our building's elevator and even with strangers he met on buses. But now, since he couldn't make eye contact, people thought he was crazy to speak into the air. They shrank from him and wouldn't reply.

Every day Paul and I went out for a long walk. He liked to call me his seeing-eye wife and refused to get a dog and go for the training he'd have to undergo to get one. I sensed that I was shortchanging my teenage son, not giving him all the attention he deserved. Except that Paul was blind and Rustin was healthy so I did the best I could—which probably wasn't too great.

Once when my husband and I were out walking together, an old woman reached a hand to his wrist and told him gently, "Don't worry, dear, someday you'll see again." Paul didn't answer her but his face hardened with anger. "Let's get out of here," he whispered to me. "I wish to hell people wouldn't try to comfort me with that shit."

We both knew she meant he'd see again in the afterlife—but Paul was a total atheist. His mantra was "When it's over, it's over." He used

15 • A Book, Some Insights, and a Giant March

to say he could stay dry on the first of AA's twelve steps: acknowledging that he was powerless over alcohol. He refused to acknowledge the existence of a Higher Power, the God referred to again and again in the next eleven steps.

That fall I handed in the manuscript of my guide. The next spring Scarecrow Press issued it in a no-nonsense format. It was a sturdy hardback designed for libraries; it didn't even have a book jacket. Still it got excellent reviews from several professional journals.

Paul was thrilled for me. The next Sunday he took a copy to church and waved it excitedly, bragging about what I'd done. I was embarrassed. It certainly wasn't a literary achievement, just a useful tool for a limited public. A week later, my sister had family and a few friends over for dinner at her apartment in Queens. My brother gave the three of us a lift. I didn't mention my new book in his car though I'd brought along gift copies for him, my father and Bernice, but as soon as we arrived and my stepmother—a take-charge, outspoken woman—saw the copy I was planning to give my dad, she complimented me enthusiastically and snatched it up.

She waited until all the guests were seated in Bernice's living room, then she hushed everybody and said proudly, "I have an important announcement to make. My wonderful stepdaughter here has written a *book* and it's been *published* and here it is!" She passed it around. Several people flipped through it curiously and made kind comments—but my brother and father were not among them. And this seemed strange and disappointing.

My father had left school at fourteen to work but as an adult, he'd taken college courses at night; he was self-taught, a zealous reader. While working at low level civil service jobs, he'd written drafts of two books—one on Ulysses S. Grant, the other on the stock market. An agent had liked his manuscript about Wall Street, but because he had neither academic credentials nor a self-made fortune, she'd reluctantly turned him down. My brother, a physics professor, had had dozens of scientific articles published. Writing was practically in our family's DNA.

Back in the late nineteenth and early twentieth centuries, my grandfather's cousin, Morris Rosenfeld[3], had spoken out in Yiddish according to his socialist lights for the exploited working class against their exploiters. He'd been acclaimed as the first and greatest of "the sweatshop poets." During the Depression, two of my mother's siblings had built a major publishing firm; my brother and I had grown up reading their publications.

Bernice had married at nineteen and had five children. Books had never carried much weight for her. But all my adult life, my parents and brother had made me feel guilty for not fulfilling my potential. Now my mother was dead—but why didn't my brother and father exult for me?

My brother didn't want to accept the copy I gave him. When I pressed it on him, he flinched as if it were toxic. (In his car driving us home, he made just one related comment, painfully competitive: "Maybe *I'll* write a book!") My father didn't exactly flinch when my stepmother passed his copy back to him but he didn't make any comments either. A few days later, I received a nice thank-you note from him—but I couldn't help feeling that his wife had insisted he send it.

Not long after, because of this guide I'd written, I gained quick promotion to associate professor. But that wasn't the greatest benefit I gained from its publication. It taught me that I needn't feel guilty anymore for the path my life had taken, that since I was a child my family had given me mixed messages. They treated me as a failure for not achieving greatly but the last thing in the world they ever wanted was for me, a girl, to outshine my brother.

That spring at CCNY, a new project came along that recalled my glory days in Berkeley. A giant march was being planned that would bring hundreds of thousands of people from all over the nation to New York to demonstrate in favor of a nuclear freeze. Along with a handful of faculty members from a mix of departments, I volunteered to help plan a campus event. We hoped to rouse student interest and convince at least some of our kids to participate in the big demonstration.

Members of our committee reserved a large lecture room, arranged for speakers, created a publicity poster and got it distributed. Remembering the exuberance of Berkeley protests, I concentrated on making the event fun so I phoned around and located a small combo that would sing and play anti-war songs for us. I also bought a batch of campaign buttons for us to distribute and picked up petitions that students could sign. On the big day, our combo would play and sing outside the lecture hall, attracting attention and luring students in.

15 • A Book, Some Insights, and a Giant March

Fliers appeared around my neighborhood inviting people to serve as staff for the coming march and rally. I showed up with a crush of others for a meeting in a cavernous hall with nowhere near enough folding chairs. Some organizer in his twenties described what was being planned and what modest roles we might play. Then he asked each of us to tell what had brought us there. One after another, women and men, young and old, said a few words about their fear of nuclear war, their hatred of the arms race, how wasteful and dangerous they thought it was. When my turn came I mentioned, just as a preface, "I lived in Berkeley during the sixties." Suddenly a torrent of applause swept through the room. I didn't have to say another word. The image of those days in Berkeley said it all.

Like scores of others, with very little training and a bright red T-shirt that labeled me STAFF, I was anointed a "peacekeeper," entrusted with the task of making sure nobody screwed up too badly near me along the line of march. The big day—June 12, 1982—saw me sitting in jeans on the curb at 4:30 a.m. at the location I'd been assigned way downtown in Lower Manhattan. My red shirt said DISARM and featured a generic human figure breaking a missile in half. At first, I was practically the only one there.

Then the multitudes started arriving. And more and more. The march itself wouldn't begin for several hours. When it did, it processed slowly, mile after mile up the spine of Manhattan with bands on floats and countless contingents with banners, with monks and nuns in their habits along with hippies and gays, with union members and religious delegations and who knows how many other delegations from a boundless variety of interest groups. Helicopters whirled their blades far overhead so observers could hazard a guess at the number of people—almost a million—in that giant flood, that avalanche of humanity that bulged against miles of sidewalks crammed with still more people, many of them waving signs supporting our cause.

At Columbus Circle we veered left onto Central Park West. Half an hour later and a mile further uptown we reached my Universalist Church. I recognized people inside, staring out its windows at our huge procession. By now many of the marchers, myself included, were desperately in need of bathrooms. Aha, I knew where the church's bathrooms were! I led a batch of us through a side door to use the facilities.

When the others surged back out, aiming to turn into the park for the culminating rally, I decided I'd had enough.

I was tired. Over the years I'd sat still for too many speeches, I figured I'd done my part for the day. The movement didn't need my wee body any longer. Home was a mile and a half away. Still walking, that's where I headed.

16

Surprises

L<small>ATE THAT FALL A COUSIN OF</small> mine offered us the use of her condo in West Palm Beach for the Christmas holidays. Once we arrived, I rented a car. One day I drove us down to Miami Beach where my parents were staying. Another day we went up to Cape Canaveral where we toured the Kennedy Space Center; the next day I drove back. But something about the air conditioning in the car felt funny. The air didn't smell right, there was something strange about it that we couldn't identify.

By the time we got back to New York, Paul and I were coming down with the flu. At least we thought it was the flu. Rustin stayed perfectly well and went back to school but Paul and I had to take to our beds. We were feverish and aching, feeble and coughing, but Paul was having stomach problems as well and every day his symptoms grew more severe. A couple of days after New Years, lying sick beside my husband in bed, I noticed something very odd about his breathing, an echoing, deep-in-the-chest sound I'd never heard before.

My health care coverage provided for house calls by physicians. I crawled out of bed to find the number to call; twenty minutes later a woman doctor was at the door. As soon as she checked Paul, she said, "He's got pneumonia. He's got to go to the hospital," and rushed to the phone. Ten minutes later, medics arrived, a man and a woman. Never in my life have I seen anyone work so fast and efficiently. They started him on oxygen, bundled him up to face the January cold, and with me tagging along, coughing as I clutched the bag that held our insurance cards, we whizzed in an ambulance north to St. Luke's Hospital.

For almost three weeks they kept him in Intensive Care on a respirator with a tube down his throat so this eminently verbal man couldn't speak. Paul loved old classic jazz. Still sick myself, I brought him a radio and tuned it to a station that played that kind of music. At last I got well enough to go back to work. My library was less than a mile away from his hospital so I could take long lunch hours and hop in a cab to see him. I'd hold his hand and talk to him or read to him. If I asked him a question, he'd blink his eyes once or twice to tell me yes or no.

During our vacation in Florida, Rustin had made a teenage scene with him. I managed to haul my son in to apologize and make peace with his stepfather. Though Paul couldn't say a word, his nods and his kindly face spoke volumes. They were friends again—I was grateful for that.

After twenty days in the I.C.U., the doctors at St. Luke's said he'd recovered enough so they could take him off the respirator. For the first time, I visited him in an ordinary hospital room. He still couldn't speak; his vocal cords had to heal first. He seemed to be breathing normally but he wasn't very responsive. A nurse came in to check on him; she and I exchanged a few words. When I turned back to Paul, there was an expression of terror on his face—at least that's how it looked to me. "It's just his hair," the nurse told me as she turned to leave. "Don't be frightened. Just go ahead, comb his hair for him." So I did. His thick wavy hair seemed to be standing on end; I combed it and he looked a little better but not much.

A moment later a social worker hurried in. She took my arm and led me behind the sheet that separated Paul's bed from the second bed, unoccupied, in his double room. The hospital wanted to release him soon, she told me, but I'd better hire a private nurse to take care of him. Insurance would help. As I left I glanced at Paul's face and it was totally changed.

He looked like the cat who ate the canary. Delighted, mischievous, even triumphant. He didn't notice that I was leaving the room. That was the last time I saw him alive. Now I believe I was blessed to see Paul as he traveled down that mysterious tunnel we've all heard about, terrified

16 • Surprises

at first, but then in bliss. Seeing light at its far end—amazing and wonderful—my faithful, blind partner *seeing* light.

HALF AN HOUR LATER A DOCTOR called me at work. They had tried for fifteen minute to revive my husband, he said. His voice was breaking; I guessed he was young, an intern or a resident. In retrospect the doctors thought he'd had Legionnaire's disease. I'd had it too; the symptoms checked out. We'd caught it from the air conditioning in that rental car in Florida. A young person like my son was unlikely to get it while Paul, twelve years my senior, with diabetes and a history of alcoholism, was doomed to suffer more severely than I.

He'd wanted his remains to be cremated. I made arrangements. My minister at the Universalist Church and I started planning a memorial service to be held on a Saturday evening, twelve days after his passing. When what the crematory called his "cremains" were ready, I went to the post office to pick them up.

I didn't believe in survival of the spirit after death—or at least I'd never given the matter much thought. Still I sent a small portion of his ashes to his relatives in Paris—he'd always loved Paris. A close friend of his, the Hindu named Gulabchad who worked at the church, asked for some so he could have them thrown in the Ganges; I obliged. I scattered the rest in the neighborhood in places that had been dear to him.

Every time friends and neighbors spoke glowingly about him, my eyes flooded with tears. But I can't say I felt terribly sad. Exhausted was more like it, exhausted and, God forgive me, relieved. At last I could release all the pain I'd held bottled up, suffering while he suffered, grieving while he grieved. Now my son and I could spend more time together.

We decided to hold an open house the afternoon before the memorial service. The effort to prepare for it kept us busy. I wrote a short biography of Paul to be read aloud by a young actress who was a member of the congregation. I couldn't read it myself. I knew if I tried, I'd break down. Still it was far easier to be a widow than to be divorced; everyone was supportive, no one was judgmental. People I barely knew hugged me and kissed me on the cheek. I sleepwalked day by day, numb, just getting by.

Paul had a fine record collection that he had cherished: old-timey Southern guitar pickers, classic jazz, the Hot Club of France, songs in French. I picked out a few tracks to be played at the service, delivered them to our minister, then shopped for refreshments for the open house.

Everything went smoothly. People brought cards and flowers. One card, brought by an older architecture student who'd become a friend, was a mite too sentimental for my taste, still I set it on a buffet in a place of honor. In beautiful calligraphy, Mary Ann had lettered a passage adapted from *Jonathan Livingston Seagull:* "Each of us is in truth an idea of the Great GULL, an unlimited idea of freedom.... Oh, Fletch, come on, Think! If you are talking to me now then obviously you didn't die, did you?" I couldn't help being touched because Paul's last name was Fletcher. This seemed like an odd coincidence.

The memorial service went well. But the next day my son and I had to resume our regular lives again, except that now there were just the two of us. Rustin had a paper due the next day for a high school class. He had to finish pasting up a chart so we could go to a copy shop and get it copied. Late on that dark February afternoon, we were standing in the living room sorting out details. The lamp that Paul used to read by wasn't turned on—but suddenly it started flashing short bursts of light that seemingly came in response to things we said. *Paul's lamp had turned on by itself, something that had never remotely happened before.*

The wiring in the building was fine. The refrigerator went on humming; the overhead light in the hall that led to our bedrooms stayed on and didn't waver. But Paul's lamp kept blinking erratically at us. My science-minded son and I both saw the same thing. We had a wild intuition that Paul's spirit was reaching out to us though our family had never discussed spirits before and I, for one, had never been remotely interested in things supernatural. My son was more familiar than I with the concept of spirits because school friends of his were dabbling in Wicca.

"Now you can visit Paris," Rustin said to the lamp. After a second, it flashed especially brightly, then it went dark again. "It can't seem to light up unless we're pretty close to it," he observed, "maybe eight feet. I think it's drawing much or all of its energy from us." (Years later, I would run across apparent confirmation of this[1] in the writings of a British physicist and inventor, Sir Oliver Lodge. After his son was killed in World War I, Lodge, a brilliant man who was knighted for his scientific achievements, reached out to his son through mediums and became a dedicated investigator of the paranormal.)

We shuttled back and forth experimentally in our big living room. At least one of us had to be near the lamp for it to light up. At last, because it had gone dark and we both had work to do, we turned our backs on it and left the room. An hour later, when we were once again near it, it blinked at us for a couple of minutes. After it went dark again, I checked the bulb that had been flashing, tightened it in its socket and made sure it was turned off.

The two of us went out to make photocopies. When we returned, though our windows were almost completely shut against the February cold, the hand lettered card that Mary Ann had brought, with its quote from *Jonathan Livingston Seagull,* had fallen down. (Later I'd hear that after a death, it's not unusual for things connected with a person who has passed, to move or fall down. Their clocks and watches also often stop. Witness the old song, "Grandfather's Clock.")

Now the lamp stayed dark. We took that as a challenge and an opportunity. Could we discover some mundane physical cause for its strange behavior a few hours earlier? We clapped our hands and stamped our feet. We plugged its cord into another socket. We loosened its bulbs, then tightened them again. Nothing we tried made it turn on.

The next day was Monday but I was free that morning. I dropped in at the Universalist Church to pick up the records I'd lent the minister for the memorial service. Gulabchad who managed the building spotted me and, his dark face beaming, rushed over to talk.

"I'm so glad to see you," he said. "I have something to tell you. Paul came to me in a dream. He took my hand. I could *feel* him with my hand. He said he was happy now so I asked him to tell me more, to tell me where he was, what it had been like, you know, to die—but then he disappeared and the next thing—I woke up."

Paul's friend, who'd been trained as an engineer, laughed. "That dream was so real. I got out of bed and looked all over the house for him. But he kept his word, you know, at least he tried to."

I couldn't imagine what he meant.

"Before you went away at Christmas, you know, he told me he didn't think he'd live much longer ..."

Paul, so psychic, hadn't confided this in me.

"... so I said to him, I said come back then afterwards and tell me what happened to you."

That's when I told him what had happened with Paul's lamp.

"You mustn't worry," he told me, speaking out of his Hindu tradition, "it's perfectly natural. For thirty days after someone dies, he can wander the earth at will."

Everything I'd learned since earliest childhood told me that Paul had taken his leave forever of my son and me, and of this friend of his who was much more open than I was to belief in spirits. Still I thought I'd better write it all down. So that day I wrote a short log of the odd things that had happened that weekend and tucked it away in a file. Afterwards these baffling experiences would stay with me as huge question marks—and pointers perhaps, to some unexpected truths.

PAUL WAS DEAD, HIS SUFFERING WAS over. No longer did I have cause to fear that his vision would worsen, that a waiter would insult him, or a friend would desert him. My habitual sense of dread faded away. People began to say that I looked younger. I wasn't even lonely. At last I could pay more attention to my sixteen-year-old son and turn my love and concern more fully his way. At work, I did my job—but just the bare minimum. People seemed to understand without a word from me that I was still healing. They gave me space.

That spring for fun I signed up for a course in filmmaking. It turned out to be more challenging than I'd expected. Just as I was getting ready to frantically rush out the door to direct a shoot with my classmates serving as cast and crew, the air conditioner started rumbling. Was Paul, a habitual punster, telling me to chill or as we said then, "cool it"? I caught my breath, turned the AC off, and left for the shoot's location nearby. All went well. Paul's influence, if such it was, seemed to be benign.

One day when I passed by the Universalist Church I stopped in to chat with Clive, its young business manager. Paul had often volunteered to work with him in his office. "It's funny," Clive said, "I can't help thinking of him. Things of his keep turning up."

16 • Surprises

He glanced down at his desk and saw with surprise a tiny earplug with a thin cord attached. Paul had used it to listen, without disturbing others, to a portable radio he carried with him.

"There," Clive exclaimed. "What did I tell ya?"

He shook his head. "It's weird. And sometimes it's like I'm being overheard. When I say something off the cuff that's not exactly right, I can just *hear* him saying it better."

THAT AUGUST I TRAVELED TO WASHINGTON, D.C. with other members of my Universalist church. We went to participate in a rally that would oppose many policies of the Reagan Administration. It was scheduled to take place on the twentieth anniversary of the March on Washington where Martin Luther King had made his "I Have A Dream" speech—an event that I'd been privileged to attend. For me it was a sentimental journey as well as a political act.

From dawn when we boarded a bus until we arrived at our destination around 10 a.m., I sat beside a man Paul and I had known for years. An ornithologist and a writer, Jim was the scion of an old and prosperous New York family. Like Paul, he had served in World War II. While we chatted to pass the time, he told me a curious story.

During the war, his mother received an emotional phone call from Cissie, originally from Ireland, who had been his nanny when he was small. His family hadn't heard from her for almost a decade but here she was calling to ask, "Is Jimmy all right?"

His mother gasped with surprise, then reassured her caller, "Well, he was injured three days ago but they tell us it's not too serious. He's in a hospital now in England and the doctors think he'll be okay. How in the world," she asked, "did you know he was in trouble?"

She'd had a terrible dream, Cissie explained. She could see Jimmy lying all bloody in a field with terrible noise and a flock of people running. Where she came from they called it second sight—her mother had had it before her. "I saw it and it felt so real," she said. "Ah, it's a blessing he's alive. I'll pray for him, that he'll come home safely."

"I heard that story when I got back," Jim told me. "It changed the way I look at the world."

So of course I told him that my son and I—and others as well—sensed that Paul's spirit had never completely left us. Jim chuckled as he quoted what Hamlet tells a friend after he's spoken with the ghost of his dead father.

"'There are more things in heaven and earth, Horatio, than are dreamt of in your philosophy.' There's second sight—scholars call it clairvoyance—that's what Cissie must have had, and then there's after-death contacts, like what you seem to be having and, believe me, there's a whole lot more."

He told me that studying the paranormal was a hobby of his. Maybe I'd like to join a society he knew of in Manhattan[2] that ran serious seminars and had a library on the subject. I took down its name and made a mental note to look into it sometime soon.

BY THE FALL OF 1983, RUSTIN was a senior at Stuyvesant High School but he'd never been one of its typical students. No public school in New York was harder to get into. Most of those who qualified were fiercely competitive but my son persisted in marching to a different drummer. He was wildly creative but never a grind.

Over the years, many of the winners in the nation's most prestigious science competition for secondary students, the Westinghouse Science Talent Search,[3] had come from Stuyvesant. Plaques with the names of this remarkable school's winners hung proudly in its corridors. Soon after he went back to high school that fall, Mr. Tarandash, who chaired the school's physical sciences department, urged his students to compete for yet another award—one that, unlike the Westinghouse, no student from Stuyvesant had ever won. The Space Shuttle Student Involvement Project was run jointly by NASA and the National Association of Teachers of Science.[4] High school kids were invited to design science projects that might be carried into space and, maybe, worked on by astronauts. My son, intrigued, rose to this challenge.

He designed an apparatus to explore the behavior of fluids in the zero gravity conditions of space. One stunt that astronauts sometimes showed off in space involved pouring water from a pitcher; instead of flowing normally, surface tension made it form into a ball which could then be rolled or gently tossed around. Rustin proposed to create, using surface tension, a spheroid of liquid that would function like a lens. Streaks of dye added to it could be filmed to show how liquid flowed in the absence of gravity.

16 • Surprises

None of this project made much sense to me but it thrilled Mr. Tarandash, his teacher. He just might have a winner in my son, he thought, a winner at last. When, in late October, Mayor Koch set up a reception to honor the crew of the Space Shuttle Challenger, Tarandash chose Rustin to be Stuyvesant's only representative.

A bit awestruck, I envied my son the formal invitation he received from His Honor the Mayor requesting the pleasure of his company at City Hall, a huge and elegant marble building and a leading New York landmark. It was just too tempting—I decided to crash, slipping in alongside him. So on October 24th, my 16-year-old and I attended this event where the NYPD's bagpipers played the Marine Hymn as five astronauts followed the mayor down a red carpet through the City Hall rotunda and up into the spacious Council Room where we waited with four hundred other invited guests. Along with the speeches we had to sit through came a yummy buffet luncheon and music by Lionel Hampton and his band. Not bad, I thought, not bad.

Late that February we learned that Rustin's space shuttle design had won him first prize for the Mid-Atlantic Region. With Tarandash as his chaperone, he flew down to Washington, DC and then on to the Goddard Space Center. A few days later he was back home, telling me about the presentations he'd had to give before teams of teachers and NASA people, the scientist he'd conferred with about his project, and men who'd tried to recruit him into aiming for a career in the space program.

Then there were the men from the Department of Defense who had sat down with him and other winners. He suspected these guys were looking for mad scientist types to dream up new doomsday weapons. His father and I had named him after a leading pacifist. This rebellious teenage son of mine was less than cooperative with the military.

17

Bonanza in Panama—for Some

IN THE SUMMER OF 1985, RUSTIN and I flew back to Panama. I wanted him to see the country where he'd been born. I fully expected to mope around there, remembering where I'd been humiliated and spurned. Instead I just felt like Rip Van Winkle. What I'd experienced there eighteen years before seemed almost irrelevant. Panama wasn't a tropical backwater anymore. In August 1977, ten years after we left, a treaty negotiated with the United States had given Panama sovereignty over the canal, but that didn't fully account for its transformation.

The other explanation was usually offered in a whisper. An avalanche of drug money had wrought magical changes. (See-no-evil, hear-no-evil government policies[1] helped a lot.) Now Panama was the entrepôt where Latin American drug cartels came to launder their profits and where often their capos happily spent them. Banks from around the world had come a-running. Signs in the airport advertised "Your Swiss bank in Panama" and claimed that another was the best place to buy krugerrands, the South African gold coins then favored by wealthy hoarders.

Downtown, Via España had a whole new look—flashy, almost classy. "Hey, Ma," my son kidded me, "How come we've flown 2,000 miles to the capital of New Jersey?"

17 • Bonanza in Panama—for Some

A giant Ronald McDonald balloon sat in lotus position outside a startlingly upscale McDonalds restaurant. Inside, each of its comfortable booths was decorated with the name and logo of a different bank: First Bank of Tokyo, Banco do Brasil, French and Saudi Arabian Bank, banks from the Netherlands, Germany, Israel and Colombia and, of course, major Stateside players like Bank of America and Citibank.

Down the avenue we found outposts of other fast food chains plus locally owned cafes and restaurants whose cuisine perfumed the air around them. Attractive shops sold stylish clothes, expensive jewelry, high-end electronics and other appurtenances of the privileged, moneyed life. Down the avenue, also, loomed the sleek new headquarters of those giant banks. Each weekday morning, battalions of young women dressed in uniforms that didn't look like uniforms, cute little wash-and-wear outfits, poured off exhaust-spewing buses to work in their offices. I wondered how many of these clerks and office assistants would have had no choice but to work as servants or prostitutes in the country I'd lived in eighteen years before.

My son and I wandered through side streets. We found the house where we'd lived in a pretty apartment but now it looked a little seedy while across the street where poor people had lived in shacks, stood a row of new four-story buildings. We skirted a giant palm tree frond, maybe ten feet long, fallen to the sidewalk. We passed a fence where blue orchids grew wild, climbing it like morning glories. All the while, we homed in on the sound of the ocean and found ourselves at Panama Bay. There, where breakers crashed and splattered over rocks and crumbling stone walls, we had a perfect view of the city's new arc of tall, aggressively modern condos—like something out of *Miami Vice*—looking out over the bay and gleaming white in the sun.

Another day we crossed the border between the city and the Canal Zone. That border, little more than a street, had long been troubled. Called J. F. Kennedy Boulevard on the Canal side, it was the Avenida de los Martires (Avenue of the Martyrs) on the other, named in honor of over twenty victims of a 1964 Panamanian uprising, bloodily put down, against American hegemony in the Zone.

Beyond it was a plaza where nowadays Kuna Indians sold their wares. Tiny brown women tended stands, looking picturesque in their tribe's native dress. Sewn onto their blouses like breastplates were rectangular molas, each one a unique cloth collage emblazoned with stylized images of animals, plants or other eye-catching objects often set off by geometric borders. Nonetheless, as they figured out what we owed for the molas and carved cowrie shells we bought from them, they acted very businesslike, calculators in hand. I wondered how much they'd learned from Peace Corps volunteers like the one I'd known years before who had aimed to help them break out of poverty.

With other sightseers, we toured the Miraflores Locks, the grand engineering achievement on the Pacific end of the canal. Now that the Panamanians had taken over, much of the area was gracefully landscaped with beautiful tall shrubs covered with blossoms. We crossed the causeway where in a fit of frustration and anger at Howard, I'd thrown my wedding ring into the Pacific. Ah well, I thought, he who laughs last, laughs best. Howard's relationship with Sally had long since ended badly.

Back in our hotel, I telephoned a man affiliated with Servas, the group that had given me leads on hosts in Europe many years before. Sr. Restrepo agreed to meet with us for a couple of hours the next afternoon, then he took us on a walking tour. He was a dignified older man who, as a longtime member of the city's upper echelons, had known my friend Felicia's sickly husband when they were both young. "He always smoked a lot," he recalled.

"I can't believe the way the city looks now," I told him as we strolled through its streets with him. "It's a whole new place. Must be a lot more choice in jobs now. Opportunities for a whole new middle class."

"Well, yes," he granted, "but there's still too much unemployment."

Lounging nearby were poorly dressed teenage boys who should have been in school but weren't.

"And the oligarchy?"

He shrugged. "They still have most of the land. And connections."

Restrepo, a sometime union leader, now held a responsible position with a big corporation. I sensed that his loyalties were divided; he didn't dare say more. Under a left-leaning strongman, General Torrijos, Restrepo had helped craft laws that increased the rights and benefits of workers. In 1981, after thirteen years of benevolent if undemocratic rule, Torrijos had died in a plane crash[2] said to have been engineered by the C.I.A. Manuel Noriega had taken his place as head of the military

17 • Bonanza in Panama—for Some

and de facto head of the government. Now Noriega's administration was watering down those labor laws, Restrepo told us, and protests were growing. He himself no longer took a role in politics but everyone in town knew that radicals were planning a two-day general strike.

A general strike? Would we be caught in the middle of one? That wasn't how we'd planned to spend our summer vacation. But then again we weren't about to hide in our hotel room either.

The next day we chanced upon a parade with lots of militant posters. It seemed like a peaceful start to the strike. All around us, stores and restaurants were open. We wondered what form this protest would take. The next afternoon we were slated to go into the Zone to visit one of Howard's former colleagues. I hired a taxi to take us to his office, but the cabbie refused to take us all the way to our destination. As soon as he stopped to let us off, a knot of people came at us from the front and the left. They were yelling at our driver and making angry gestures. Someone threw something at the taxi's windshield. It glanced off harmlessly but the driver looked alarmed. I paid him quickly and hopped out. It was easy for me, I was seated on the right. But my son, rushing to follow me, had hardly gotten out of the cab before the driver started up again. Rustin was almost dragged.

We scurried the next two blocks to the Institute's headquarters. The man we'd gone to meet seemed embarrassed to face me. He'd split with the wife I remembered and married a younger woman. Her pretty face and two kids who looked like him smiled at us from a picture on his desk. Soon my son and I caught a bus back to the neighborhood where we were staying. It detoured around streets blocked off by police motorcycles parked sideways. We watched as an officer threw a canister—perhaps of tear gas—at young men running away down the middle of the street. Then the bus moved on and the scene slipped from sight.

Near our hotel, shops were still open but their salespeople looked frightened. In the computer store where we browsed, a salesman was smoking frantically, his hand shaking. That evening the local TV news featured pictures of burning cars lying on their sides and reported that members of the National Guard and Panama City's new police force were being treated in hospitals. Rioters, the announcer said, had thrown stones and handfuls of nails at them. Many of the demonstrators, he said, had come from the university. He didn't say if any of them had been injured.

The next day, my son and I enjoyed a good and tranquil breakfast in a pleasant cafe. We assumed that the general strike was over. Once again we went walking. In the center of town we came to the Panama Hilton; three of its tall floor-to-ceiling windows had been smashed. Piles of broken glass were everywhere; one window had a bullet hole at the base of the break. Across the street stood a stately old church, a landmark often visited by tourists. It was undamaged but Rustin spotted deep tread marks on the sidewalk beside it.

"Looks like the government brought in tanks, maybe an armored personnel carrier. Must've been cracking down on whoever was raising hell outside the hotel."

After lunch we walked over to the University to see what the students had to say about the strike. But once we got there, we were too shaken by what we saw to try to start a conversation in our limited Spanish. Apparently the strike wasn't over. Most of the scattering of students we saw wore kerchiefs masking their faces. Sitting on curbs or slouching in knots of two or three were edgy, angry young men and a few girls. Lying nearby lay frightening weapons for *mano a mano* combat, lengths of rebar—heavy steel reinforcing rods, menacingly ridged. The street was littered with wooden slats hammered through with big nails at regular intervals and upended to puncture tires.

A car drove up, stopped at a safe distance from the nail-studded slats, and a middle-aged woman got out. She pleaded with her son to come home with her. Rustin and I walked on ahead. At an intersection further down the road was an improvised barricade—a bedspring, wooden lawn ornaments, a sign from a bodega. A fellow in jeans with a kerchief over his face was stopping traffic, signaling approaching cars to turn around and go back the other way. My son and I turned around too.

This didn't look like Berkeley. It sure wasn't nonviolent. As soon as we could, Rustin and I left for beautiful Costa Rica, Panama's neighbor to the north. Costa Rica was democratic and peaceful; it didn't even have an army. It had abolished its army in 1948.

OFTEN A REVISED EDITION OF A reference book is issued seven years later. By 1986, I figured it was time for me to put together a new architectural

17 • Bonanza in Panama—for Some

guide that would include projects that had been built in the interim and would supply more information about all the projects covered.

Soon much of my free time was taken up by work on this revision of *Highlights of Recent American Architecture*. I wrote the three leading publishers in the field and asked if they were interested in giving me a contract. I applied for a research grant as well as—given the college's strained finances at the time—an unpaid leave of absence from my job. A book contract came through, along with a small advance. So did a modest research grant and that year's leave of absence.

In the fall of 1988, I went back to work. Early the next year, my new guide came out.[3] It was a thing of beauty with a classy jacket and glossy paper that made the most of its 247 photos. I cherished a fantasy that my publisher would hold a book party for it and I'd get to meet some of the famous architects whose creations I'd written about. The thought of a festive room throbbing with their clashing egos filled me with (perhaps morbidly) expectant delight.

But it was not to be—there was no party. Nonetheless this new publication of mine gratified me in other ways. It assured my promotion at the end of that year to full professor and in the corridors of CCNY's architecture school, it gifted me with an unexpected benefit.

It had long been my custom to post on a prominent bulletin board, the book jackets of any new works that members of our faculty had written. My first architecture book hadn't had a jacket and I'd made no special effort to publicize it. But now I had an artfully designed jacket to post that named my latest publisher, a leader in the field. Suddenly the attitudes of the professors I worked with turned more appreciative, even a bit cowed. It dawned on me that probably some of them—maybe most of the minority who wrote books—had been turned down by all the major houses. Now even though I was a woman and a librarian at that, the teaching faculty treated me with more respect.

Soon librarians and computer experts started collaborating to create a new electronic database for architectural research. Following my example, they supplied access to information about specific buildings by location, building name and building type as well as the name of the architect.

18

Nicaragua—A Rougher Taste of the Third World

IN MID-NOVEMBER 1989, AN EVENT IN El Salvador made headline news. Some time before dawn, twenty armed men in uniform blew open the back door of the residence of six Jesuit priests[1] and shot them dead. They also killed their housekeeper and her 15-year-old daughter. They massacred all eight because the priests, humanitarians associated with a major university, opposed the government and gave moral support to guerrilla forces fighting to overthrow it.

In keeping with liberation theology—a growing force among Latin American Catholics—these churchmen believed their mission was to act as Christ had on behalf of the poor. There was plenty of poverty in El Salvador, a crowded country, much of it mountainous, about the size of Massachusetts with about as many people. It was ruled by an oligarchy, not unlike the Panamanian ruling class I'd heard about from Felicia but with a conspicuously more vicious record. In El Salvador, the small circle of rich families who owned most of the land historically had used most of it to grow coffee for export but, even as the economy diversified they hung on to power and, ruling with an iron hand, kept most of the population hungry and powerless.

Everyone knew that rightwing death squads were supported by the Salvadoran government. Nonetheless, the Reagan administration endorsed it and was vowing to send it more military aid. But then the Salvadorans overplayed their hand. Eight days after the massacre of the priests, the Salvadoran National Police arrested a young American named Jennifer Casolo and charged her with having a massive cache of weapons buried in her backyard. Casolo worked for Christian Education Seminars, based in Texas; it was her job to guide American members of Congress and religious groups around this war-torn Central American nation. When word got back to the United States that she'd been arrested, leading legislators and human rights activists sprang into action. A former U. S. Attorney General, Ramsey Clark, flew to San Salvador to press for her release.

After keeping Casolo in police custody for fifteen days, the Salvadorans released her. Soon she was touring the United States giving talks about what she'd been through and what she'd witnessed. When I learned that she'd be speaking at Riverside Church, I was eager to hear her.

Standing behind a lectern, Jennifer Casolo didn't look very imposing. She was 28 years old and less than five feet tall but an air of innocent earnestness and devotion to lofty principles radiated from her. If weapons had been found on the grounds of her rented house, Casolo said, they must have been put there before she moved in—or rightwing Salvadorans had planted them there to incriminate her. Hauled off by the police, she'd spent three days sleeping without blankets on the floor of a small isolation cell. Then she was transferred to a cell with five Salvadoran women, all political prisoners. At night she faced grueling interrogations; she was sleep-deprived and sometimes blindfolded but otherwise, because she was an American, she was never tortured. The Salvadoran women were not so lucky.

She could hear them being brutalized[2] at night "... the beating and screaming ... would go on for hours. Many times ... I heard flesh hitting flesh, cries and sobbing, choking and vomiting." As for the six priests, she said, "I knew them, I loved them. They were innocent people. Now they are martyrs."

During her program at the church, a flier was passed out. It asked for donations to some organization that was working for a just and peaceful resolution to struggles going on in Central America. I sent them a small gift. Two or three months later I got a letter from a sister group called Witness for Peace. It invited me to join a delegation of theirs that would visit Nicaragua, another troubled Central American nation, to see what was happening there and to help in a small way to rebuild it after a devastating civil war. Recent developments in my life conspired to make me do just that.

CUNY was promising bonuses to senior faculty like me who would take early retirement in 1991. By now I'd been with the university over twenty years. Meanwhile I'd heard from my ex-husband Howard that, though by now Berkeley was dauntingly expensive, he was thinking of retiring and moving to Eugene, Oregon.

Berkeley had changed my life. I'd never forgotten the feel of the place-—the political fervor and the parties, the hiking and camping and laidback spirit. Bitter as my breakup with Howard had been, over the years we'd reconciled. He'd split with Sally, then Paul had died. All the while, my son's father and I had stayed in touch. Maybe we'd both retire to Eugene, we said, a university town in the state just north of California. Eugene's passion for political action on the left made it seem like Berkeley North. Rents there were fairly high, Howard told me, but buying a house was cheap. If you rented out part of it, you could live rent-free.

I flew to Eugene, scoped it out, then put a down payment on a property there near the Willamette River and a picturesque park that ran beside it. Legally one tax unit, it comprised two smallish houses connected by a carport and one of these contained a wee mother-in-law apartment. All for far less than what one modest house would have cost in Brooklyn or Queens. *Then Witness for Peace invited me to join a delegation to Nicaragua that was scheduled to leave from Eugene.* I couldn't resist. This, I figured, was one way to meet Oregonians who might help me settle in when I moved west.

I joined the group in Mexico City where our delegation was staying at a Quaker-run hostel. Witness had sent me a packet of articles to read and a list of things to bring. Solid walking shoes and boots for mud were recommended. We'd be arriving in the middle of the rainy season. At the hostel our team of eleven got acquainted with each other, did non-violence trainings together and, guided by our delegation leader and a few invited speakers, we reviewed Nicaragua's history.[3] American influence had often loomed large.

In 1910, the United States supported an insurrection against a dictator. Soon America sent in the Marines. They occupied the country

18 • Nicaragua: A Rougher Taste of the Third World

almost continuously from 1912 till 1933, usually at the request of whatever strongman was in power. For five years a Nicaraguan general, Augusto Sandino, led a guerrilla war, first against the government and then against the Marines. U.S. troops finally left in 1933 but first they trained and equipped a National Guard not unlike what ran Panama when I lived there. They put Anastasio Somoza García at its head.

Members of the Guard killed Sandino. By the late 1940s, Somoza was the nation's largest landowner. He also owned or controlled banks, power companies, the national railroad and numerous businesses. In 1956 he was assassinated by a 27-year-old poet—but not much changed. Somoza's eldest son, Luis, took over the post of president; another son took over the National Guard. Opponents were tortured and imprisoned. After Luis died of a heart attack, another member of the family became president.

In 1972 a major earthquake struck the capital, 90% of Managua was leveled. Thousands were killed or injured, a quarter of a million were left homeless. A bounty of international aid flowed in to help the nation rebuild—but almost no rebuilding took place. Most of the aid money ended up in the pockets of the ruling Somoza and his buddies.

His blatant corruption and brutality, along with his failure to rebuild Managua, led many middle- and upper-class Nicaraguans to support the Sandinista National Liberation Front, generally called the FSLN or simply the Frente, named after the national hero who thirty years earlier had battled the Nicaraguan government and the U.S. Marines. The Frente—much more than a political party—was also a guerrilla movement which staged bold and often successful military actions.

Early in January 1978, the editor of the leading national newspaper was assassinated. Pedro Joaquin Chamorro was a member of the oligarchy but he'd also been a forceful opponent of Somoza. The business community organized a general strike demanding that the ruler resign. Another anti-Somoza faction seized the entire Nicaraguan congress and held it hostage until Somoza paid them a $500,000 ransom and released 59 political prisoners. Bands of semi-armed civilians attacked installations of the National Guard. Somoza's troops put down this revolt—but only at the cost of thousands of lives. This bloodbath unified the forces fighting against him.

The Organization of American States and the United Nations charged Nicaragua's National Guard with violations of human rights. After a brief but bloody campaign, the Sandinistas took power on July 17, 1979—a date reverently referred to by FSLN loyalists as The Triumph of the Revolution. The nation was in ruins. An estimated 50,000 had died in the conflict, more than one in five were homeless, and the national debt of this country of roughly 2,300,000 people was over a billion and a half dollars.

Several Latin American nations endorsed the new government and, conditionally, the Carter administration decided to work with them. Meanwhile Somoza fled to Paraguay[4] where, in 1980, he was blown away with a bazooka in his white Mercedes by leftist guerrillas from Argentina.

The Sandinistas set to work immediately to improve the lot of the common people and assure fairer treatment of women. They focused especially on land reform and improving health care and education. Before 1979, 4% of the landowners had controlled over half the arable land. The new government confiscated Somoza's huge agricultural holdings plus unused land that belonged to other absentee landowners and turned most of it over to FSLN supporters to farm communally. They also nationalized some factories, especially scores that the Somozas had owned. Their most striking achievement was a literacy campaign that in six months taught basic reading skills to over half a million people and led UNESCO to award a prize to Nicaragua.

During those first years after The Triumph of the Revolution, infant mortality went down, food production went up, most of the people ate better and got to drink cleaner water. Women headed several ministries. Roads were built or improved. But serious trouble was brewing across the border. In Honduras and Costa Rica, opponents of the FSLN regrouped. This mixed bag of dissidents came to be known as the Contras, short for "counter-revolutionaries" in Spanish. When, in 1981, Ronald Reagan became president of the United States, they gained a powerful friend. He hailed them as "freedom fighters" and gave orders for the C.I.A. to secretly finance, arm and train them.

As quickly as schools and health clinics were built in Nicaragua, bands of Contras set out to destroy them. Incredible as it seemed to me when first I heard this, teachers and health workers were targets of

18 • Nicaragua: A Rougher Taste of the Third World

choice; so were the farms set up by the FSLN. Settlers said, "We have to live with our machine guns on our shoulders." People lost their lives, others lost limbs; crops and buildings were systematically destroyed.

The Contras fought very dirty[5]—kidnapping, torturing, mutilating, killing, raping, burning. An endless list of atrocities was chalked up to them. When the government, desperate for money, compelled farmers to sell their produce to it at fixed rates instead of bargaining for higher prices elsewhere, many of them turned against the FSLN and linked up with the Contras. One major task of Witness for Peace workers stationed in Nicaragua was researching and documenting the terrible things that were taking place.

In the United States, most Democrats were outraged by Reagan's support for the Contras. They pushed through an amendment to the defense budget which forbade the U.S. government from providing military support to forces working to overthrow the government of Nicaragua. To get around this, the Reagan administration came up with the devious scheme that would become its most blatant scandal: the Iran-Contra Affair.

Americans were being held hostage in Iran; U.S. policy banned the sale of weapons to that country. Still Reagan authorized a series of just such sales, stage managed secretly by the CIA. In return, American hostages were released and the U.S. used the profits from these weapons sales to subsidize the Contras. Many of these "freedom fighters" were involved in the drug trade. U.S. planes that carried arms to the Contras often flew back to the States loaded with Contra-marketed cocaine.

WHEN I SAW JENNIFER CASOLO SPEAK, the Sandinistas were struggling to keep their war-torn nation afloat. A month later they held honest elections. Maybe because the United States strongly hinted that the war would end if the Sandinistas were defeated, they lost to UNO, a coalition cobbled together from fourteen parties that opposed them. The new president, Violeta Chamorro, was the widow of the newspaper editor who'd been assassinated by Somoza in 1978—the event that set off the uprising that eventually brought the Sandinistas to power. When my Witness for Peace delegation arrived in Nicaragua, the nation was suddenly at peace but it faced an unpredictable future.[6]

My first sight of Managua was shocking even though I'd heard about the damage from the earthquake. Square miles were covered with little but rubble—but in its outer districts, the city still lived. There we stayed for a couple of days in the modest headquarters of Witness for Peace, getting briefed about what was going on. Everyone was war weary. Now people hoped that the rich and powerful United States would pull the country out of the mire where years of low intensity conflict—property destruction, killings, and a commercial embargo—had left it. But whether that would actually happen, remained to be seen.

Our leader, Pam, a slim pretty brunette in her early forties, taught us basic skills for getting by in this Third World nation. The dogs we saw weren't pets, they were feral; if necessary we should kick them away. Once we got into the countryside, we'd have to carry our own potable water; Witness for Peace staff would refill our canteens. Soon we'd be heading for a village in the northwestern part of the country where we would help to build a schoolhouse.

Witness had a battered old bus that bounced and jounced north as it carried us over rocky roads or over tracks that were barely roads at all and wound for many miles through rugged hills. The driver picked his way slowly, often threading between steep hillsides and down-slopes. Lucky for him but unlucky for the local farmers, the route wasn't wet and slippery. Although it was the rainy season, the whole region was in drought. Flecked with low brush and stunted trees, the land around us was baked dry by heat.

At last we arrived at Santa Teresa, population around 500, a cluster of small, mostly mud brick houses surrounded by farmland, about sixty miles from the border with Honduras. Most but not all of its people had supported the FSLN. Hard feelings and suspicions remained between families. Years of grinding conflict, destruction and declining income had worn people down.

Members of our delegation were assigned to stay, two by two, in the homes of local families. My roommate in Maria Rosa's house was Lynn, a tall, attractive young blonde who didn't speak a word of Spanish so I, with my limited survival Spanish, was assigned to be our spokesperson when smiles and gestures didn't work for her.

Maria Rosa was around my height and in her late forties with dark curly hair cut short, skin the color of *café con leche,* and a sturdy,

18 • Nicaragua: A Rougher Taste of the Third World

slack-breasted, thick-waisted body that spoke of much childbearing and hard physical labor. She was relatively well off. Her little house was a striking example of fine hand-hewn construction—good enough to make it into one of the books I had in my architecture library. Under its tile roof, its wooden exterior walls were slotted together, tongue and groove, and topped by a lattice of shakes that kept out rain while it let in air and light. All this rested on low concrete bordering walls and a concrete foundation. Hand-cut beams and pillars supported a wide porch. Almost the whole back of the house was storage, entered only by a sturdy door inside. Its central room, about 18' by 24', was divided into one smaller and one larger area by a wooden partition, less than 6'-high, with photos and diplomas hung on it at eye level.

Its toilet was an outhouse, conveniently supplied with an old book on an obscure subject from which you tore out pages as needed. In this country where many of the men had been killed during nine years of conflict, our hostess was lucky enough not to be a widow. Her husband didn't live with the family but she said that was because he was working somewhere else—she wouldn't say where. Hopefully she sometimes received remittances from him.

Witness for Peace paid our hosts with small quantities of basic foods: beans, rice, sugar, cooking oil and coffee, not much more than what we, their guests, were likely to eat. Though rice was a staple of the Nicaraguan diet, for the moment it was a luxury in Santa Teresa since it didn't grow in this area. Because of the drought, even much of the local bean crop was failing. To make things worse, skyrocketing inflation was robbing people of the value of whatever cash they might have. When I returned to the States I would bring home as a souvenir a 20 cordoba note on which numbers overprinted on it by the government made it worth instead 500,000 cordobas. Officially, half a million cordobas were worth around $10; on the black market they went for less than half that much.

The first night we all had beans, tortillas and rice for dinner. We ate in shifts because our hostess had only three plastic plates in three different bright colors. The rice was probably a treat for our Señora and the two children she had at home. (She had seven in all but the older ones had moved out.) She shared with Lynn and me the best she had. In return we were supposed to share whatever goodies we'd brought along. Late that evening as I snacked on my stash, I gave her a handful of raisins and some dried peach and apricot halves. She accepted them gratefully. I wished I'd brought more.

In the morning, her 12 year-old daughter ground corn for tortillas in a small hand grinder. I tried to help—but the crank was much harder to turn than I'd expected. Maria Rosa chuckled gently at how hard it was for me. Soon we had visitors, two half-grown pigs who ducked their heads in the door and were rewarded by our Señora with bare corncobs newly stripped of their kernels. Back out they went into her yard where they'd already eaten every sliver of greenery that dared to peek out of the ground. Around her yard as around her neighbors' yards, fences strung with barbed wire kept the animals in.

"That's her savings account, the pigs," Pam would tell me later. "Their value isn't affected by inflation. If she gets desperate, she can always sell them."

While our hostess made tortillas from the freshly ground corn, I watched two cows outside browse listlessly. Bumps on their sides signaled the presence of worms; most of the farm animals in the countryside had parasites. For breakfast, once again we ate tortillas and beans. No rice this time. Still, the tortillas were delicious and, unlike any I'd ever seen before, they popped open in the middle the way some heated pitas do, so you could tuck beans inside them. Maria Rosa made coffee. I drank water from my canteen. Soon it was time for Lynn and me to walk to our work site.

I'VE ALWAYS BEEN POLITICALLY PROGRESSIVE, I thought I didn't blame the victim, I thought I knew how to think outside the box. But even as I took off for Nicaragua, flaming liberal that I was, I assumed I'd be meeting with simple peasants, with people intrinsically different from me. I was wrong. With Maria Rosa as with many others I'd meet, I would come to sense how alike we were. And how subtle and complex and hardworking *they* were. Only the different physical and political realities we faced made our lives acutely different.

The schoolhouse we'd come to help build was set in a field beside a smaller structure temporarily being used as a school. This smaller structure had once been a clinic but after the original school—located elsewhere in this tiny town—was destroyed by Contras, the townspeople

18 • Nicaragua: A Rougher Taste of the Third World

had turned the clinic into classrooms and made do without a health care center.

By the time we got there, the first rows of mud brick had been laid already along lines marked by tall wooden posts fixed in the ground at regular intervals. Heaps of bricks as well as sand, gravel and small rocks for concrete lay on the ground, being replenished as the work went on. A dozen men and women seemed to make up the work crew. Children hung around for fun, restless, skinny kids. Girls and boys carried loads of rock to our work site, heavier loads than we American grownups cared to carry. When, in my clumsy Spanish, I asked little kids why they weren't in school, they looked at me in puzzlement and didn't answer. Turned out that, despite the best intentions of the Sandinistas, now only half the nation's kids finished sixth grade. Unlike many other Third World nations, no school fees were required—but some families couldn't afford notebooks and pens.

When we started working, folks told us we could *put* bricks in place but we mustn't actually *set* them with mortar. Singing, we passed the heavy adobe bricks from hand to hand. A construction brigade of six women had been hired to do the actual bricklaying for twenty days; most of them were widows. With help from international groups they'd been trained in building skills. But by the end of our first day their contract was up and, after a committee of local people formally thanked them, they left. Then we volunteers were free to lay brick ourselves.

That first day, I volunteered to shape metal rods to reinforce the concrete, twisting them into a square around thick nails that had been hammered into a heavy wooden table. A genial, work-worn man named Alonso taught me how to do this. Someone from Witness translated as needed. Alonso ran the project—but only in the most tactful way. He was funny and smart and never made anyone angry. A man like this, I thought, would be successful anywhere. A mason by trade, he was being paid the equivalent of $12 a week by the community—but he might not get all his money right away.

One afternoon it rained, it poured, a tropical downpour that made everyone exultant. Maybe, we all hoped, it marked an end to the drought. But the earth sucked up the rain. Soon it was dusty again and it never rained again while we stayed in Santa Teresa.

One morning Maria Rosa invited us to walk with her into the campo to see the hectare—about two and a half acres—she farmed. Lynn said no thanks but I was eager to see it. It wasn't more than half a mile away but it was hard hiking over rough country without roads or even trails. When we got close enough to see her patch of land, she pointed to it from across a small gully. Her corn crop didn't look healthy and I didn't know how to say anything complicated so I just said, *"Mucho está amarillo."* Much of what should have been green was yellow. I asked if it would turn green again if they had more rain later that season. Smiling sadly, she shook her head no.

That afternoon, my roommate and I went out to sit for a while on the Señora's porch. A few feet from our bench, a little boy in torn pants was playing at being a wheelbarrow. He walked on his hands while a little girl held his legs. Both were laughing. When our hostess emerged from her house to pull eggs from chicken roosts on a table near where we were sitting, the little girl let go of the boy's ankles and the two scampered down from the porch to the dusty ground. Then a fellow we hadn't met before stopped by to talk to us. He'd brought along a boom box playing a tape of Latin music. He swayed to the music suggestively as he invited my companion to dance. He was hot to dance with Lynn who was tall and young and blonde. Nobody in Santa Teresa looked remotely like her. But Lynn didn't speak Spanish and this trip of ours was beginning to scare her. She whispered to me that she didn't want to dance. I guessed she was frightened by this pushy young man.

Maria Rosa didn't say a word, she let me do all the talking. I stood up and started trying to explain that my friend was sick, that was why she didn't want to dance. "Sick" I'd learned long ago was a safe excuse in much of Latin America where healthy-looking people often suffered illnesses, passing or chronic, from dirty water and poor sanitation. He looked at her skeptically and then back at me. Meanwhile our hostess positioned herself so she was facing me but her visitor couldn't see her expression. She was encouraging me to fend him off—but she didn't dare send him away herself. I wondered how dangerous it would be in this tiny, politically divided village, for her to offend this neighbor of hers.

In time he left. That evening, our hostess cooked a special treat for us. Had someone in this town where no one seemed to have refrigeration just slaughtered a calf? Along with the usual beans and tortillas

18 • Nicaragua: A Rougher Taste of the Third World

she served us morsels of veal she'd braised with garlic and the juice of a *limon*, that cross between a lemon and a lime so common south of the border. (A small limon tree grew behind her house.)

The next day—it was a Saturday—one of Maria Rosa's older sons came home to visit from his technical school in Managua. We chatted in broken English and broken Spanish. When I mentioned the delicious veal his mother had cooked the night before, he said, "Yes, some people here eat meat once a week and some people eat meat twice a week." That seemed to cover Santa Teresa's culinary and social ladder.

THE AFTERNOON BEFORE OUR DELEGATION WAS due to leave Santa Teresa, the community held a fiesta to thank us for our few days' work on the school. Dozens of grownups and loads of children were there. Community people made short speeches thanking our delegation. Two men, pretty good musicians, played guitar and sang together. At the edge of the crowd, one of the local widows sold what passed for cookies; they tasted like crackers with a crumble of something sweet on top. Hanging from a rafter in the simple pavilion where the party was being held, a piñata waited. It was tiny by American standards, smaller than a basketball, still the children were excited and impatient for it to be broken open.

Alonso took charge again. He blindfolded people, one by one, and spun them around before he handed them a stick—a tree branch trimmed of twigs—to swing at the piñata. The fellows with the guitars played lively music so each person with the stick could dance as they whacked away blindly. All the while Alonso finessed the situation, prolonging the suspense so nobody broke it open too soon. He gave me a turn—he probably guessed I was aching to try—but while people laughed and clapped as they'd done for all the others, I wandered far from my target and swung wildly at the air.

At last someone smacked the piñata open. Hard candies, only hard candies, fell to the ground, bouncing, rolling, scattering. I thought of how scornfully most American kids would have viewed this event, this minor diversion: the piñata contained no toys, no brightly colored surprises. Still Santa Teresa's children were thrilled. They scrambled all over, reaching wildly for one candy here, another there. Sucking on one, clutching the couple more they'd managed to grab. I thought of little boys and girls I knew in the States, kids with roomfuls of toys, kids who ate desserts and treats every day. Kids who grew fat, kids who were dissatisfied. I wished they could see these other children and maybe come to understand.

SOON WE PACKED UP TO LEAVE. I'd brought along cheap rubber boots for the muddy ground I'd expected. Maria Rosa looked at them with longing but, following the rules of Witness of Peace, I couldn't leave them with her. It was just too dangerous to favor certain members of the village over others. Jealousy bred violence. But if we took photos, we could send them back to our hosts. People in the countryside had very few pictures of themselves.

When I pulled out my cheap, disposable camera, my hostess lit up and ran to put on a new sky blue tee shirt printed with shiny gold decorations. After I got back to the States, I sent copies of the shots I'd taken of Maria Rosa and the two kids she had at home to Witness for Peace headquarters in the United States to be hand delivered to her. Regular mail to Nicaragua was unreliable.

From Santa Teresa we went to Condega, a larger town. Now we were traveling with a couple of community people as well as our driver and other Witness for Peace staff. Along the way we stopped at a popular barbecue restaurant that featured whole roast pig. Sixteen of us crowded onto wooden benches, facing one another across long tables. Our waitress gave us plates, provided stacks of tortillas, and set out bowls of vegetables—cooked yucca, cabbage and carrots as well as beans—and invited us to help ourselves to the pork.

The carcass of a pig, already a third demolished, lay on a giant platter on a table at the front with a couple of implements that didn't include a sharp knife. After my first taste, I was ravenous. Like all the others, except for our two vegetarians, I yanked handfuls of meat greedily from its side. After almost a week of beans, tortillas, a little rice, a smidgeon of egg and a few morsels of veal, I was desperate for something else. Almost anything else. And when they didn't refill the bowls of vegetables—largely monopolized by our suffering vegetarians—I was bitterly disappointed. How did people live, I wondered, on a steady diet of beans and tortillas?

18 • Nicaragua: A Rougher Taste of the Third World

That evening we met with a group of UNO supporters. Most of the men wore sombreros that made them look typecast for slightly paunchy Mexican landowners or banditos. Someone from Witness for Peace translated their speeches to us. One told how, because he'd collaborated with the Contras, he feared being kidnapped or killed by Frente loyalists. "Last week someone killed one of my dogs," he said. Others complained about inflation: 1100% in the past six months. All hoped that soon international aid would lift the nation out of the economic abyss which nine years of war had plunged it into. Then a skinny, hollow-cheeked man walked to the front. He seemed to burn with some dark code he was driven to live by. What stays with me is not so much what he said as the effect this man had on the others.

Nobody dared to say a word. No one whispered to a neighbor, everyone paid strict attention. I sensed fear all around, as if we were all in aspic, each of us glued and frozen in place, surrounded by terror. For this was, somehow, a terrifying man, an evil man who might do anything. Afterwards Pam told us that he'd been responsible for the massacre of twelve people, two families in the area. Our delegation would be leaving soon, we would be out of his reach. But I pitied the people we'd seen at the meeting who had to go on living in his presence.

FROM CONDEGA WE WENT TO A larger town in the highlands, surrounded by mountains. Here we visited the handsome, airy headquarters of an environmental group. Architects, I thought, would have applauded its one wall of roughhewn stone, another wall earth sheltered. Its skilful design let breezes sweep through and welcomed lots of natural light.

Their concerns sounded familiar. When Sandinistas proposed to let a Costa Rican company log in a pristine area, these activists had mobilized international organizations to protest until it was declared a protected forest reserve. They worried about the dumping of toxic waste and the overuse of pesticides. They were working to save sea turtles on the Pacific Coast. As we sat around their beautifully finished long wood table, I felt as if I'd never left home.

Next we visited the headquarters of COSEP, an organization of businessmen who came from a range of parties. ("COSEP" stands for Superior Council of Private Enterprise, in Spanish.) In the last days of Somoza, many of them had opposed him; some had even helped to finance the Sandinistas. Most were independent coffee and cotton growers who now felt they'd been mistreated by the Frente.

Nicolas Bolaños, a large coffee grower now a member of Nicaragua's legislature, sat down with us. He was a plainspoken man who seemed basically truthful. In 1980, he told us, when first the FSLN took power, six seats in the Assembly were reserved for COSEP members but as the years went by, they came to feel betrayed. They were always outvoted. Some had land confiscated. All were forced to sell their crops to the government at below market value. At last, in the late eighties, Bolaños boycotted the Frente system of selling coffee; in retaliation the government seized 95% of his land. He left the country, belatedly following the lead of many others who'd left long before. But right after the election, he returned and the Sandinistas gave his land back to him.

Still he was angry and indignant. He sneered at their efforts at land reform, giving Somoza's lands away only to supporters willing to live on state farms. "There's plenty of land in Nicaragua," he said, "but we need people who know how to make it productive." When he came back, he said, his farm was ruined. An airplane, tractors and other farm equipment had disappeared. Much of what hadn't disappeared was rundown and broken. He was proud of his skills as a farmer and manager, proud of what he'd built, and quietly furious at what he viewed as theft. Besides—he repeated what we'd already heard several others say—after the election the Sandinistas had given away houses, vehicles and land to a privileged circle of the party faithful. People called it *piñata-ismo*. Troubled at heart, we thanked him politely.

Back in Managua we visited the Center for Popular Education, an ambitious program with a staff of 15, modeled on the teachings of Paolo Freire, the influential Brazilian author of *Pedagogy of the Oppressed*. It was run by an ex-nun and an ex-priest who met with us in an attractive atrium with a fieldstone floor. Through it a refreshing breeze was blowing as they described recent developments in Nicaragua.

The Frente, arguably naive about finance and credit, had given farmers no-interest loans. Now, our hosts told us, if borrowers didn't pay back the money they owed, they could lose their land. Then they'd have to work for the rich landowners who'd come back from Miami to reclaim their estates, or else crowd into the cities or go abroad hoping to find other work. Teachers were being fired, especially pro-Sandinista ones, and even the ones who kept their jobs had to get by on less. Formerly, in addition to their skimpy salaries, teachers had received baskets of food—rice, beans, meat and oil—but now those baskets had been discontinued. And now sex education was banned in schools. The only birth control program that remained provided condoms and ostensibly was a campaign against AIDS.

The ex-nun was white, the ex-priest was black, both were trim and well-spoken and looked to be in their forties. I wondered if they were life partners, lovers. I wondered if that—and their support for family planning—was why they had left the Church. But surely it was their work that was central to their lives.

They trained teachers and had helped to build a women's cooperative that produced nutritious soybean products and ran a natural medicine clinic. Their Center also ran workshops that dealt with youth problems, petty delinquency, unwed mothers, and gangs. They sent agronomists and technicians to the countryside. The sanity of it all and the hardheaded hopefulness of this center's efforts were reassuring toward the end of this often unsettling trip.

OUR DELEGATION DEBRIEFED IN MANAGUA, THEN we packed our bags and flew to Mexico City where we could change planes and hurry home. But I didn't fly straight back to Eugene. I checked into a hotel that overlooked the Zócalo so I could play plain American tourist for two days. Could watch professional Indians in extravagant costumes perform traditional dances in that grand plaza, and then walk around and shop and buy pretty things. This giant city looked rich and vibrant compared with Managua. Its citizens looked healthier and prouder than the struggling people we'd left behind. The Contra War had worn Nicaragua down. Now, second only to Haiti, it was the poorest country in the Western Hemisphere.

I thought about Maria Rosa. I think of her still. Intelligent, cautious, hardworking, concerned about her kids. In her artfully crafted little house with her beans and tortillas and her dry, brown yard. With her pigs and her privy and the fear she had to live with. There but for the grace of God go I.

19

The Man Who Gave Away a Fortune

In June 1991 I moved to Eugene. Because the two houses I'd bought were occupied and I couldn't decide where I wanted to live, I rented an apartment and waited for my furniture to arrive. I'd left over half of it in New York, in the rent-stabilized apartment that my son now occupied.

Soon his father moved to Eugene as he'd said he might. We avoided intimacy, it was easier just being friends, cluing each other into places we'd discovered and things to do in town. Summer in Eugene was dry and sunny. Flowers bloomed everywhere, there were towering trees, clean air and a sense of tranquility. No one was in a frantic hurry, no one was impolite. People said it was a healing place.

I hooked up with a local writers group. Howard, zoologist that he was, hung out with environmentalists who, in ardently green Eugene, were in ample supply. At last I decided to move into one of the houses I owned. A ranch style home set behind an older bungalow, it contained two apartments. Each had one bedroom and a separate entrance, but the larger one also had a small backyard that boasted a giant oak for shade. That was the one I claimed for myself.

The men's group at the Unitarian Church in town did moving jobs as a fundraiser; they transported my stuff into my new apartment. That's how I met Todd, the youngest of the Unitarian moving crew. Todd was a vegetarian, politically progressive, and a part-time student at the

19 • The Man Who Gave Away a Fortune

University of Oregon who supported himself by working as a handyman. For modest fees he repaired and improved my fixer-upper. When he took breaks from his chores, I served him lunches and dinners and listened to stories about his classes and housemates and the girlfriend with whom he went on long, athletic bike trips.

Todd could fix almost anything, build shelves, set tile and refinish floors, and he was tolerant enough to respect my taste. Sometimes together we rummaged through the organized chaos that was Bring Recycling, a high-minded if messy Eugene institution, mostly open to the elements, where people brought used sinks/doors/windows/you-name-it that someone else might find a use for. It was fun and engrossing to transform my new place. On weekends I drove around from yard sale to garage sale, picking up secondhand furnishings. In the process I learned a lot about Eugene.

One Saturday afternoon I bought a dresser from an old couple. After I got it home, I found at the back of one of its drawers a crumpled piece of brocade that must for ages have lain forgotten there. It was deeply wrinkled; I tossed it on top of the dresser, not certain what I should do with it. The next time I glanced at it, its wrinkles were unbending. The fabric was relaxing, taking up more space, displaying its original patterns, asserting itself. And it seemed to me that, starting out here thousands of miles away from New York, I was like that piece of brocade, no longer crammed into a job or hemmed in by the expectations of people who'd known me for years. I didn't have to conform to the rituals of my past.

It was exciting, it was freeing—but often it was lonely. I forced myself to reach out for new friends, going to events listed in Eugene's free weekly. That's how for the first time I came to see Charles Gray. Someone I'd met at church had mentioned him to me. This man Gray, he reported in awestruck tones, had been a millionaire but he'd given away all his money to get by on what he felt was his fair share of the world's wealth. Lately he'd been living in Nicaragua, working to help the people there but soon he'd be speaking in Eugene, he was on some sort of tour.

When I saw his name listed in the weekly's calendar, I showed up early at the Friends Meetinghouse where he was speaking. There I ran into Pam, the woman who had led my delegation in Nicaragua. She spotted me in the small crowd that was settling into pews in the structure's unadorned main room and greeted me warmly.

"So you've finally discovered the Quakers! Here, come sit with me."

"Charles and Dorothy," she tipped her head toward a couple sitting quietly in the front row of pews, "a few years ago they were long-termers with Witness for Peace but then they moved on. Now they're running a women's health clinic in a community of mostly displaced Sandinistas."

Charles Gray was tall, white-haired, and good-looking in a gaunt sort of way, his wife, Dorothy Granada, was short, dark and chunky with a pretty face. They took turns speaking about the country I'd visited two years before. Mostly now it was at peace, they agreed, but sometimes bands of ex-Contras roamed and stole and menaced. Like most of the Sandinistas, many of these ex-Contras were desperately poor. If one of them turned up in need of medical care at Dorothy's health clinic for women, they would try to help him as best they could.

Under the Sandinistas, health care had been a priority and shipments from the USSR had provided medicines and other needed supplies. But now the Soviet Union had self-destructed and the new Nicaraguan government had cut support to the bone for the paltry number of public clinics that remained. Dorothy and her assistants—like the healers at the Center for Popular Education—did their best with herbal remedies, acupuncture, massage and what standard medicines they could obtain. Meanwhile Charles helped local people build inexpensive systems to collect and store rainwater so they wouldn't have to fetch it from the local river. He taught them how to purify it with a few drops of chlorine. And, because he was skilled as a carpenter, he taught them how to make furniture for their children's school. It all sounded commendable—but one thing seemed odd. The looks the two exchanged were less than cordial.

I didn't stick around after the program to talk to them but a couple of weeks later I attended a Sunday service at the Meetinghouse. These Quakers sat for an hour in silence broken only when a worshipper felt inspired to speak briefly. Their silence helped me meditate, something I felt I needed. I started attending services here fairly often. Soon an announcement on the bulletin board attracted my eye: "Attenders are invited to join the Quaker Economics Study Group." Economics had

19 • The Man Who Gave Away a Fortune

long been an interest of mine. Studying it had been my father's hobby, almost his passion. He'd been a devout socialist—he was definitely not into greed. Still one side effect of his fascination with economics was that he'd guided and encouraged me to play the stock market with more than the usual amount of skeptical savvy. That was part of the reason I could take early retirement and move to Eugene.

When I showed up for the group's next meeting, I was startled to discover Charles Gray there, already a member. He and his wife had separated at the end of their fundraising tour. Now, respected but very nearly penniless, he was living less than a mile from me, managing a complex of eight apartments owned by a Quaker, in return for housing in one of them.

This little committee was striving to look at global problems through the lens of traditional Quaker teachings like simplicity rather than ostentation, social justice, commitment to responsible stewardship of the earth, and opposition to war. How, they asked, should today's Friends view the *economic* violence in the world? How should they view the web of policies and practices that increased the gulf between rich and poor and, by glorifying high levels of consumption, threatened to dangerously plunder the planet? I went to their meetings and read articles they gave me. Soon I was a regular in the group.

I'd drive to the Meetinghouse in my new Honda Civic, the only car I'd ever owned. I'd bought it soon after I arrived in town. I hadn't wanted to buy a car, I'd hoped to just use public transit and walk but I soon realized that if I wanted to have a life here, I'd have to have a car. Eugene's buses ran infrequently after dark and, during my quirky childhood, I'd never learned to ride a bike. Charles arrived at meetings on an old bicycle that someone had given him.

One evening before the committee came together I found myself sitting in a room across from Charles and another woman. Gioia was in her mid-thirties, bosomy and a bit plump, the mother of a five-year-old daughter. Sometimes, she said, she worked as an editor. "I'm living in my RV, me and my kid. Don't know just how long I'll stay in Eugene." Her unusual first name, she said, had come to her on a vision quest. From the way she kept glancing at Charles sitting beside her I sensed some sensual tie between them though this man was at least thirty years her senior. I dismissed the idea as too odd to believe.

Oregon's gray and rainy winter came on. Now the committee set out to compose a statement of principles that in time might be adopted by the whole denomination. Charles and I volunteered to work together on one of its sections. I bought a bike carrier so I could give him a lift back to his apartment, not far from where I lived. Often after our meetings he chose to come over to my place instead for a couple of hours so we could work together on the piece we were drafting until he pedaled home. As Charles and I worked together over the coming months, our friendship grew.

THE MORE I LEARNED ABOUT HIM, the more impressed I was. Charles knew a huge amount about social movements and economics. He'd grown up poor, the youngest of four children in a fatherless home. Almost by chance, he said, when he was twenty-one he'd married into a wealthy and socially prominent family in Eugene. He hadn't learned until the day after their wedding that his bride, Leslie, was an heiress.

He'd earned a doctorate in sociology and taught at the college level. In the mid-Sixties, after he, Leslie and their two teenage children took a six-month around-the-world tour, they moved to New Zealand. They were fleeing the threat of nuclear conflict—New Zealand seemed relatively safe from radioactive fallout—but after three years he and his wife returned to America. (By this time, his son and daughter had each coupled off with partners in New Zealand. Conflicted, they were reluctant to move back to the States.)

When Charles got back, he set up his own think tank and organized actions against the Vietnam War. But by the Seventies, the trappings of wealth were making him more and more uncomfortable. He stopped driving and talked Leslie into turning the home she'd grown up in, her family's mansion, into a co-op with eight or ten other people, all involved in a Quaker-spawned experiment called Movement for a New Society.

I learned his story little by little, sometimes from him, sometimes from others. But first we grappled with more prosaic matters: this extraordinary man was lean and hungry. Dignified and reserved though his manner was, whenever we came back to my place, Charles was literally hungry. At first I made herbal tea and put out cookies—but I quickly sensed that wasn't enough. When I put out cheese, bread and

19 • The Man Who Gave Away a Fortune

fruit, he ate them with gusto. Soon I was heating up leftovers from my fridge: *boeuf bourgignon,* stir-fried veggies, ziti with clam sauce. It was fun to have a man around, particularly such an interesting, improbable man. That solemn look of his started fading away. A new light came into his eyes, new energy and fire. It was fun to watch him relax and stretch out, like that piece of brocade I'd found in my secondhand dresser.

In 1976, he told me, his wife and he had decided to give away half their relatively modest fortune, worth about a million dollars at the time, to set up a foundation. "It was her idea, really," he said. (Though later she'd tell me it was *his* idea but she hadn't been opposed.) Unlike most philanthropists, Charles and Leslie didn't choose what causes this new institution would support. Instead, they brought together a band of their fellow leftwing activists at a resort up the McKenzie River near Eugene. Over a weekend they collaborated in planning how it would run. Several of these activists would go on to serve on its board.

This new foundation didn't bear the Grays' name; instead they gave it a mouthful of a label, the McKenzie River Gathering Foundation, naming it for the ritual of its founding. Each year it collected additional donations from progressive donors. Gradually it would evolve into what it is now, "MRG," the leading source of seed money for grassroots organizations working for positive social change in Oregon.

In the mid-Seventies, Leslie's family mansion morphed into a crash pad. (Around this time, I'd learn later, Charles came out boldly in favor of open marriage. Leslie's own parents had split up when she was ten; her mother had never remarried. Leslie would endure much to stay with Charles.) After a while Charles and his wife moved out and rented a two-bedroom apartment nearby. But still he wasn't satisfied, he urged his wife to join him in giving away the rest of their shared fortune. At last Leslie said no, enough was enough. In 1977, after thirty-one years together, Leslie filed for divorce from Charles.

Now week after week, as the winter wore on, this extraordinary man visited me. We worked together on statements to bring to the Quaker Economics Group; sometimes, also, we hugged each other chastely. Often he would stretch out on my couch and I would lie down beside him, both of us fully clothed but cherishing each other's warmth. I didn't press him, this worldly man who seemed to have turned ascetic.

More than once in a meeting, he'd mentioned that he was a Gandhian. I assumed that, like Gandhi, he'd sworn off sex.

I knew he'd married Dorothy around 1980. In the late Eighties he'd moved with her to Nicaragua. One evening, I asked him what he'd done in the years between. He answered with a combination of defiance and pride, "We organized a fast, a fast to end the arms race. That was in 1983. We called it the Fast for Life. A lot of people around here remember that."

Aha! I thought, maybe that was one reason why some folks at the Meeting seemed to view him with awe. "You fasted here, here in Eugene?"

"No, down in the Bay Area, in Oakland. We knew we could get a lot more press coverage down there. It took years to organize, it was an international action, a Gandhian action. I've been a Gandhian ever since I read his autobiography when I was sixteen. We had people fasting with us in Japan and France.[1] And thousands of people did sympathy fasts, shorter fasts, here and all over the world."

"So what happened? What do you think was its impact?"

He turned away. He seemed to be retrieving the story from some dark place deep inside him. "We would have had more impact if we'd had better luck. When twelve of us had been fasting almost a month and the media were getting interested, a South Korean plane was shot down by the Russians. Maybe you remember? Everyone on board died. Two hundred and ninety-six people."

The story sounded vaguely familiar.

"It was a civilian airliner that had strayed into Soviet airspace. The Russians didn't ask questions, they didn't try to warn it. They assumed it was a spy plane and they shot it down. And of course, people around the world were shocked, they were appalled. Here in America, Reagan made a big thing of it. The Russians had played right into his hands, they gave him a first-rate excuse to beat the drum for the arms race."

He scowled. Then he went on, regret and sorrow in his voice and eyes. "Friends of ours, people who supported us, they urged us to end the fast. They said that, just then, we didn't have a ghost of a chance of having an impact."

What an extraordinary effort, I thought. And what a disaster. Funny, I'd never even heard of the Fast for Life.

19 • The Man Who Gave Away a Fortune

"In the Bay Area, Japan and Europe too, they gave us lots of coverage but back east—nothing. The staff we had that was working with the media, they said the big news services were waiting for one of us to die. Maybe then they might consider it worth reporting."

"My god." I sighed. "How long did you fast?"

"Forty days. Dorothy quit after thirty-nine. She was beginning to go blind so the staff we had—we had lots of volunteers, we had every kind of medical help—anyhow, they said it didn't make sense for her to do this to herself. Afterwards, a couple we knew down in Santa Cruz gave us a little place to recuperate so we lived there for a while. That was before we went to Nicaragua."

By the time they went down to Nicaragua, the Contra War was raging. They went as long-termers with Witness for Peace, committing themselves to stay at least six months as staff. Charles's face clouded over. It hadn't been pretty. He didn't go into the details—he changed the subject.

CHARLES AND A LONGTIME PEACENIK FRIEND towed a secondhand travel trailer down from Salem. He parked it on the property of a dedicated environmentalist who was building an intentional community on an acre of city land about a mile from me. Now Charles quit managing that apartment complex and set out to live in this tiny space as simply as he possibly could. Shoehorned into his new quarters—seven feet wide and twelve feet long—were a single bed, a closet, a small table, and a minimal kitchen. Rob, his new landlord, hooked up a hose that supplied him with cold water and let him use the bathroom in a communal cottage nearby.

"It's got everything I need," he said. "I'm happy as a clam." He loved the feeling, he said, of "walking lightly on the earth."

One week he didn't show up for our meeting on Quaker Economics. When he returned he told us that the Oprah show had flown him back to Chicago. They were doing a program on simple living so they'd picked him up from the airport with a limousine and put him up in a fancy hotel so he could stand up in the audience and say a couple of sentences. The program was broadcast a few days later. We watched it together on my TV. Charles looked tall and handsome when Oprah called on him to speak but he wasn't on screen more than twenty or thirty seconds.

How did they know to contact you?" I asked him.

Oh, he said, his story had been written up in a couple of books. The best known was *We Gave Away a Fortune*.[2] Published the previous year, it contained short biographies of over a dozen philanthropists.

Once again we lay down together on the couch. This time he let down his guard a bit, we kissed. Turbulence stirred inside me. I was hopelessly drawn to this brilliant, audacious man, no matter how eccentric his life style was. But then he sat up abruptly, looking troubled.

"There's something I have to check," he said.

Charles got up and walked around the room. Then he acknowledged some unexpected realities. "I've been thinking about getting tested for HIV. Gioia slept with some guy who was shooting up drugs and then I...." He cocked his head, waved a hand and let me guess the rest.

So *that's* what's been bugging him, I thought. It was almost funny. This paragon, Charles Gray, wasn't the saint a lot of people liked to think he was. Weeks passed before he got the results—negative for AIDS. Finally we dared to make love, we melted, merged and simmered together. I felt I'd been sent across the continent to offer him safe harbor. And he'd been sent north thousands of miles to make me feel whole again. It was crazy. To much of the world we probably looked too old to be capable of passion; I was 59, Charles was almost eight years older. It didn't matter.

We told each other stories out of our past, we let down our defenses. He and Leslie had both been virgins when they married, he said. Then they'd had two children, less than a year apart. They'd had a good life together. For a long time he'd been faithful to her but over the last fifteen years of their marriage, he'd loved many women. He'd fallen in love with each of them he said, but later I'd ask myself, had he really? Did he think his philandering didn't sound so bad if he said it was based on love? Was it partly a way, I wondered, for him to declare his freedom from Leslie with whom he'd started out young and innocent and to whom he owed so much?

With Dorothy it had been different, he said. He'd learned to be faithful to her. It upset her too much if he strayed, he explained. (Others would tell me later that Dorothy had a ferocious temper. Just how much he strayed from her, I will never know.)

19 • The Man Who Gave Away a Fortune

Oh well, I thought, who was I to judge him? What sedate, conventional man would want to take me on, adventurous and wayward as I'd been much of my life? I'd been married four times and had had adulterous flings myself. Though once I bonded to a man, it was my pattern to stay faithful to him unless he was blatantly unfaithful to me. Margaret Mead called it serial monogamy.

After that, Charles started staying over at my place a couple times a week, having dinner with me and staying for breakfast. I'd been lonely too long to make demands on him, to hold out for a greater show of commitment. Every time he climbed on his bike to leave I felt a bit bereft. Charles never said he loved me, I didn't think he did and in my heart I didn't believe this affair of ours would last.

20

Living on Less

CHARLES HAD CALCULATED WHAT HE CALLED the World Equity Budget—the amount of income a person could honorably live on if everyone on the planet had an equal share of a sustainable world economy. He settled into his condo-minimum, living simply in accord with his ethical beliefs. He had a minute income: his Social Security based on the few years when he'd worked at normal jobs. He paid Rob miniscule rent proportionate to the amount of land his trailer occupied, and contributed to the commune by working in its large garden. Fortunately, that garden supplied him with lots of fresh, nutritious food.

Sometimes Charles did handyman jobs outside the commune. In keeping with his World Equity Budget, he charged about a third of the going rate, though when he helped me out by fixing a leaky faucet or a cupboard that refused to stay closed, he worked for free. He started introducing me as his partner to folks around town—though I sensed that there were many aspects of his life he didn't share with me. Nonetheless, when we were together, he listened patiently to my rambling stories and often he enriched my life with adventures. Because I was too timid a driver to explore the wilder parts of Oregon, he renewed his long lapsed driver's license. Then with him at the wheel of my car, we took off to the coast or the mountains to go hiking and car camping

20 • Living on Less

Charles bought a bike for me at a yard sale and taught me how to ride it. We took to cycling together on a wide paved path that stretched for miles along the river, but sometimes that bike seemed haunted. It would make odd scraping noises that stopped as soon as we took note of them. When Charles checked it, he could find nothing to explain them. Hesitantly I told Charles about the apparently paranormal events I'd experienced years before. He accepted my tales dispassionately, not openly belittling yet skeptical. Soon we would both be confronted by an even more puzzling happening.

Charles's sister, her husband and their daughter, a vegetarian, lived in town and had welcomed me into their family. More than once I'd had dinner with them. When it was my turn to reciprocate, I planned to make eggplant parmigiana, garlic bread and a salad. Charles volunteered to help. A couple of hours before his relatives were due to arrive, I pulled a grater out of a kitchen drawer and laid it down on a counter. It was nothing special, just a flat piece of stainless steel with sharp-edged slots for shredding vegetables and such. I was planning to use it to shred mozzarella. Later Charles could use it to grate a carrot to garnish the salad. But for the moment each of us was busy with other tasks.

Soon I was ready to shred my cheese—but now that grater was nowhere to be found. My new partner and I looked high and low: on counters, in drawers, in and under bags of produce. At last we gave up in desperation. I sliced up my hunk of mozzarella with a knife, Charles took a potato peeler to his carrot. Our guests arrived, we sat down to eat in the nook that adjoined the kitchen, then I got up to fetch dessert. *There on the counter lay the runaway grater, just where I'd left it in the first place.*

I didn't touch it. I just came back to the dinner table with a store-bought Key lime pie and a stunned expression on my face. "Is something wrong?" Charles whispered. I put down the pie and beckoned him to see where the grater was lying. Now he'd experienced for himself one of those spooky occurrences I'd told him about. Was Paul, the punster, at it again? By calling our attention to that common kitchen tool he seemed to be saying that my new partner was *greater*, better for me than anyone else I'd fancied I might partner with in the ten lean years since he died.

231

Activist Odyssey

A TEAM FROM THE BBC APPEARED at Charles's travel trailer. They checked him out for a program they were planning to film about the choices people made about money. Then the series host, Angus Deayton, and five skilled technicians with British accents crowded into his tiny home to hear how he'd given away half a million dollars and see how he was living now. A whimsical profile contrasting his lifestyle[1] with that of two other Americans would be broadcast the next year.

"He restricts himself," Deayton reported on the program, "to what he calls the World Equity Budget: $160 a month, about a hundred pounds." Charles showed them his carefully kept accounts, listing what he'd spent for the past sixteen years, usually less than the WEB ordained so he could give symbolic reparations to needier folks. "I've got everything I need," he said with a warm smile. "I've got my books, I've got my office, I've got my dishes and my sink and my stove and my storage for clothes and storage under the bed. And got a good bed. What else do you need?"

Outside the trailer he displayed the simple-living way he did laundry: sloshing clothes around a bucket with a toilet plunger. Then he pulled out a roll of adding machine tape and treated them to a graphic demonstration of the excruciatingly unequal distribution of incomes in the world. He'd done this dozens of times before, in schools, churches, synagogues, and public meeting halls. For the BBC he handed one end of the tape to Deayton and started unreeling it, walking out into the yard he shared with his neighbors in Rob's urban commune. He'd marked it off in symbolic fifths, from the world's poorest fifth to the richest.

In 1994 the poorest fifth of the world's population—represented by the first 4-1/2 inches of the tape—lived on an average income of $463 a year. The second fifth's average annual income was just over a thousand dollars, the third $2,094. The next to the richest fifth had incomes of about $4,500. The incomes of four-fifths of the world's population were represented by less than four feet of Charles's tape. But as he approached typical incomes for Americans and Brits—even the poorest—he started walking further out into the yard. "Now," he said, "you're getting into the richest fifth of the people of the world. That starts at about $7600 but the average is about $15,679. The thing you have to remember about the richest fifth is that that goes on practically to infinity!"

20 • Living on Less

Charles's figure receded into the distance, heading for the line that marked the richest 1%. The reel wasn't long enough to symbolize the incomes of the very wealthiest. "How much paper did Charles have?" the program's host would ask amiably. "He'd already passed the Duchess of York, and Donald Trump was just the other side of the hedge. But did he have enough to reach Andrew Lloyd Weber? Apparently he'd be somewhere in the middle of the Pacific Ocean." Brit that he was, Deayton would make no mention of those American multibillionaires, Warren Buffett and Bill Gates.

CHARLES WAS BRILLIANT AT WHAT HE did, I thought, and what he did was useful. Many idealistic sorts who heard him speak were shamed into restructuring their lives to get by on less. But it bothered me that it wouldn't work for everyone to live as he did. He relied more than he liked to admit on the generosity of others—people who lived more conventionally. His landlord worked as a plumber and builder; he was paying off a mortgage and cheerfully risked trouble with the local authorities for letting Charles park his trailer on his land. His sister and I had him over for meals. Each year at harvest season, he collected fruit from other people's trees and dried it to stash away for coming months. And old friends of his brought over gifts of prepared food and an old computer to use for his writing projects. There was no way he could have lived as he did if he had young children to care for. I refused to let him lay a guilt trip on me.

I recognized that the planet couldn't support everyone in high style. I just wished for a world where everyone had what they needed to live a safe and simple life without costly frills. Lots of those frills, it seemed to me, served mostly to show others that you outranked them or indulged some sick need to spend and spend. I went on living in my modest way and did what I could to support him—and other causes in which I believed.

CHARLES AND I WERE ACTIVE IN a local Witness for Peace group organized by Pam Fitzpatrick with whom I'd toured Nicaragua. We participated in grassroots campaigns like one that publicized dire conditions in that ravaged nation by collecting basics like beans, aspirin and pencils to help meet its people's needs. In the summer of 1995, I visited there again with another Witness for Peace delegation. This one focused on the policies of the World Bank and the International Monetary Fund and how they were transforming post-Sandinista Nicaragua.

I'd always heard the World Bank was a good thing; I knew scarcely anything about what it was up to. It claimed that one of its major goals was reducing poverty. But what I saw with my own eyes soon changed my opinion.

After the fall of the Sandinistas the Bank along with its sister institution, the IMF, had stepped in to work with Chamorro's government to restructure the Nicaraguan economy. It offered loans—ostensibly that was the carrot. The stick was the "bitter medicine" it required, "structural adjustment" designed to help the nation pay off the huge international debt it had built up during the Contra War. This was supposed to strengthen the country's economic health.

The Bank and IMF date back to the closing days of World War II. At meetings in Bretton Woods, New Hampshire in 1944, delegates from the Allied nations—those opposed to Hitler's bloc—designed new ways to regulate international commerce and finance that might guide reconstruction after the war. Decades later, after oil-producing nations formed OPEC and raised oil prices, the Bretton Woods institutions started playing a different role.

That jump in prices, often called the Oil Shock, had strange consequences. Poor countries slipped into debt, trying to pay for oil they couldn't afford. Meanwhile oil producers, primarily Arab states, were flush with cash and eager to invest it. During the Eighties and Nineties, the Bank found an ingenious way to accommodate them while opening the door to vast profits for transnational corporations and ensuring low prices for Western consumers on products exported from the Third World.

Claiming that the policies it pressed on poor nations in exchange for loans would improve their situation, it promoted Structural Adjustment Programs all over the Third World.[2] Often these featured giant projects like constructing dams—usually built by American firms—which typically displaced thousands of local people, had unfortunate environmental effects, and produced power used primarily by multinational corporations for enterprises of their own located nearby. The cost of these projects, paid for by loans to the governments of poor nations, increased their debt burden and made them all the more desperate for more borrowed money. Soon Third World activists talked of being "SAPed" and painted anti-Bank slogans on the walls of their towns.

Twelve years of structural adjustment in Mexico,[3] first implemented there in 1982, saw its minimum wage fall by 60%, infant mortality triple, and legions of small and medium sized businesses and farms go under due to competition from cheap imports—typically from American agribusiness—and interest rates set oppressively high. Meanwhile, between 1988 and 1994, the number of Mexico's billionaires grew from 2 to 24.

This was largely because those on cozy terms with the folks running the government acquired public assets—giant enterprises like banks, mining companies, and electric power and telephone utilities—at fire sale prices when they were privatized as structural adjustment ordained. The World Bank demanded that the private sector control such enterprises; if the government owned them, it was forced to sell them off. Presumably it could raise lots of money that way—but the Bank didn't require the government to auction its valuables off to the highest bidder so too often, corrupt officials sold them cheap to their wealthy friends. Then one hand was expected to wash the other.

Often, as in Panama when I lived there in the Sixties, the ruling elite was made up of people who came from a few powerful families and had gone to school together when they were kids. Old chums ran both the government and the business sector. No wonder buyers of government assets obligingly kicked back millions[4] to the ruling party. All these circumstances contributed to a spectacular Mexican debt crisis in December 1994. Meanwhile illegal immigration to the United States skyrocketed as poor Mexicans, most of them displaced from small farms, fled north across the border looking for jobs.

The structural adjustment program foisted on Nicaragua included the privatization of most enterprises that had been publicly owned during the Sandinista regime but it didn't involve big dams or other massive projects. As in Mexico, it pressed Chamorro's administration to cut spending on health and education and to lend no money to small farmers. Campesinos by the hundreds of thousands were forced to get by on a few months' work a year for large landowners, move to the cities, or clear land in the rainforest to homestead. Large farmers were granted loans—but only if they *didn't* plant "basic grains," that is, the corn, beans and rice that ordinary people lived on. Instead they were pushed to plant specialty crops for export. Theoretically, according to World Bank economists, this would increase the nation's income and increase its ability to pay off its international debts. But it also made it dependent on imported food—largely from the United States—to feed its people.

The loans the government received from the Bank didn't enable it to provide benefits to its citizens. Instead they were earmarked to service the nation's debts to creditors abroad, typically paying *just the interest* on these debts. Since they couldn't afford to pay down the *principal*, they'd be obligated to pay more and more interest down the road. What a trap, I thought, what a disingenuous trap.

WHEN WE ARRIVED IN MANAGUA IN July 1995 it looked very different from what I remembered. Five years after the defeat of the Sandinistas, its downtown streets teemed with the expensive cars of "Miami boys" who had returned to reclaim their holdings; billboards advertised costly goodies for them to buy. Crime had increased. The wealthy lived behind high metal fences, their homes guarded by big, fiercely barking dogs or even by armed men. And you couldn't sit in a sidewalk cafe without having skinny, barefoot kids try to sell you lottery tickets, candy, cigarettes, whatever. Often they were the sole support of their families.

According to a goodhearted woman we met with at the modest offices of the U. S. Agency for International Development, only 47% of Nicaraguans who wanted to work were fully employed. Only 42% of Nicaraguan children were getting most of the calories they needed. Many were so severely undernourished that the staff at USAID thought they were doomed to suffer lifelong damage. Unfortunately there was little they could do about this. In 1991 and 1992, when AID worked in concert with structural adjustment programs, it was generously funded. But by 1995 when it had switched its focus to grassroots development, its budget had been slashed to a tenth of its former size.

Most Witness for Peace delegations get to stay with local people for a few days. On this trip we traveled northeast to Matagalpa, a good-sized city. There we stayed in a large hillside settlement of squat but solid cinderblock homes without running water built by the Sandinistas for the mothers and widows of fallen soldiers. The *Madres* we talked to said that, hard as it had been to live in a nation at war, it was harder now to get by. The pensions of widows hadn't been raised to keep up with inflation, jobs were almost impossible to find, and most had no men at home to help them out.

Theoretically elementary school for their children was free but notebooks and pencils had to be bought and uniforms and shoes were often required. Since teachers no longer received a basket of food as part of their pay, to supplement their starvation wages they demanded fees for letting students use textbooks or for giving them tests. Somehow most of the kids in this barrio got to go to elementary school but for most families, education past sixth grade was out of reach.

One day our delegation visited a center funded by Finland. (All over Nicaragua we would run into programs funded by foreign countries and organizations.) It provided lunch, classes, therapy, arts and affectionate attention to a hundred children who worked in the city streets each day. Some sold fruit, lottery tickets or enchiladas their mothers made, others shined shoes or carried loads to help support their families. The staff at the center called them *"las hormiguitas,"* the little ants.

The *doña* of the house where I stayed had lost her husband and three sons in the Contra War. Her daughter and three grandchildren lived with her in a fairly large house. The daughter had added three rooms to it while she worked as a maid for a wealthy woman. But now she was unemployed and her husband was vaguely described as living and working somewhere outside the country. This was hardly unusual when even in Costa Rica, just south of Nicaragua, wages were more than three times as high; lots of Nicaraguan men left their families to find work elsewhere. If those families were lucky, remittances from their men helped to keep them afloat.

The threat of theft was real and constant. During the five days our delegation stayed in this barrio, thieves stole cooking pots, a hand mill for grinding corn and a couple of live chickens. And illness was far harder to deal with than it had been while the Sandinistas tried to provide everyone with medical care. One evening a member of our delegation came by, his face drawn with concern. "The lady I'm staying with has a terrible open sore on her leg," he told me. "She's had it for weeks. We're taking up a collection so she can buy medicine."

Money our delegation donated paid for drugs and bandages for this woman's leg and to treat the racking cough of a child in another home. Then it was time for us to leave, to visit hopeful projects elsewhere in the country. We met with a spokesman for a partnership of Nicaraguan churches that with money donated by a Wisconsin group, had made almost $3,000,000 worth of low interest loans to women, collectives and small businesses. Elsewhere, on a cooperative farm in mountainous country, planned with the help of university agronomists, we met with men and women who were working together to grow organic coffee, reforest the land with mahogany trees, experiment with natural pesticides and practice other environmentally friendly techniques.

Soon it was time for us to fly back to Washington, DC and meet with officials who might, with luck, learn something from us about what was really happening in Nicaragua at the grassroots. The man from the World Bank lectured us non-stop so we had virtually no time to say our piece. The man from the State Department was diplomatic—what a surprise! The man at the office of the AFL-CIO swapped with us scary stories of his own.

We were painfully aware that most of our friends and neighbors back home were uninformed about the grievous conditions under which Nicaraguans were forced to live. When we joined this delegation we had promised Witness for Peace that we would do our best to tell others about what we learned on this trip. And so we did.

A newspaperwoman from Missouri sent each of us a copy of a moving full-page article, complete with color photos, she'd done for her city's daily. A minister from the United Church of Christ collected slides from us all, then showed the best of them to his congregation and to his denomination's Board of World Ministries.

Back in Eugene, I did what I could. Charles helped. Longtime grassroots activist that he was, he saw opportunities for me to spread the word that I never would have found for myself. I was interviewed on local radio and reached out to Eugene's most popular journalist with facts he featured in one of his daily columns. I contacted the minister at the U-U church I'd attended for over twenty years in New York, asking how I could share my story with my old friends there. He suggested that

I write a short piece for someone else to read aloud; then he scheduled it as part of the church's most popular service, the one each year where Catholic peace activist Dan Berrigan was the featured speaker.

I was part of a growing movement. In 1985 the International Rivers Network, a watchdog group furious at the ecological destruction wrought by projects conceived by the World Bank, had been founded in Berkeley. It started a publication called BankCheck to keep an eye on their nemesis. In 1994 a brilliant and determined couple (a Kenyan woman and her white American husband) had founded Fifty Years Is Enough, commemorating the half-century since the World Bank and IMF had been established. Based in Washington, D.C., they agitated in their eminently literate, non-violent way against the destructive policies these institutions were imposing on poor countries—dealing with regimes that often enriched the most prosperous and powerful of their citizens at the expense of the vast majority. Around this time, Oxfam International, founded in Oxford, England,[5] established a headquarters also in Washington, D.C., to influence the World Bank and the IMF. (Oxfam is a global NGO which works to tackle the root causes of poverty and create lasting solutions.) Thanks to efforts like these, accounts of the toxicity of these policies spread around the planet.

Legions of nuns, many of whom had lived and worked in the Third World, organized protests. Church ladies of other persuasions got the message too. Together they created the Jubilee campaign for the forgiveness of debt, based on the principle of Jubilee described in the Old Testament. Every 50 years, slaves were to be set free, land was to be returned to its original owners, and debts were to be forgiven. In 1999, the global Jubilee 2000 campaign would urge that the debt of the 41 most impoverished nations in the world be canceled. By 2000, over 21,000,000 people from 155 countries had signed the Jubilee 2000 petition.

In 2005, an activist newsletter would report[6] that "After years of campaigning ... power has backed down. What they once deemed as impossible is now the position of the group of 8 of the world's wealthiest countries .... 'all the debts owed by eligible heavily indebted poor countries to [the International Development Agency, an arm of the World Bank], the International Monetary Fund and the African Development Fund should be cancelled.'" Unfortunately, to qualify for cancellation of debt, these countries had to implement punishing "reforms" such as steep cuts to their spending on health and education. As a result, this report continued, "only 18 of the over 60 countries who desperately need debt relief are currently eligible."

When in 2013, the threat of bankruptcy loomed over Greece and Spain, their creditors—many of them their European neighbors—were forced to reconsider the policies which the international financial institutions routinely applied to heavily indebted Third World countries. As reported in *The New York Times*,[7] "economists in the I.M.F.'s fiscal affairs department concluded that efforts to curb budget deficits increase inequality, especially if they take the form of spending cuts. It suggested that targeted government spending and progressive taxes could offset some of these effects."

Unfortunately, these suggestions had little effect. When late in 2018, Angela Merkel announced that she would retire from being chancellor of Germany, a long and thoughtful article by Peter S. Goodman[8] in *The New York Times* faulted her among others for, earlier in the decade, having forced the bitter medicine of structural adjustment on European nations struggling with overwhelming debt. "Like many national leaders," Goodman asserted, "Ms. Merkel ... catered to domestic political interests at the expense of broader European concerns.... She adamantly opposed debt forgiveness to Greece, even as it teetered toward insolvency, and even as joblessness exceeded 27 percent—a special source of outrage given that German banks were primary lenders in Greece's catastrophic explosion of borrowing."

Quoting the Nobel laureate economist Joseph Stiglitz, the article continued, "She was at the heart of the design of the flawed Greek program, which not only imposed austerity, but most importantly resisted restructuring the debt in order to save the German and French banks. The rhetoric that she used suggested that the crisis was caused by irresponsible behavior by Greece, rather than irresponsibility on the part of the lender."

"In place of public spending to soften the edges of the crisis," Goodman said, "Ms. Merkel used Germany's power as the largest economy in Europe to force troubled governments to slash support for pensions, health care and education. In the process, the moves helped lengthen and deepen a devastating economic downturn."

21

Helping the Homeless

For years I'd thought I should write about the mysterious communications I'd sensed after Paul's death—but I dreaded revisiting in memory that long painful period when he was going blind, to set the scene for what happened later. Now that over a decade had passed, that pain had faded. The next time I visited New York, I stopped by the mansion that housed the American Society for Psychical Research. I'd joined it at the recommendation of Jim, my old friend whose former nanny had learned from a dream that he'd been wounded during World War II. The ASPR had a library and a small bookstore so I started my research there, buying a few of their books and chatting with a fellow who worked there about my new enterprise. He recommended a shop nearby where I could find some relevant titles and suggested I check secondhand bookstores as well.

Soon I was shipping boxes of books to Eugene. Back home I morphed into a more dedicated student than I'd ever been before, poring over one volume after another, highlighting passages and scribbling comments in the margins. Then I typed up notes on what I'd read and filed them away in a fat loose-leaf binder.

By now Charles had experienced enough of what might be manifestations from Paul to be open-minded about the subject. What was more, often when we were at some casual gathering and I mentioned what I was working on, other people shared tales of their own. One sometimes got advice from her dead mother in vivid dreams, a man smelled his wife's perfume whenever he visited her grave, a third said that when she was a little girl, she saw her aunt visit to say, "Don't worry, things will be all right." Then her aunt disappeared, the phone rang, and her family learned that she'd just died.

"I think you're on to something," Charles said—even as he concentrated on his own activities. One day he told me mildly, "I think I'll do something for the homeless here in Eugene, a grassroots project." He didn't say what he planned to do.

Charles was very nearly homeless himself. Still within the eighty-four square feet of his travel trailer he had light and heat and shelter from the weather; a few paces away he had access to a bathroom. All this was far more than what several hundred Eugeneans had.

He hooked up with a group called the Homeless Action Coalition. It worked to improve conditions in Eugene and in Springfield, its more working-class neighbor. In different ways, its leaders had backgrounds in social service. Wayne, a dark-haired man who played upright string bass in a folk-rock band, had been an emergency room technician until the constant pressure of trying to save lives had left him partly disabled with PTSD. Tom, whose curly blonde hair hung down to his shoulders, was a Vietnam vet ordained years before as a Southern Baptist minister. His mission now, he felt, was to minister to the homeless. With these two at his side, Charles started attending City Council meetings and getting to know the folks on the city's planning board.

The man in charge of housing for Eugene advocated building more units for low-income people but years went by with more talk than action. Meanwhile people slept in the rain or huddled in doorways. (Virtually all of these, given Eugene's population, were white and American-born.) Wayne and Tom pressed the county to establish a year-round campground where folks could set up tents or park the vehicles that were their improvised homes and use toilets and showers supplied on site. But the county had tried something like this before and said it hadn't worked. It was hard to provide security for the residents.

Prodded by HAC, the city set up small shelters for teen runaways and homeless women and children. Other desperate people stayed reluctantly at the Eugene Mission, a longtime community resource, which charged $2 a day and let the penniless work for their keep. Single women felt safe there but both men and women resented the Mission's rigid rules at that time, its paltry food, and daily fundamentalist services that all residents were required to attend before they were allowed to eat dinner. (The Mission's policies have since improved.)

Homeless men who didn't have vehicles camped surreptitiously behind stands of trees, or on the narrow strip of land that lay between the river and the park that ran for miles beside the Willamette. That strip was a miniature wilderness where thickets of wild Himalayan blackberry sprawled, forever being cut back yet still threatening to crowd out an Oregon abundance of native vines, shrubs and trees all jostling one another, competing for sunlight. During Eugene's dry season, mid-June through mid-October, nighttime temperatures rarely dropped below the fifties. During those temperate months, people could live in the open fairly comfortably. Come fall and winter, nights were much colder; few days were completely dry and the ground stayed muddy.

The police had orders to keep homeless people from settling in anywhere. At any hour of the day or night, cops prodded them to move on. I was glad to know that my partner was working with the Homeless Action Coalition, but I knew very little about what they were doing though by this time Charles was staying over at my place three or four nights a week.

In the spring of 1997, he surprised me with an announcement. He'd decided to move in with me and he wanted us to get married. "I'm sick of not knowing where my stuff is," he said lightly, "I never know where I've left anything."

I'd long wanted him to move in with me. Soon he did. It was easy, he had few possessions. Still clinging to much of his World Equity Budget, he went on riding his hand-me-down bicycle around town and wearing secondhand clothes, some of which he'd decorated with embroidery. His favorite shirt bore, along with tiny butterflies and birds, the outline of a bike and the caption, ONE LESS CAR.

I figured we could just go down to City Hall to get married but Charles wanted us to have a real wedding with lots of guests and meaningful vows we made to each other. This sounded sweet—but there was a hitch. For years we'd kept up with my young friend Todd, the part-time handyman who'd helped me when I first moved to Eugene. He'd often come by to share meals with us until he decided to join the

Peace Corps. For the past couple of years he'd been stationed in Kenya. Now in letters with foreign stamps and Peace Corps return addresses he urged me to visit him there.

Todd's tour of duty was about to end. He wanted to go on safari and travel around without responsibilities. He invited me to be his traveling companion. When Charles was rich, he'd done a round-the-world tour with Leslie and their kids. He'd been to Africa, he'd even visited a game park there. No way would he indulge himself in anything like that again. So he told me, "Sure, go. You know you want to."

If I traveled with Todd, I wouldn't have to stick to the tourist track. Thanks to his Peace Corps training, he spoke two local languages and I'd be able to stay briefly with a Kenyan family. Besides, who could resist the lure of going on safari? Not with a gun, of course, but with a camera. If I timed it right, I might even see the fabled annual migration of well over a million animals from the plains of western Kenya to the Serengeti south of it in Tanzania.

Charles and I decided to get married in late July in a Quaker ceremony at the Meetinghouse. He wore an old shirt he'd trimmed with embroidery. I wore a flower-trimmed straw hat just so I could toss it in the air when the service ended. Three weeks later I flew to Nairobi where Todd met me at the airport.

His home place was up in the highlands, 5,000 feet high, cool in August. The day I arrived, people in the community he'd been serving were giving him a party. He took me as his guest. Men and women made speeches thanking him for the things he'd been doing: building systems to collect rainwater, developing and distributing improved cook-stoves (at $5 each) that burned less fuel and gave off less smoke, and generally working to make their lives easier and better. There was nothing exotic about their dress except that the women wore skirts instead of the pants I was wearing, skirts almost to their ankles that looked old fashioned and rather maidenly—maybe first pressed on them by missionaries. They served us tasty stews with lots of beef and goat meat. I was surprised to see Todd eating them enthusiastically—he'd been a vegetarian as long as I'd known him.

"Oh that," he said. "Yeah, I guess I should've mentioned. It's from local animals, that's how most people make their living around here. It's all natural, organic." He went back to putting it away.

21 • Helping the Homeless

At his home site I met my hosts, Mr. and Mrs. Henya, and their five children. As in Nicaragua, their toilet facilities were in a privy but this time, thanks to Todd's efforts, there was a charming bathhouse where you could shower with rainwater collected in a giant tank he had built, fed by a system of gutters that led from the roof of the Henyas' house. He had also run hoses close to their home so they didn't have to haul water for cooking or washing. They could even use a little to water their crops. Mr. Henya was a skilful mechanic employed by the Peace Corps but he and his wife also tended a small farm.

They were members of the Kikuyu tribe, the biggest ethnic group in Kenya. About the only thing I'd ever heard about the Kikuyus was that they'd been central to the Mau Mau rebellion that had led to the freeing of their nation from British rule. In the Fifties, the American media usually referred to them as "the dreaded Mau Mau" and made them sound like bloodthirsty savages. Greatly outgunned by the Brits who had no desire to yield power and land, nonviolence had not been the Mau Mau's style.

The Henyas, however, proved to be agreeable hosts. Both spoke English, both had attended high school. Like my peasant hosts in Nicaragua, they were determined that their children would get a good education but school fees were a constant, often desperate worry. They explained proudly that the Kikuyu were the first tribe in the country to convert to Christianity; they considered themselves more modern and Westernized than other Kenyan tribes. I wondered what their beliefs were about ghosts and the afterlife. They sidestepped my questions and said perhaps older, more traditional people could answer them for me.

One evening, for my benefit, they invited an elderly couple over. We six grownups gathered around a big table in the small house Todd had built for himself on the Henyas' property. For the present I was staying there in a comfortable room of my own but when he moved out, in a matter of weeks, it would belong to them. Even now, most afternoons after the Henya kids came home from school, they gathered around this table to do their homework.

The view from Todd's house was spectacular. Two of its windows looked out across the Great Rift Valley to its opposite bank 35 miles away. This mammoth trench, a seismic fault line, slashes 1500 miles through East Africa, south from Ethiopia to Mozambique. As diplomatically as I could manage, I asked our visitors about their beliefs. Since they spoke little English, the Henyas had to translate for me. Finally the elderly woman conceded that, yes, she believed there were ghosts but you didn't have to fear them if you were a Christian. Christ would protect you.

If when they were alive you'd had a good relationship with the person who died, you might see them in visions, might talk with them in dreams. She described complex burial rituals and taboos between family groups when someone was in mourning. She was telling more than I could take in though, confused, I went on taking notes. She didn't fear witchcraft, the old woman said. She felt safe because she'd been cleansed by the blood of Jesus.

Soon the tables turned. The others wanted to know who I was and where I came from.

How much land did I own? they asked. I told them about the modest house I lived in, the other small house I owned alongside it and the less than a quarter acre on which they were built. Then how many animals did I own? I had to be a woman of means, they thought, if I could fly all the way from America to holiday in Africa on little more than a whim. But I had to confess that I didn't own cattle, not even goats or sheep—just two cats. (I couldn't help grinning as I told them this.) The Africans looked perplexed. Only land and animals spelled security to them.

I tried to explain that I used to have a very good job and I'd always lived modestly so now I had other assets. I tried to explain about banks and pensions. I didn't dare mention stocks and mutual funds—too insubstantial to seem real to them. Our ways of life seemed mutually incomprehensible. They reserved judgment, I changed the subject.

One day Mrs. Henya asked me, "How do you get water where you live? Do you have donkeys?" More than once, traveling through the countryside, I'd seen a small donkey loaded with a plastic cask of water, being led by a woman. Poorer women carried such casks on their backs, partly supported by a strap across the forehead. "No," I said, embarrassed by the vast gulf between her world and mine, "it's much easier where I come from." I couldn't bear to try to explain how much easier it was.

21 • Helping the Homeless

TODD AND I LEFT TO RETURN to Nairobi. The largest city in Kenya, it's located high in mountains, aloof from tropical heat and malaria. Corporations and non-profit organizations from around the world chose it for their offices. Some of its streets, lined with cafes and fashionable shops, wouldn't have looked out of place in New York or Paris. At 8:45 on a weekday morning, its downtown bustled with cosmopolitan looking, stylishly dressed businesspeople rushing to work, nine-tenths of them black.

In Nairobi we signed up for our safari and joined a small band of tourists to drive into the Masai Mara Game Reserve. There, men who ran the safari herded us into Land Rovers with fenced open tops so we could stand in them and take photos or simply gawp. A family group of elephants, three or four moms and their sisters plus young'uns of varying sizes, ambled across the track ahead of our vehicle. Gargantuan, they blocked our way until they passed by. So many sights all around us. (We tourists briefly part of the menagerie.) Giraffes grazing the upper stories of trees, any number of deer-like animals—antelopes and gazelles, impala and tiny dikdiks—a lion twenty feet away from us humping a lioness, and a troop of small monkeys cautiously creeping across the grassland. Our guide phoned other guides; they exchanged news of where the rarest and most fascinating creatures might be seen.

Then he drove cross country to where the migration—yes, the great migration!—was taking place. A seemingly endless procession of wildebeest trotted across the savannah accompanied by much smaller numbers of zebra running alongside. At first they seemed unaware of anything but the urgent need to move on across the floor of the valley, yet clearly they took note of us. The stream of animals diverted some yards away from where we stood. They veered to a slightly different track, still lurching forward on and on. Then we too moved on, to the banks of the Mara River, the only source of water left for game during this dry season.

Hippos were soaking themselves there, just their backs and heads visible. We loafed along on the river bank, past a crocodile lazing in the sun. I walked so close to it that our guide winced visibly but he hesitated to reproach me. (He was a black African well-schooled not only in the lore of an endless list of local wildlife but in how to deal tactfully with palefaces like me.) I was acting like an idiot, I realized right afterwards, but it all seemed so unreal at the time. What did I know about watching out for predators?

I left my tour group to walk fifty feet further along the bank of the river to where the beach ended in a tangle of low vegetation in front of me and an arm's length away on my right. A few yards farther on, mostly obscured by shrubbery, I could barely make out what seemed to be a troop of baboons. Curious, I moved closer to the edge of the bushes. Then suddenly, fiercely, I felt eyes on me.

When I turned to my right I saw to my horror, lightly screened by shrubs, what must have been the alpha male of that troop of baboons, determined to protect them from (he thought) potentially dangerous me. Standing up he was a little shorter than I was but he looked tough, *very* tough—broad shoulders and long muscular arms under shaggy fur—and he was baring his teeth at me, huge teeth, three times as large as a human's. This alpha baboon was glaring furiously at me. He didn't look friendly.

Should I run? Or would that make him run after me? Instead I lowered my head respectfully, backed away several feet, then turned and slowly rejoined the other tourists. A few days later, when Todd and I went to Mombasa, the two of us had a different kind of adventure.

Mombasa is an extraordinary and ancient city, very unlike Nairobi. A major port, it sits on the Indian Ocean on trade routes from India and the Middle East. Indians and Arabs make up much of its population. Muslim calls to prayer resound near its harbor where massive wooden doors, elegantly carved in Moorish style, guard the mysteries of buildings in its Old Town. Across the road lies Fort Jesus, a major tourist attraction. A ponderous stone fortress built by Portuguese in the 16th century, it has a dark history of involvement with the slave trade.

That summer Kenya's president of almost twenty years was once again running for office despite rumblings about his corruption and state torture of his opponents. Rumors of violent conflicts fifty miles up the coast from Mombasa reached us in Nairobi where we had to catch our train. Nonetheless, since troubles had only been reported in rural districts some distance away, we bought roundtrip tickets to the port and traveled southeast out of the mountains.

Todd led me on a tour of the city's points of interest: Fort Jesus and places to shop nearby for African crafts. Further on, in the center of

21 • Helping the Homeless

town, we stepped into a big indoor market with stalls that sold every kind of food—meat, fresh vegetables and grains, canned and bottled goods and fragrant spices. Almost instantly, vendors crowded around us. They left their stalls to press their wares on us like something out of an Indiana Jones movie. But why? I looked around. We were the only ones shopping there. How could this be? We made a quick exit.

After a late lunch we ambled over to Peace Corps headquarters to say hello and hear the latest news. But as soon as the slim, tanned woman on duty spotted us she yelled, "Todd, what are you doing here? You've gotta go back! Haven't you heard?"

The violence up the coast had spread to Mombasa. Men with machetes were attacking people. Someone had been hacked to death in that indoor market not long before we arrived. No wonder there weren't any customers there—word spread fast.

"Well," Todd assured her, looking a bit rattled, "we've got return tickets for tonight on the train."

"Damn good thing," she replied sharply. Then she relented enough to turn hospitable. "Stick around for a while. Sit down, make yourselves comfortable. You two better stick around till it's time to go."

When we got to the station, both first and second class were sold out and hundreds of frantic people were waiting in a line so long we couldn't see its end, hoping to crowd into the third class section. Most of them were carrying bundles, most of these bundles were balanced on their heads. It all looked like something I recalled hazily from some ancient movie—amazing to see how accurate those images had been. Now it was really happening and Todd and I were minor characters on the sidelines, fortunate ones confident that we'd get on the train.

EUGENE'S TRANQUILITY GATHERED ME BACK. CHARLES told me about HAC's latest project to help the homeless in town. They called it their Campaign for Legal Places to Sleep. For some time HAC had been urging that people be allowed to sleep in vehicles parked in specific industrial areas or church parking lots and be allowed to camp in backyards where the homeowner or tenant had given approval. But a majority on the Council were reluctant to act.

Charles devised a petition that stated the campaign's basic goal: "I support the Homeless Action Coalition campaign for legal places to sleep." It had room for supporters to sign their names—but its layout differed from the usual plan. After each signer supplied name, address and phone number, there were several boxes to check off. Would they put up a lawn sign? Were they willing to engage in a nonviolent demonstration? Responses from just eight people filled a page instead of the usual twenty or more.

I asked him why he'd used this strange format. He just granted me an enigmatic smile and said, "I think it'll work." Then he and his colleagues at HAC enlisted volunteers to collect signatures. Naturally I was one of their recruits. Charles loved to make signs; piles of plastic poster board and squat tins of waterproof paint filled him with glee. He created a sandwich board for me to wear. HELP THE HOMELESS it said, Campaign for Legal Spaces to Sleep. It saved me lots of explanations as, armed with a clipboard and pens, I prospected for signers outside the library or at the main bus station and the Saturday Market. It wasn't hard to get people to sign in our mostly liberal town. Sometimes folks who looked middle class offered stories of how they themselves had been homeless for a while.

I collected 200 signatures; they filled twenty-five pages of Charles's odd form. When our little crew had amassed fifteen times that many, Charles decided it was time to present them to the City Council—but first he told me he had some work to do down at the HAC office. Up for a vote that night were changes to local rules, designed to improve conditions for houseless persons.

Outside City Hall, at least fifty HAC supporters were picketing in their favor. As soon as the meeting-room doors opened, they crowded in; some signed a list to address the Council. Charles and Wayne signed up too while Tom cradled a big, mysterious bundle. When I asked him what it was, he just chuckled and winked at me. "You'll see pretty soon. Stick close, we need you."

The meeting began. Two of the councilors observed dourly that they'd received many calls about this issue, maybe as many as twenty-five. Most of their callers opposed the proposed changes. When at last it was Charles' turn to speak, Wayne yielded his three minutes to Charles, giving him six. Charles, calm and dignified, stepped to the mike. Tom beckoned me to join him where he'd gone to stand, over to the right of the platform from which the Council presided, then he finally unwrapped that heavy bundle of his. There were the petitions—but instead of just stacking them, Charles had scotch-taped each of them, one after another, to a roll of newsprint, several hundred feet long. (Later Tom would recall with a chuckle, "Charles was methodical ... and diabolical.") Since eight signatures filled a page, our 375 petitions took up 400 feet.

This taped-up scroll was bulky and clumsy. Tom handed me its free end. He didn't say what I should do with it—he just raised one hand in the classic signal for "wait" as Charles began his speech.

"The fact underlying this campaign," he said, "is that every human being must sleep, therefore every human being has a fundamental right to a place to sleep. Any law that denies that right is immoral and inhumane and probably unconstitutional."

Only when Charles intoned, "Tonight we're here to present to you concrete evidence of the wishes of the citizens of Eugene about this issue," did Tom start unrolling his humungous, sloppy cylinder and whisper, "Go for it!" Grinning, he flicked his hand toward the floor to my left. That's when I started presenting our petition to our honorable elected officials by dropping yard after yard of it in front of the podium where they sat.

Back and forth I shuttled to where Tom stood at my right, grabbing lengths of paper from him as he unrolled it. The stiffness of the paper plus the petitions on it made it impossible to pile the ribbon of sheets into a tidy stack. Photographers from the nightly news and community TV closed in on either side as this rustling white hillock jiggled around like a living thing. The pile of petitions grew higher and higher—to my knees, to my hips, heading up toward my waist. Council members started giggling nervously. It was theater, of course, shameless, barefaced theater. But it worked and that was what counted. That night the City Council voted to approve ordinance changes that the Homeless Action Coalition had been demanding for years.

By now I'd immersed myself in scholarly literature about the paranormal and was eager to write about the startling experiences that I, and others close to my former husband Paul had had after he passed. Like most of my friends, I'd been brought up to think that belief in ghosts was medieval, like denying that the earth was round. But I'd come to believe that *dismissing* the possibility that there might be an afterlife might be our era's way of denying another fact.

Different as the world's faith traditions were, I suspected that they had a common source. Over thousands of years, humans all over the globe had gained fleeting, partial insights into higher planes or alternate realities from near-death experiences, afterlife encounters, mystical visions and the meditations of seers and philosophers. Religions differed—but the roots from which they derived were the same.

Starting in the late nineteenth century, an intrepid band in Europe and the United States had done rigorous studies inquiring about what they called "survival," survival of the human spirit after death. Best known among these were the British gentlemen and occasional ladies who worked under the auspices of the Society for Psychical Research, founded in 1882 by intellectuals associated with Cambridge University. Soon the SPR attracted leading figures from elsewhere. Among its presidents in those early days were the American psychologist William James; the Nobel Prize-winning French physiologist Charles Richet; and a sometime British prime minister, A. J. Balfour. Probably its most famous member was Sir Arthur Conan Doyle, the creator of Sherlock Holmes. In 1922 after years with the society Doyle left it, impatient with its equivocal stand on whether some human essence could survive beyond the death of the body. He'd come to view survival as an established fact and spent the rest of his life arguing for its reality.

When I'd visited the American Society for Psychical Research in New York, someone at their bookshop had recommended I read a book by Ian Stevenson. Dr. Stevenson headed a well-funded program at the University of Virginia that studied aspects of the paranormal. I wrote him there and he kindly answered my letter. Mentoring me, he suggested more for me to read and recommended that I join the SPR, still going strong in London. Then he put me in touch with the editor of its journal.

In July 1998 an article of mine appeared[1] in the *Journal of the Society for Psychical Research*. It focused on a series of physical events for which there was no conventional explanation—like the turning on and off of electrical devices and the movement of objects—which suggested that my late husband's spirit had used them to communicate with myself and others.

Not eager to appear completely off my rocker, I introduced these seemingly outlandish tales with a brief survey of books and articles[2] by physicians and social scientists, plus one doctoral dissertation in psychology, which supplied evidence that over half of all widows in the United States and elsewhere sensed their late partner's presence after death at least once, and that the percentage was almost as high for widowers. That doctoral dissertation and also a best-selling book by medium James Van Praagh,[3] confirmed that flashing electric lights often seemed to signal a spirit's presence. Lights *topped* Van Praagh's list of "ways spirits let their loved ones know that they are around them without the use of a medium." Other electrically operated devices came next on his list. Before such devices were invented, the clanking of chains was associated with the presence of ghosts. Like electrical gadgets they could be manipulated by magnetic fields.

I started interviewing people who believed they'd sensed contact with the dead. My first subjects were a dozen men and women personally known to my husband or me; we could vouch for their good health and sanity. Then I started looking for other interviewees.

When I lived in New York near Columbia University, I'd seen ads for research subjects posted on the walls of bus shelters. I typed up a flier briefly explaining how common it was to sense apparent contact from beyond the grave; it listed my first name and phone number. I tacked copies on bulletin boards around town inviting calls from volunteers who'd had such experiences and were willing to talk about them. Soon a few people phoned. The most important response I got came from a journalist with the local paper. She did a long profile on me and my work; it supplied my name and telephone number. Lots more people called me after that. Often one informant recommended someone else who also wanted to be interviewed.

Back in the late nineteenth century, the Society for Psychical Research had done a similar and far larger study. Still the SPR's scrupulous researchers wondered: Was there any significant basis for the perceptions people *thought* they had? Reports of what they called "crisis apparitions" argued strongly for this.

In those days when news of loved ones in faraway places might take weeks or months to arrive, people often reported that they'd sensed the presence of a relative or close friend at what they later learned was *the same time* that person was in serious danger: wounded on a remote battlefield, thrown from a horse or lost at sea. Eighty reported that they'd sensed a distant loved one's presence within 12 hours of that person's death. Often they could confirm this recollection by a diary entry or a letter they had written. The SPR called these phenomena "death coincidences," the strongest evidence they could find for real psychic perception.

"The fact that each of us only dies once," its researchers observed dryly, "enables us to calculate ... the probability that that death will coincide with any other given event"—such as someone faraway sensing the dying person. Leaning over backward to be conservative in their calculations, they figured—determined two different ways—that the odds against these death coincidences occurring by chance were 400 to 1.

My interviews soon turned up many such stories, including that of the little girl who saw her aunt. By the time I'd interviewed 61 people, I'd collected 14 stories of death coincidences. I reported on them in another article, published in the same journal[4] the following year.

WHILE I TRIED TO DEAL RATIONALLY with the numinous and spiritual, my husband worked on more concrete issues. Charles loved statistics and demystifying them for the general public. During the Vietnam War, he'd organized a team—and wangled official permission—to paint a quarter-mile-long graph of the national budget on the main street that led into the University of Oregon campus. Most citizens were startled to see how short the bars for social services and foreign aid were while the bar for the military ran on and on.

Now he started comparing the revenues of multinational corporations with the budgets of countries. Only the seven most prosperous nations had budgets larger than the revenues of Exxon-Mobil, GM and Ford. Charles turned his data into a colorful poster, "Corporate Cash, Few Nations Can Top It." Activists around the country bought it and a couple of publications printed articles[5] that included his chart.

254

22

Solidarity in Seattle

EARLY IN 1999, CHARLES AND I started meeting with a newly formed "simplicity circle." Following guidelines proposed by a Seattle woman,[1] nine or ten of us—we were the oldest—met weekly to talk about adopting a more sustainable lifestyle, aiming to use as few of the world's resources as possible while enriching our lives with simple pleasures. Of course, Charles had figured out most of this for himself when he chose to go on the World Equity Budget.

Voluntary simplicity meant valuing time more than money. It meant working and playing more with family and friends, and building community by reaching out to our neighbors. Using less water, paper and fuel, driving less, walking and biking more. We gloated about finding attractive clothes and furniture at Goodwill or St. Vinnie's. Three of the guys enjoyed dumpster diving. Late that spring we learned that another kind of challenge was brewing.

The World Trade Organization was slated to have a major international meeting in our own Pacific Northwest beginning on Tuesday, November 30th. Every two years it held a "ministerial," a gathering of trade representatives and other higher-ups from well over a hundred member nations. Demonstrations were being planned against it. We were invited to join them.

This organization had been formed just four years earlier,[2] but its origins could be traced back to the Bretton Woods meetings that spawned the World Bank and the IMF. After what I'd seen of their impact when I traveled in Third World countries I had my doubts about this new international institution. It claimed to be working to increase "free trade" around the world but it was definitely not for "*fair* trade." Fair trade, as progressives then understood it, meant ensuring fair pay for workers who produced useful products under humane working conditions. Often these workers banded together in cooperatives.

By contrast, the World Trade Organization was set up to enforce the rights of multinational corporations, if necessary at the expense of the environment, consumers and workers. On the theory that increasing trade was always a good thing, it favored globalization for profit, whatever the human costs.

A WTO panel—no appeal permitted—had ruled in Venezuela's favor against a U.S. regulation that required gas refiners to produce cleaner gas. Another of its panels had blocked an American law designed to protect endangered sea turtles from being caught in shrimp nets. One of its latest agreements set scary limits on the safeguards relating to food safety that any government could impose on foreign companies. And soon an agreement, to be enforced by the WTO, aimed to throw control of municipal water systems open to international corporate bidders.

Didn't sound good. Didn't sound fair. By September most of us in the simplicity circle had decided to participate in the coming demonstrations. One of our number—a darkly handsome young man nicknamed Win—headed the local chapter of a national organization, Alliance for Democracy, that was involved in the planning. Periodically he traveled north to Seattle for meetings with the Direct Action Network that was organizing the coming action. Like all the actions I'd ever been part of, this was to be nonviolent.

Soon half a dozen of us from the simplicity circle were meeting with like-minded folks from Eugene. There were University of Oregon students who had come together to campaign against sweatshops, pressing the school's administration to stop authorizing the use of the U of O logo on items like caps, sweatshirts and hoodies made by grossly underpaid, mistreated workers in the Third World. There were miscellaneous older activists too: a professor, three artists, and a partner in a company that packaged herbs.

Every week or so, twenty or more of us crowded into the unpretentious living room of a successful real estate broker, Mary Ellen, whose environmentalist son had converted her to the cause. We talked and argued and speculated but that wasn't exactly the point. We were getting to know each other, forming an affinity group. We called ourselves McKenzie Free, naming ourselves for a beautiful, wild river that tumbled down out of the Cascades to the edge of Eugene.

Remember that provocateur who infiltrated the Brooklyn Black Panthers, who turned some of them against their fellows and tried to turn the community against them? Affinity groups provide some protection against that kind of treachery. That fall, all of us in McKenzie Free came to know each other by sight and name and style. That meant that when we took to the streets of Seattle, we would be a lot less likely to be taken in by some untrustworthy stranger who might try to lead us in foolish stunts that might jeopardize our cause. And we were primed to work together smoothly.

Mary Ellen and I collected slogans for anti-WTO bumper stickers. We sent them off to be printed. Soon many cars in Eugene sported our mottos:

<blockquote>
FAIR TRADE
NOT FREE TRADE
</blockquote>

<blockquote>
THE WTO IS A
HAZARDOUS WASTE
</blockquote>

<blockquote>
We the People
NOT
WE THE CORPORATION
</blockquote>

And most relevant of all:

<blockquote>
Participate in Democracy
STOP the W. T. O.
</blockquote>

LATE IN OCTOBER WE ALL TROOPED off to a nonviolence training. There we formally agreed to the guidelines of the Direct Action Network: we would use no violence, physical or verbal, toward any person; would carry no weapons; would not bring or use any alcohol or illegal drugs; would not destroy property.

Early in November we received a tentative schedule of events slated to take place before the WTO meetings. One of them was a program of lectures to be held in Benaroya Hall, a stately place, home of the Seattle Symphony. I sent a check for two tickets off to the International Forum on Globalization which had organized this event. That afternoon and evening, a procession of world-class intellectuals with spirited views on where the world was tending gave brilliant talks on their areas of expertise. But each of their talks took twice as long as might have been expected because of the way our mostly middle-class, middle-aged audience responded.

We were high on solidarity. High on unanimity. (Though a show of hands testified that about a fifth of us were from Canada.) It was electric—glorious, empowering—to be surrounded by a couple thousand strangers who felt as we did, cared as we did, and probably like us were planning to put their bodies on the line for what they believed in. Almost every sentence won a burst of applause and every minute or so the stomping crowd of us charged to our feet to give the speaker a standing ovation. Not that what the speakers had to say was cheery. Much of it was grim. Still their insights and their indignation sparked fires in us all. Charles and I strode out into the night energized and strengthened.

Each day daring climbers dressed the city up for the coming event. Two young women scaled a retaining wall near Interstate 5 to hang a SHUT DOWN THE WTO banner. Then men from the Rainforest Action Network hung giant arrows from a 170-foot-high crane near Seattle's signature Space Needle. One labeled DEMOCRACY pointed forward; the other, labeled WTO, pointed back in the other direction.[3]

We met regularly with our affinity group, hearing reports-back from Win, our spokesperson. Sometimes we convened sitting on the sidewalk downtown. Win kept attending meetings with the DAN, the local collaborative that had been coordinating planning for almost a year, housed in a converted warehouse. There, artists were making signs and giant puppets and more closely guarded preparations also were underway.

One day I attended a training session at the warehouse. One of the things I learned and later reported back to my group was that whenever possible, we shouldn't talk to the police at all. Looking around at a roomful of mostly fresh faced young people, I couldn't imagine why—until they started speaking up. Many of them had traveled from far parts of the world to join us. Their accents would immediately give them away.

On Monday evening, a pro-WTO organization treated official delegates to an opening reception and gala. In an action led by an interfaith coalition, we joined with 5,000 others in a "human chain to end Third World debt,"[4] encircling the site of the gala more than once. We hoped our drums and chanting could be heard inside as we called on the powerful, industrialized nations that ran the WTO to cancel the debt of the world's poorest countries.[5]

As the big day approached, we learned that our goal was to nonviolently block access by WTO delegates to their ministerial. The DAN had envisioned a circle around the convention center and cut it into thirteen "pie slices," each to be held and blocked off by a cluster of affinity groups—but we didn't know exactly how our group would do this or exactly where we would be posted. Even Win didn't know where we'd be, or at least so he told us. Maybe we'd be stuck blocking some highway somewhere, out of sight of the central action. After all, we weren't local activists; Eugene was 300 miles away.

Charles and I, elders that we were, were not slated to be in lockdown, directly blocking access by WTO delegates to their meeting. Only those who were to physically block our sector knew just how they would be doing this. We took on other assignments. Charles, old hand that he was at dealing with media, was press officer for our affinity group. I, typecast as a solid citizen, was picked to obtain legal help for any team members who were arrested. Since they weren't supposed to give their real names if arrested—this was part of "jail solidarity," another mode of resistance—each chose a nickname instead. I memorized these from notes, then destroyed the notes.

My favorite job involved those bumper stickers Mary Ellen and I had had printed plus my partner's predilection for fitting me with waterproof placards. Charles had devised an ingenious sign that displayed all eight of our stickers, housed multiple copies, and advertised that they were for sale for a $1 donation. It folded in half for convenient packing and I could hang it from my neck with a soft silk scarf. It was well before dawn on November 30th when Charles and I set out to join our group.

The city had authorized marches into the center of Seattle from two different points. Our group was supposed to start from a park near the Pike Place Market at 7 a.m. but, along with hundreds of others, we rendezvoused there hours before. In dim and foggy pre-dawn light we barely managed to find our comrades in McKenzie Free. Someone distributed kits for us to use if we were tear-gassed. Then cops appeared and I heard a shout, "They're taking our towers!"

Sturdy metal tripods are often used by activists to block logging roads into old growth forests. One protestor sits on top while others are locked to its base. Figures I could barely see in the fog hauled a couple off and were prowling suspiciously around our equipment when one of our campus members started shouting, "We know about the law against prior restraint!" Instantly, she gathered a little circle of women around her and three of us chanted with her as loud as we could manage, "We know about the law against prior restraint! We know about the law against prior restraint!" I hadn't a clue what I was chanting about but the cops backed off. Then I found out. It was illegal for them to confiscate something just because they thought it might *later* be used for some illegal purpose.

Our young ringleader had been arrested the previous summer during an action in the heart of Eugene, trying to protect old trees from being cut down. Tear gas had flooded the streets; she'd been banned from participating in protests for a year. Still she'd come with us to Seattle anyhow and it was a damn good thing she did. If she hadn't, our cluster might never have held its "slice of the pie."

Well before 7 a.m. our affinity group started up the line of march. Hundreds of others were parading alongside us, many with signs and banners, thousands more were following after but we found ourselves particularly burdened down. We were carrying a long float the cops had been snooping around before we four women started yelling. It wasn't much of a float as floats go. It bore a papier-mâché octopus with lots of hands grasping money but that figure took up less than a fifth of its surface. Still the float itself was terribly heavy. Sixteen of us struggled, bearing it on our shoulders out of the park onto Pike Street, past the market and then up the street. It came as a welcome surprise to many of us when half a mile further on, the order came to put it down.

At the far side of the intersection of Sixth and Pike, policemen stood lined up facing us in full battle gear. Instantly people who knew more than I did about the overall plan sprang into action. Quiet and unarmed they ranged themselves, a human barrier, between us and the uniformed figures so the cops couldn't see what was going on. In moments the octopus was discarded, our float became a raised platform and a dozen or so activists locked themselves to a framework of pipes hidden underneath. Meanwhile a cluster from Olympia, Washington fastened a matching barrier to ours with Kryptonite locks while an impenetrable mass of protestors on foot surrounded the platforms and jammed the sidewalk.

Now the intersection was blocked and it was a major intersection, the one that authorities probably had expected to keep clear for delegates to use. The convention center was less than two blocks to the northeast. Three blocks west was the hotel where the U.S. Secretary of State was staying.

Well dressed men with fiercely determined expressions pressed past me where I stood some distance away from the platforms with my display of bumper stickers across my chest. I was making an occasional sale but mostly I was making a statement. A swarthy fellow with the face of a sheik stopped to read the captions on my stickers, then glared at me. I granted him half a smile. "Just doing my bit for free enterprise," I said. From the fury in his face I sensed he wished we were back in his country and he could have me flogged.

Many of these men who were probably delegates were wearing long jackets of supple dark leather to ease them through the Seattle rain. But nothing eased them past the solid mass of protestors who blocked their access to the convention center. Soon nearly three thousand of our closest friends were jammed into this intersection and the four corners around it. The next street over took the brunt of police attacks, probably because the people locked down there were more exposed than ours.

Clouds of tear gas started sweeping up Sixth Street. I pulled a kerchief up over my face and backed out of the intersection into a side street; after a while I learned to start sprinting as soon as I saw that telltale cloud. It didn't bother me much. I was grateful that I was free to dodge away and, like everyone else, I was running on adrenalin. But we heard that at other corners, the cops were shooting plastic-covered ("rubber") bullets that could knock out teeth or maybe even an eye.

As the morning wore on, word spread that federal officials had deemed the streets too dangerous for Secretary of State Madeleine Albright[6] and her trade representative to travel to the opening ceremonies. By 10 a.m. the morning session had been cancelled. Now, though the battle to block the meetings was still raging, it was easier to enjoy the carnival rollicking through the streets.

Joyous and insistent, the wham-wham-wham of drumming, most of it from upended plastic buckets whacked by any kind of stick. It punctuated chants.

> Ain't no POWER like the power of the PEOPLE
> And the power of the people can't LOSE! [*WHAM!*]
> Ain't no POWER like the power of the PEOPLE
> And the power of the people can't LOSE! [*WHAM!*] ....

Handmade signs broadcast the anger and wit of independent thinkers.

CORPORATE GAIN
GLOBAL PAIN

What Slave Made Your Shoes?

THIS IS MOST OF THE MONEY OF THE WORLD LINED UP AGAINST MOST OF THE PEOPLE OF THE WORLD

TREES SAY NO TO WTO

DO YOU SEE THE EXODUS OF OUR JOBS YET?

W T O
GET YOUR PAWS
OFF OUR LAWS[7]

AND STILTWALKERS AND GIANT, CARTOONISH PUPPETS that loomed overhead. Teams of people dressed up as Santa Clauses or sea turtles. And lots of guys threading through the crowds, photographing or filming the action. But none of them got to record the huge scope of it. Access was banned to all the tall buildings[8] from which they might have filmed the multitudes.

It was 11 a.m. before I saw violence from anyone aside from the police. Four booted figures dressed completely in black, with black balaclavas covering everything but their eyes, slipped past me into a side street lined with stylish shops still open on either side of Nordstrom's. Carefully made up and chicly dressed saleswomen were hovering nervously near the doors of their stores.

Three of the ninja-looking figures were tall and slender, the fourth was short and rounded—probably three young men and a woman. Each of the street trees near the corner was bounded by four wedge-shaped metal grates that covered otherwise bare soil. Laid together they formed a latticed circle around its trunk and a neat square where they met the pavement. In thirty tightly choreographed seconds the figures in black grabbed up the steel grates from a couple of trees and tossed them into the gutter, tossed waste containers beside them into an instant barricade and moved on up the street. Broke windows as they went and quickly disappeared. The saleswomen ducked inside. The carnival went on.

I'd been on my feet since four in the morning, most of it standing in rain. Nature called. I ducked into Nordstrom's and looked for a restroom. I must have been a sight in those ladylike precincts, wet as a river rat, with bumper stickers arrayed in front, a daypack on my back, and a kerchief tied around my neck, barely pulled down from my face. As soon as I left the ladies room, two women employees rushed to lock it behind me. Soon they closed the store.

Outside, more teargas, wafts of pepper spray and who knew what else. (Later the police would use concussion grenades.) Now I noticed a new set of black clad figures squirming up the side of a nearby building. Black Bloc, someone told me they were called, supposedly anarchists, supposedly from Eugene. Violent toward the trappings of the corporate world, otherwise determinedly non-violent.

I hadn't noticed till then the sign over a store at the corner: Niketown. Nike was widely despised for using Third World sweatshop labor to make its expensive sneakers and sportswear. The guys in black started laboring to pull its sign down. Some of the demonstrators did as we'd been trained to do. They pointed and chorused, "No violence." Then others of us started intoning "Om-m-m", another thing we'd been trained to do. The sound of thousands sighing "Om-m-m" was gentle and calming. But the fellows from the Black Bloc, who hadn't thought to bring tools, went on yanking at that recalcitrant sign.

After a while things quieted down a bit. I chatted with Brookrod, who'd organized our simplicity circle and who stood holding a poster beyond the densest crush of people. Rumor had it that the WTO had canceled its afternoon session but many members of our affinity group remained in lockdown and, as members of the media, foreign and domestic, pressed through the streets trying to figure out what was happening, I watched my husband many yards away holding his ground and briefing them.

I made my way over to him. "Brookrod and I are thinking of joining the labor march. Wanna come?"

The United Steelworkers had paraded in force the previous day. Today they were staging a conventional march and rally not far from downtown. I could sell my bumper stickers anywhere—or give them away to anyone who promised convincingly to display them.

He shook his head. "No, thanks. You go. Think I'll stay here, think I'm still needed." He grinned, "But we're doing good, eh? Damn fools at the WTO, they should never have picked Seattle for their meeting. Guess they didn't know its history."

In 1919, Seattle had the biggest general strike ever in the United States. Trade unions fighting for pay of a dollar an hour for skilled workers shut the city down for five days without any of the dire consequences that had been predicted, without depriving children of their milk or the sick of hospital services. What a proud tradition, I thought, for rebels to be honoring today!

Brookrod and I strolled across town to join the labor demonstration. As we lined up to get into the stadium, I ran into acquaintances who'd come up from Eugene. I told them about life as I'd come to know it at the corner of Sixth and Pike. Then a woman I didn't know struck up a conversation with me.

22 • Solidarity in Seattle

"Never thought I'd be with you folks today," she said quietly. "I was supposed to be at the meetings. The W.T.O. meetings."

"You were?" I eyed her suspiciously. She looked remarkably ordinary. Forty-ish or a little older, short brown hair cut simply, dark pants and a light brown, thigh-length coat.

"Don't worry," she smiled. "I'm with an N.G.O. I was supposed to be an observer." She wouldn't say what organization she was with. But she had inside information and she seemed to want to share what she knew.

"They're meeting," she said, speaking slowly and thoughtfully. "You know, they're holding meetings at other places in town. But maybe it doesn't matter. These disruptions—this enormous show—it's changed things."

"What has it changed?"

"It's changed a lot of minds."

"Whose minds?" I asked.

She smiled faintly. "Oh, not the big guys, not the G-7. The little guys. The representatives from the poor countries, the 'unimportant' countries, delegates that thought they had to take orders from the countries that run things."

I'd heard about something like this before, though never on an international scale. I'd heard that at conclaves of corporations and lesser institutions the big guys might caucus ahead of time and decide how things would be and then they'd tell the others and the little guys would rubberstamp it.

"But now that's all changed," the woman said. "These demonstrations—they've given them backbone. They're refusing to agree." And it turned out that what she said was right.

I could describe the union rally, though it was like other rallies. I could say how exciting it was when afterwards those rugged, blue-collar steelworkers with their matching, professionally printed signs joined the anarchic-looking protests. I could tell you how for a golden time when the police halted their attacks, dance and music and poetry readings blossomed on improvised stages in downtown Seattle. I could write lots of things but they wouldn't matter as much as what that woman I met on the union march told me. Because she was right.

That day in Seattle, representatives from those countries whose opinions weren't supposed to count heard rumblings in the belly of the beast—the great and powerful U.S.A.—that signaled that they weren't as friendless and helpless as they thought. When the American Trade Representative walked into a plenary session, the African delegation booed her. "And as the day came to a close," one observer reported, "a coalition of delegates from over 70 countries in Africa, Latin America, and Asia ... stubbornly refused to sign onto an agenda in which they saw they had little voice."[9]

Time and again after that, the World Trade Organization tried unsuccessfully to push a plan they called the Doha Round. Supposedly designed to help developing nations, it was far more likely to help giant food exporters from rich countries like the United States flood their markets with cheap, genetically modified grain. At stake was the welfare of small subsistence farmers who in much of the Third World made up the majority of the people. What happened in Seattle in 1999 gave Third World nations the courage to resist.

As 2015 drew to a close, the World Trade Organization ended the Doha round of negotiations. "This was not unexpected," *The New York Times* observed, "given how fruitless these discussions have been."[10]

23

On the Road with the Zapatista Caravan

THE BATTLE IN SEATTLE MADE FRONT-PAGE news in Eugene and, as word spread about the role our group had played in it, the Eugene chapter of Alliance for Democracy attracted new supporters. Charles and others wrote fact sheets and policy papers, I contributed a flier on sweatshops, and he built a rack on which to display them all. We hauled a folding table, literature and my husband's rack around to local events that were likely to draw in progressives. But soon many of our members drifted away to other causes or dropped out for personal reasons and the chapter fell apart.

Charles got restless. "We could go down to Mexico," he said one day. "We could study Spanish. There are some good programs around that aren't too pricey."

"Sounds like a great idea," I said. "It'd be like a vacation, only better."

But neither of us pursued it so we didn't go. Then early in 2001 I received a tempting request via email. The Mexico Solidarity Network was looking for volunteers to serve as international observers on an unarmed caravan of the Zapatista leadership to Mexico City from their stronghold in the remote Mexican state of Chiapas. The country's new president, Vicente Fox, had said observers would be welcome. This was a rousing change from the previous president who, three years earlier, had thrown hundreds of American activists out of the country.

I'd never heard of the MSN but I'd heard quite a bit about the Zapatistas. On New Year's Day 1994, an indigenous movement that called itself the Zapatista Army of National Liberation had appeared out of nowhere in the nation's southernmost reaches, site of the ancient Mayan empire. Their spokesman, not indigenous himself, called himself *Subcomandante* Marcos. It was a title that implied he answered to these Indians; they were his commanders.

Long before Columbus, their forebears had prospered in the region. Their traditions were strong; their culture extraordinary. They wanted to live in keeping with their traditions—but they needed government services too. They were blessed or cursed by riches of petroleum that lay under their land. Like many of Mexico's Indian groups, they proposed to maintain that land in *ejidos,* properties traditionally owned and shared by the community. If the government wanted their oil, they demanded sovereignty over it—but the government didn't see it that way.

On January 1st, 1994, something else happened. That was the day that the North American Free Trade Agreement took effect in the U.S., Mexico and Canada. The Zapatista uprising that day was no coincidence. Marcos predicted accurately that NAFTA would destroy the small corn producers of Mexico. They could never compete with cheap U.S. imports, grown as they were with chemical fertilizers and herbicides and subsidized by the American government.

When, seven years later, I received that email inviting international observers to join their caravan, the Zapatistas had been almost completely nonviolent since their brief military showing in 1994. Harassed by the regular army, forced further back into their mountains, those masked campesinos had faded for me into mythic, possibly tragic figures. Solidarity with the Zapatista rebels seemed like little enough to offer. Particularly if riding along with them would carry us through the heart of Mexico.

I showed Charles my email. "It'd be a whole lot better than language school. We'd be helping them out, doing accompaniment. They won't be armed, that's part of the deal and President Fox says it's okay with him."

He looked doubtful.

23 • On the Road with the Zapatista Caravan

"Hey, Fox used to be a high exec with Coca Cola so he probably watches his step with Americans. Aw, come on. It'll be fun," I said. "It'll be an adventure."

Grudgingly at first, my partner came around. At our Valentine's party I jubilantly announced to a roomful of friends that soon we'd take off for the Zapatista caravan. A woman I knew who edited a counter-culture paper in town asked me to send her progress reports. "Sure thing," I agreed, and made a mental note to keep a log.

Two weeks later we were in San Cristobal de las Casas, a beautiful mountain town of neat little houses clinging to the hills, most of them roofed with curved red tiles. There Charles and I boarded a rickety old bus with frayed seats and no restroom that would take us on a great loop of a route that passed through many of Mexico's poorest states.

For many a mile, glowing brown faces welcomed us. Men and women waved to us or raised their arms to signal support with V-signs or clenched fists or thumbs up gestures. Classes of sweet-faced children dressed in matching school uniforms shouted Zapatista slogans while their teachers, stationed behind them, watched intently. (The government had been cutting back on its support for schools.) And at each rally the banners posted by local organizations blared all manner of slogans. DOWN WITH THE ECONOMIC POLICIES OF FOX AND HIS ALLIES/ NEVER MORE A MEXICO WITHOUT OUR INDIGENOUS BROTHERS/ TRUE PEACE WILL BE THE FRUIT OF JUSTICE AND LOVE.

As we traveled through the country, more vehicles joined us. Still the Comandancia kept receiving death threats. And even as Charles and I traveled hundreds of miles, our lives were oddly circumscribed. For most of our waking hours, we sat side by side watching scenery flash by. When the caravan stopped for rallies, we ran frantically through unfamiliar streets, trying to find bathrooms and buy provisions for our next meal.

By the time we neared Querétero—a small state northwest of Mexico City—we no longer saw supporters along the road. We were on a highway now, well-paved and remote from villages. It sliced across the sandy drab soil of the nation's arid high plateau and Querétero's governor meant to scare us off. All Zapatistas deserved the death penalty, he declared, and if we crossed the border he'd throw all us caravanistas in jail.

Half a mile from the border, the whole caravan pulled over and stopped so the governing council could decide what to do. When Tom, our group's leader, came back he told us they'd decided we'd all try to cross. The Italians of Ya Basta were well-disciplined, robust revolutionaries traveling in two sturdy new vehicles. They and some other internationals would lead the way. Mexican citizens would come next. Snugly tucked into the middle of our cavalcade would be the bus that carried dignitaries like that member of the National Congress who had dined with Charles and me one evening. The Comandancia would come right after them, we and other internationals would follow. More Mexicans in buses plus a mélange of supporters in private cars and vans would round out the procession.

For a few hours the previous day, our MSN bus had held a place of honor, riding right after the Zapatista leaders. As the caravan started up again, we rumbled into place four buses behind it. We were in hilly country now. From my seat midway back, I watched our progress through the windshield as the bus driver eased us slowly down a long, steep incline. At the foot of this hill, still a couple hundred feet away, another steep hill began. Two lanes went the way we were headed but clearly local officials were maneuvering to slow us down. One of the lanes halfway up the hill was blocked by a police car parked across it. In the second lane, another was just creeping along.

Suddenly we were all jerked to attention. The whole bus shook with a series of furious impacts. "Get down!" someone shouted. We kept on rolling. Again BOOM ... BOOM ... BOOM. Paramilitaries must be shooting at us, I thought. But it couldn't be just guns. What could it be—mortars?

At the foot of the hill we slowed to a stop. We felt no more concussions. Then another voice shouted from up front, "Get out of the bus!"

I wondered if we were going to be taken hostage or worse. Maybe in the long run, prison would be safer. But the order seemed to come from one of our fellow caravanistas, so we grabbed our daypacks and rushed out the door. Soon Charles and I were linking hands with others to start a protective ring around the Comandancia bus. Four bloodstained women stumbled past us. We looked around for paramilitaries. No sign

23 • On the Road with the Zapatista Caravan

of them yet. Instead swarms of police in three kinds of uniforms had materialized from out of nowhere. Lots of photographers too, equipped with all sorts of cameras and videorecorders, had piled out of the caravan to witness it all.

The cops didn't arrest us. They just closed off the road—except for two ambulances that came screaming up a few minutes apart. The first one stopped behind our now empty bus; we couldn't see who it picked up. The second one backed into our cordon; it barely stopped in time. Then the blood-stained women, who had been following the Comandancia in an SUV, hobbled past us and climbed into the second ambulance.

It was eleven in the morning, a beautiful warm day, not a cloud in the sky, and our protective circle around the Zapatista leaders kept growing—first one ring, then another and another and another with hundreds of volunteers. Figures I couldn't see clearly through the crowd were coming and going from the bus we'd been riding on. "Can you tell what they're doing?" I asked Charles, much taller than I.

"I think they're taking things out and laying them on the side."

Then a tow truck appeared and hauled our bus away. Nobody came over from our delegation to tell us what was happening.

I was thinking of Crazy Horse's war cry at the Battle of Little Bighorn, "This is a good day to die."

Or not.

THE SUN ROSE HIGHER AND THE day grew hotter, people started passing water bottles around. Prudently, Charles and I passed them on and sipped from our own. Hundreds of us in six rings around the bus shouted one Zapatista chant after another until someone from the guiding council, crouching near its open door, asked us to please be quiet so they could decide what the caravan should do next.

At 1 p.m., Josh, Tom's assistant, ambled over and pulled everyone from our group out of the cordon. "We're starting up again," he said wearily. Except that our MSN bus was gone.

"Get your things. We pulled them out of the bus before the tow truck came."

"What happened?" everyone asked.

"Get your stuff. Then I'll tell you."

We rummaged in the pile of belongings by the side of the road. Charles found our big hiking packs that had been stored in the luggage compartment underneath. I looked for a light jacket and a paper bag of mine that had contained oranges and cheese. My jacket and bag were gone but I found a smaller bag with oranges and grabbed it.

"So what happened?" someone asked.

"No one was shooting at us," Josh said. "The brakes failed on our bus. The brakes failed and the driver was trying to slow the bus …"

"Because we were going down that hill…."

"Yeah, so he pulled out onto the shoulder and started whamming into the side of the buses ahead of us to slow us down but we just kept rolling. I could see it all from where I was sitting. That's why I yelled 'Get down.' I figured we'd crash.

"So then," he made a face, "so then there were these two motorcycle cops riding ahead of us. He whammed into them. One of them musta died instantly. The other's not doing so great. Then he hit that black Suburban the media people were riding in, the media people for the Zapatistas. They were all wearing seatbelts, damn good thing. And by then he was at the foot of the hill. So he spun their car around but they weren't badly hurt and that's where the bus stopped."

"And where's the driver?"

Josh snorted, "He took off like a shot. Ran for his life. Musta figured the *federales* would blame it all on him."

CHARLES AND I WAITED BY THE side of the road for new transportation. Half an hour later we and what was left of our belongings were jammed into a van that belonged to Pastors for Peace. Then it was hurry-up-and-wait until at 3 p.m. the caravan was finally underway again, heading for the capital of Querétero. We arrived there six hours late but we still had a small rally. Given the local political climate, most of our supporters were probably afraid to show up.

The next day, the Pastors for Peace van had to head elsewhere. We switched transport again, climbing onto the Little Yellow School Bus, a cheerfully decorated mobile project out of California that supported schools for Zapatista communities in Chiapas. Half the people on it were Mayan. As we rode, our new companions told us that the incident we'd suffered through was front page news in all the Mexican papers

23 • On the Road with the Zapatista Caravan

and the biggest story on TV.[1] The media blamed the Comandancia. They said its bus stopped suddenly and vehicles trying to avoid running into it killed the man on the motorcycle. The other motorcycle cop was in terrible shape, his condition grave. Why hadn't Marcos phoned the policemen's families, they demanded, to apologize for the harm his people had done?

That afternoon at a rally in Acámaro, Marcos told the crowd that all the comandantes deeply regretted the death of the policeman. They realized that he was helping them by escorting them. But they also wondered if what happened was an accident. When Charles and I rejoined our delegation—now riding on a replacement vehicle that Tom had managed to rent—it was clear that many on the caravan were wondering that too.

Were our brakes sabotaged? The day before for a little while, our bus had been stationed directly behind the Comandancia. That night volunteers took turns guarding it but might someone have sneaked past them and vandalized it, thinking that again it would be following the Zapatista leaders and would smash into their vehicle? The government had towed the culprit bus away. We'd never be able to inspect it. The fellow who yelled, "Get off the bus," had feared it might catch fire and explode.

OUTSIDE MORELIA THAT FRIDAY WE PASSED huge green agribusiness fields that looked very fertile. Farm workers waved to us from those fields or from beside the shacks where they lived. They looked desperately poor.

Morelia is a beautiful city with stately old stone buildings, some dating from the sixteenth century. Once we arrived there, Charles and I settled into a comfortable hotel. That weekend the MSN buses would be making a side trip into the campo to join indigenous groups having a conference there. This excursion, Tom told us, would be strenuous, accommodations minimal. The two of us were more shaken and weary than we cared to admit. Besides, I'd promised to send back accounts of our travels to my newspaper publisher friend back in Eugene. That seemed like a good excuse for us to drop out of the caravan for the weekend.

On Saturday, after tangy *huevos rancheros* and lots of *café con leche,* I braved a local cybercafe. Armed with the log I'd been keeping, and struggling in semi-darkness with an unfamiliar Spanish keyboard, I managed to send the makings of an article[2] back to Eugene. That afternoon, I collapsed into bed and didn't stir for four hours, partly catching up from a week of sleeplessness. Dinner in a restaurant down the street was the most exciting event of our evening.

The next day we discovered a political rally that felt like a fiesta rollicking along in the central plaza beside the cathedral. Vendors sold soft drinks and donuts, giant balloons and soap bubble kits. Schoolkids fumbled through traditional dances while a worried-looking teacher supplied music with a portable keyboard. Then professional performers appeared. A joyously blaring mariachi band. Spanish dancers in elegant costumes. During breaks in the entertainment, speakers railed against the way the government's neo-liberal policies were eroding the constitution's guarantee of free public education.

Our caravan returned to town the next morning. At 10 a.m. we spotted the MSN's replacement bus, paid our hotel bill and, with our big hiking packs on our backs, headed out the door. The woman at the desk called "safe journey" after us, *Qué le vaya bien*.

As we got closer to Mexico City, the caravan grew. On Tuesday alone, 20 buses and over 100 cars joined the parade. Charles and I no longer felt needed. That evening we arrived in Cuernavaca, just south of Mexico City, where Tom had arranged for us all to stay in a large, rundown old motel called Los Canários. Los Canários means The Canaries and we heard lots of sweetly singing birds on its grounds. I spotted an odd expression on my partner's face. "I think I stayed here before," he said. "I came here with Leslie and the kids a very long time ago."

"How long?"

Charles showed plenty of emotion about the woes of other people. But when it came to feelings about his own life, he played the strong, silent type—and sometimes that made me feel lonely, shut out of his world. Still I sensed that staying here brought back memories that troubled him.

"How long?" he repeated my question. "Must be forty-six years ago. We were on our way to a work camp where we were going to chaperone. This place looked a lot fancier then than it does now."

"You were rich then and you were going first class."

23 • On the Road with the Zapatista Caravan

"Well, something like that. It wasn't expensive by American standards. Anyhow when we got to the work camp we had to rough it and that was fine."

"That was one of the things you did for the Lisle Fellowship?" I ventured. I'd heard part of this story before. The Lisle Fellowship had been set up years earlier to bring together people from different backgrounds—multi-class, multi-ethnic, multi-faith.

He nodded and I gathered that the subject was closed. He'd disappeared into that private world where I wasn't invited.

I thought of my own capricious travels in Mexico when I was young, decades before I met Charles. Driving through a forest fire with my husband Robert and improvising to keep house for him in Mazatlán. Then Howard who would become the father of my son. Braving giant roaches and a resident iguana to stay with him in San Blas; careening across the country with him to Mexico City, chaotic and beguiling with its crowded boulevards and grand museums.

The next day we heard that several people were leaving our delegation.

"We could take a breather," Charles said. "We could meet the Zapatistas in Mexico City."

"Sure, I'd love that."

We took a comfortable public bus to the neighboring town where the national hero, Emiliano Zapata, was born and raised. A museum about him was in the planning stages; for the present the main exhibit was the remains of his childhood home enclosed in a small contemporary building. On that building's walls, in grainy photos greatly enlarged, Zapata and his men, abundantly mustached and wearing wide sombreros, rode to victory on horseback in the Mexican Revolution. Outside on a long freestanding wall, there was one of those heroic murals that Mexicans do so well.

The next day we traveled to Mexico City. For a change, winds had blown the smog away and the air was wonderfully clear, so clear that both the mountains that tower over the capital were visible. Popocatapetl and The Sleeping Woman are heavily snow-capped and almost 18,000 feet high.

Once, I remembered, when Howard and I were tourists here thirty-odd years before, we'd driven in his battered old Chevy to the end of a winding narrow road that went up Popo. On foot we climbed a short way further to an alpine hut poised several thousand feet below the summit. There we chanced upon a pair of climbers who'd just conquered the mountain, who had fought their way through a storm that was raging up at the peak. They were exhausted and exuberant, emotionally transported. Howard was a rock-climber and something of a mountaineer; he seemed unnerved and challenged by these men. While for me it was thrilling just to meet them, to sense their triumph and their joy.

Now as Charles and I wandered the city, I felt the burden of too many memories, his and mine, memories of the lives we lived before we knew each other. And there was another ache. While we were on the caravan we were part of the making of history. Now the two of us were outsiders again.

We miscalculated the schedule of the Zapatistas and missed their dramatic entry into the city. When a vast rally to welcome them filled the capital's great central plaza, we loitered at the edge of the crush. We retreated to crowded streets where vendors sold cheap toys and souvenirs, then made our way back to more gracious boulevards. We never ran into members of our delegation. Soon it was time for us to fly back home.

Later we heard that the Comandancia had finally addressed the National Congress, demanding full implementation of the San Andrés Accords. But most members of Congress didn't deign to attend. They preferred not to listen to these dissidents, these upstarts, masked and strangely dressed. Nonetheless, a conservative newspaper reported[3] that, according to a poll, "rebel leader Subcommander Marcos ranks higher in popularity than President Fox." The great majority of Mexicans didn't think of the EZLN as a guerrilla group. Half saw it as primarily political; 22% called it a social movement. That movement wouldn't readily go away.

In 2006, a presidential election year in Mexico, the Zapatistas staged a campaign which, according to *Encyclopaedia Britannica*,[4] aimed "to form a movement among other indigenous and resistance groups in the country and to create change outside the scope of electoral politics." Afterwards, they shrank back into mostly rural areas they controlled in Chiapas. In 2014, their long-mysterious leader acknowledged what had long been suspected, that his name was Rafael Guillén Vicente and he was the Jesuit-educated son of a prosperous mercantile family that owned a chain of furniture stores in Tampico. In 2018, when once again the nation was due to elect a new president, the Zapatistas changed course and nominated a candidate of their own, an indigenous woman who partly due to financial impediments, failed to get on the ballot.

That July in a dramatic turn of events, Mexico's citizens turned out in force to elect a firebrand leftist[5] with a reformist agenda, Andrés Manuel López Obrador, commonly known as AMLO. Though he and the Zapatistas had often been at odds, these masked rebels probably helped create the political climate that ultimately brought AMLO to power in a landslide.

24

Winding Down

Back in Eugene, Charles and I collaborated on a fuller, more polished article[1] about the caravan. The city's daily newspaper gave it a two-page spread and dressed it up with great photos of the Zapatistas. Folks in town were impressed; they seemed to learn something from what we'd written. It had been a great ride but I doubted that I'd ever again dare to join an expedition as stressful as that. Since my teens I'd longed to See the World, to experience Life in capital letters. To learn firsthand about different kinds of people and to fight for positive social change. But now I felt too old and battered to court perilous challenges.

Back in New York, unthinkable disaster struck on September 11th. My only child was still living in the city. He'd built a career as a computer consultant for publishers there but he dropped whatever he was doing to present himself as a volunteer at Salvation Army headquarters, less than three miles north of where the Twin Towers had stood. He thought they'd send him to work at Ground Zero. Instead they assigned him to organize their logistics, sorting truckloads of donated food, protective gear and other supplies that were pouring in and sending them where they were needed—not just to "The Pile" downtown but to the Medical Examiner's Office at East 30th Street where doctors and technicians were working around the clock, struggling to deal with an avalanche of corpses.

24 • Winding Down

Later it was good to be in touch with my son who sometimes, for months or even years, gave me the silent treatment for reasons he would never explain to me. Though he had close friends, both men and women, Rustin had never settled in with a life partner and he hadn't given me any grandkids. Still he seemed to be healthy and to enjoy his life. I cherished what little contact I had with him.

I kept busy, returning to a project I'd started two years before. By this time I'd interviewed almost eighty people who believed they'd had afterlife encounters. I started analyzing those interviews. The next year a book of mine would come out about everyday people who'd sensed contact with the dead.[2]

IN SUBTLE WAYS CHARLES'S DRIVE TO transform the world was waning. Together we participated in demonstrations against the Second Gulf War but my lifelong activist husband no longer played a leadership role and, when people asked him to give speeches at political events or talks to groups, he gently refused. Several days a week he took the aging Honda we shared and drove it out to an organic farm we were helping to develop. He helped build a greenhouse, enlarged a crumbling shed into a small cabin, and built a rustic bridge over a wee creek. In myriad ways he took part in an effort to create a beautiful and productive place on previously undeveloped land.

Sometimes I worked there too. I cleared invasive wild blackberry vines and Scotch broom, painted the cabin, helped build a fence to keep out deer, raked and watered and weeded. None of these jobs took much background or skill. But I didn't have the enthusiasm for work on the farm that he did. I kept finding things to write about.

Articles of mine on aspects of psi were published in obscure journals, in Italy and Spain as well as in Britain and the United States. I gave talks to small or middle-sized groups and delivered papers at little known conferences. Once in a while, I collected an honorarium but mostly I paid for my research and travel. They were what Internal Revenue calls hobby expenses. The IRS was right—I did what I did for love.

I realized that plenty of close-minded skeptics made fun of such studies. Still public opinion was changing.[3] Polls showed that a majority of American women and more and more young people—as many as 65% of those ages 25-29—now believed in ghosts. About half of these said they'd sometimes felt they were in the presence of one. Soon, since advertisers were eager to reach these consumers, many television series—particularly *Medium* and *Ghost Hunters*—as well as dozens of personal accounts from celebrities broadcast on the Biography Channel, would focus on apparent contacts between the living and the spirit world. In 2011, following up on older mainstream movies like *Ghost* and *The Sixth Sense,* the prizewinning Spanish film *Biutiful* and Clint Eastwood's *Hereafter* would depict communication between everyday people and the Other Side as aspects of matter-of-fact reality.

By 2015, a scholarly article would report[4] that "Currently, over 3,000 paranormal investigation teams exist in the United States [using] a wide variety of methods ... to find evidence of ghosts and, therefore, life after death." A 2017 poll would find that 50% of Americans believed in ghosts.[5] The next year, a Canadian publication would report what they called "a surprising sociological trend."[6] According to a study done at the Universithy of Lethbridge, Canadian millenials and Gen X-ers were more likely to believe in an afterlife than older people. When asked if they believed "We can have contact with the spirit world," 53% of those 18-29, and 57% of those 30-49 answered yes.

Charles started complaining of arthritis. When we went camping and slept on thin air mattresses, he had to take aspirin to get through the night but he was determined to keep roughing it as he had much of his life. In town he started biking less; more often he drove our car or took a bus. For exercise, he went on walks in the park beside the river. One day he reported to me, "My stride's getting shorter."

"What do you mean?" I asked. "Do you suppose it's your arthritis?"

"I don't know. I'm just not comfortable stretching out as much as I used to."

"You ought to go see your doctor," I said. He didn't want to but I persisted. When he came back, he told me that his doctor thought he might be suffering from pressure on a nerve. He referred Charles to a physical therapist but, just to be on the safe side, he urged him to go in for an MRI. Charles refused; he thought it would just be a waste of Medicare money. "Nowadays," he told me, "doctors order too damn many tests." Instead, he went for therapy; it seemed to help.

I got an invitation to give a talk in Spain the following year. A woman who'd featured an article of mine in her multilingual journal there was planning to hold her second annual international conference

24 • Winding Down

in April of 2006. Dr. Anabela Cardoso was a linguist, fluent in six languages. For years she'd been one of Portugal's highest ranking women diplomats; now she'd become an expert in the extraordinary field called instrumental trans-communication. It had to do with messages apparently received on electronic devices from "beings in an unseen domain of reality" participating in a cosmic experiment: communication from another dimension.

I thanked Dr. Cardoso for her invitation but respectfully declined. I didn't understand her field, I explained. I knew zip about electronics and, given my own difficulty identifying certain consonants recorded against a background of white noise—the most common way ITC messages were received—I couldn't confidently endorse her findings. Still she persisted. Two chapters of my book on the paranormal dealt with other people's experiences that involved lights, radios, telephones and the like. A paper about these, she insisted, would be perfect for her conference.

It was tempting to have an excuse to visit Spain, a place where I'd never traveled. Most of all I wanted to see the Alhambra. Fifteen years spent as head of an architecture library had left me enchanted by images of this architectural marvel, a thirteenth century palace built by the Moors.

I told Charles I'd like to leave him for ten or twelve days to attend Anabela's conference and then tourist around a bit, making sure to visit the Alhambra in Granada. I figured I'd sign up for a short tour to start as soon as the conference was over. Instead he said, "I'll go with you," and insisted that we take an extended vacation in Spain together, starting in Vigo where the conference was to take place.

Vigo, located on the Atlantic not far from the border with Portugal, is home to shipbuilders and car factories as well as a spirited cultural life. Our accommodations, arranged for us by Anabela, were in a hotel not far from the center where the meetings were to be held. The day before the start of the conference, Charles helped me scout out its location up a steep hill before we went to dinner together. But the next morning he didn't come with me. His arthritis was bothering him, he said; he thought he should sleep in. I didn't press him though he was habitually strong. I wondered if his pain was a stress reaction. Did it bother him that I was hogging the limelight while he was just along as my companion? Never before had he traveled to a conference with me.

At Anabela's request I'd sent her a copy of the paper I was planning to read. Now I learned that she'd made extraordinary preparations. There would be simultaneous translation of all the papers; mine would be translated into Spanish and French. Many distinguished European scientists and scholars would be participating. Yet she'd scheduled me to be the keynote speaker, the first speaker on the first day of the conference.

I felt honored and amazed. As I gave my presentation, flashbulbs exploded and I could see photographers creeping down the center aisle to get more and different shots. Suddenly, briefly, in this faraway place I was a celebrity—probably because Anabela had described me (too generously) to the local media as a distinguished author coming all the way from the United States. Then the excitement ended, I finished my talk.

The next morning after Charles had walked me halfway up the steep hill to the conference center, he stopped at a small park tucked in along the way. "It's pretty here," he said. "I think I'll stay here awhile. Maybe I'll join you later." But he never did.

"How's your husband?" Anabel asked me. "I saw you with him last night at the hotel when you were leaving for dinner. He looks like such a charming man. Is he coming to the cocktail party tomorrow? We'd all love to meet him."

"Oh, yes, the party tomorrow. I'll certainly try to bring him. But I'm afraid he hasn't been feeling well," I explained.

The next day Charles didn't attend the final meeting. As we traveled on to Madrid, my husband's discomfort seemed to wane a bit. Still we stopped in a pharmacy so Charles could buy the strongest painkiller they would sell him without a prescription. From there we took a train to Granada where we had tickets we'd bought months before over the Internet to visit the Alhambra on May the 4th. What I hadn't realized from the photos I'd seen of that architectural treasure was that it was sited on a high hill and was part of a grand complex that had served as a fortress long before the Moors.

There were other buildings to see, elaborate gardens, and a strictly defined route by which to make your way from one to another. You had to climb several flights of stairs. Throngs of tourists chattering in a

24 • Winding Down

dozen languages rushed past us. But Charles labored along ever more slowly. Every few minutes he had to stop.

Then something happened. I don't know what happened. Suddenly this vigorous man whom I'd loved and relied on for thirteen years was in excruciating pain. His face contorted, he doubled over. He had to sit down, he had to rest. I found a seat for him in a palace that had been built beside the Alhambra by a conquering Catholic king. It was a somber stone pile that recalled castles all over Europe. Hanging on to me, Charles managed to hobble to a bench I'd found for him there and sat down gingerly.

"What time is it?" he asked me once he'd caught his breath. "Isn't it time for you to go?"

I looked at my watch and then at my ticket.

"Yah, you're right."

There was just a half hour window during which I would be allowed to enter my longtime destination. But leaving him seemed like a betrayal.

"For God's sake," he blurted out, "we've come all this damn way. Go on. Go!"

I handed my ticket to someone at the entry, then I was inside a place of dreams. A place of serenity, of grace and balance like early Mozart. My architecture books had shown designs rendered in tile and artfully molded stucco on its walls and ceilings: abstract, mathematically inspired patterns, verses in elegant Arabic script. But those books hadn't prepared me for its airiness, for the way its welcoming halls flowed harmoniously into courtyards lush with green plantings, where water trickled from understated fountains and ran on through slim channels to shallow pools inside and out. They hadn't prepared me for its almost feminine feeling, for the way its towering, intricately ornamented ceilings were supported by pairs or quartets of dainty columns, for the way screens of lacy fretwork beguiled the eye.

It was an ultimately gracious place. You could sense the benevolence of the rulers who reigned here in the Golden Age of the Moors in Spain. From the city's highest hill they had smiled down on a realm where Jews and Christians and Muslims lived together in peace. Here for a few bright centuries, while most of Europe lay swaddled in medieval ignorance, scholars and scientists made bold advances in physics and astronomy, botany and medicine. Intellectuals and artists dared to think new thoughts and make breakthroughs to a richer life. Until in the same era that spawned the Spanish Inquisition, the marauding soldiers of Isabel and Ferdinand snuffed out this last outpost in Europe of the Moors.

The Alhambra was even more beautiful than I'd expected. I looked at my watch; there was still time for Charles to see what I had seen. When I went back to him, he got up and, apparently no longer in such terrible pain, walked for a minute or two in this Moorish palace. But that was all he could do. The pain came back on him, that frightful pain. I sat him down again, this time on a bench outside another building, and tried to find a way that he could be taken away in an ambulance.

But nobody seemed to speak English and I didn't speak much Spanish and I could barely understand the accent here. Though I tried and tried, what people seemed to be saying was that he'd have to get out on his own two feet; we'd have to follow the long route that tourists customarily took out of the complex. Clearly Charles was in agony; it was racking to watch his struggle. Somehow we got out, I found a taxi that took us back to our hotel, and my suffering husband went to bed.

At last we went to a hospital emergency room. There a kind young physician gave Charles a prescription for strong painkillers and something to help him sleep on the flight back. As soon as we arrived in Eugene, we phoned Charles' doctor; he scheduled an MRI immediately. Its results shocked us. Charles didn't have arthritis, he didn't have pressure on a nerve, he had fourth stage cancer of the bone and it was centered in his pelvis. It had already metastasized.

Charles' doctor recommended an oncologist. This man was old and set in his ways. Cancers like this one never started in the bone, he said, it was crucial to determine where it had started. So began a series of tests. For weeks Charles stayed at home with me, then when he could no longer stand up, he went into the hospital.

Finally his oncologist gave up looking for that primary cancer that had to be there somewhere. He recommended radiation—but Charles kept getting worse. By his third or fourth session, he could no longer travel to the radiation facility in a wheelchair; he had to be carried in on a stretcher. A young relative prodded me to look up my husband's sort of cancer on the Internet. An hour's search revealed that according

24 • Winding Down

to the latest research, a small percentage of large cell lymphomas of the bone *started* in the bone.

Charles dismissed the oncologist. He resigned himself to dying—though all over town good people who loved and revered him were praying for a miracle. Then this man who for many years had seemed unfailingly strong and able, decided to return home and go on hospice. But before he left the nursing home there were many things to arrange.

Hospice supplied a hospital bed and set it up in our living room, the only large space available in our modest house. His children flew in from New Zealand and moved in with their mother in town. Then, because in Eugene and elsewhere he'd been a public figure, I thought he deserved a celebration of his life *before* he died, something he could enjoy and be a part of. I called a friend who was a marvelous organizer. She took the job on cheerfully and recruited others to help her. As soon as the time and place were determined, I worked out how we'd take him to the event, on his way to coming home.

Charles could no longer sit up in a wheelchair. There was a hole the size of a half dollar in his pelvis; it could no longer support his weight. We made plans to have him moved in a reclining chair, like a chaise lounge, in which he could lean back and be transported in a van equipped to carry disabled patients. But now that he was so fragile and vulnerable, how could we transfer him from this chair to his bed? An attendant in the nursing home taught me a trick: if we put a sheet on the reclining chair before the nursing home staff moved him onto it, four men, each holding a corner, could use the sheet to lift him onto the bed.

I traveled with my husband in the van to the hall where over a hundred people were waiting for us. During the Seventies, Charles had been part of a group of traveling players that did political theater throughout the Northwest. Two of his fellow actors bantered about the man whose life they were celebrating.

"One thing we all know about Charles," said Peter, "is that he's a unique individual."

"Hey, wait a minute," Gwen burst out, "did you say he was a eunuch individual?"

The audience roared.

"Anything but that," said Peter, "but he's one of the most unusual people you're ever likely to meet."

He ticked off campaigns Charles had been involved in from early adulthood. Doing sit-ins with CORE, organizing for United World Federalists, building housing to integrate a Denver neighborhood. Then Leslie, Charles's first wife, took the mike.

Gwen showed Leslie a picture and asked her, "Can you tell us about Gull Haven?" Gull Haven was the ramshackle retreat that she and Charles owned on the Oregon coast. There they'd hosted many activist friends. And there during the Seventies he'd been wildest and happiest, host to non-violence trainings but also the master of the games.

"Can I tell you about this?" she answered dryly, as if anything she said would be an understatement. "This is going off the track but how many people here have been to Gull Haven?"

Three quarters of the audience raised their hands. They laughed and cheered—people in their settled fifties and sixties joyously recalling their salad days. Leslie, always discreet, talked about pacifist seminars and peace workers camps they'd held there, led by Quaker trainers who came out from the East Coast. Her listeners fidgeted, looking restless.

Till a middle-aged man exclaimed, "Hey, remember how we used to go skinny-dipping and then walk around naked on the beach? And then the neighbors had the gall to complain." Whoops and guffaws filled the room. "But they couldn't even see us without binoculars. So they were peeping Toms. We should've sued!"

Leslie looked mortified.

Peter and Gwen moved the celebration on. One person after another told of working on projects with Charles. Forcing the decommissioning of a nuclear power plant, setting up the McKenzie River Gathering Foundation, refusing to pay federal taxes for war. One longtime ally read a report on Charles's efforts to end the arms race with his Fast for Life. Then Peter passed the mike to Charles in his reclining chair. He thanked people for coming, then made a pitch for one more cause.

"The ambulance drivers that carted me back and forth to the radiation center have no health insurance. They're subcontracted by the hospital, those little vans that cart people around. They themselves have no health insurance and they're young people with families—that shows the state of our health care system. And the drivers are angry, as well they should be."

24 • Winding Down

Charles paused, gathering his strength to finish his last speech ever. "Since I've been flat on my back I've become aware that there are so many loving people, caring people everywhere around us. And the love is eternal." He started crying, still he went on with a quaver. "Whatever happens, that love is more powerful than any bombs. The guns'll rust, the love is always there. Thank you so much for coming."

I recruited four men to move him into the hospital bed that now dominated our living room. They were all old friends, dear to both of us. Then the closing chapter of his life began.

At first I shared his care with relatives and a couple of close friends, occasionally rolling him gently from one side to the other to keep him from getting bedsores, adjusting his pillows, and powdering him with cornstarch to keep him comfortable. He'd often said that when he thought his end was near, he'd go on a dry fast, abstaining from water as well as food. Yet even after he stopped eating he remained surprisingly strong. The bed had a bar attached that curved high above his shoulders and was called a trapeze. When we asked him to, he would reach up to the trapeze and lift himself easily so we could change the pads and sheets underneath him.

As volunteer helpers dropped out, I hired attendants to cover some of the shifts around the clock. But probably because the agency that supplied them knew Charles wouldn't remain their patient long, they sent us their less desirable aides. I reserved to myself the task of giving my husband his medicines several times a day: morphine for general pain and another special pill for pain in the bones. The pill for bone pain had to be taken with food (a tablespoonful of pudding) so he could never fast completely—we both knew that probably slowed his death, his release, but it couldn't be helped. Visitors dropped by; he chatted with them easily, clearheaded and gracious as ever except when he had to sleep. Day by day he got thinner.

A journalist from *The Eugene Weekly*, a popular left-leaning paper in town, asked if he'd grant her an interview. Charles agreed. For three hours she questioned him about his personal history and beliefs; he gave her lucid, diplomatic answers. But the next time friends asked to visit, he told me to turn them away. From then on, only members of the family were welcome. I took on more and more shifts, spelled irregularly by his children and Leslie.

Activist Odyssey

For many hours, day and night, the two of us were alone. All the world knew that Charles had done much good in his life. Still the symbolism of his cancer—centered in his pelvis—struck both of us. Was he being punished for damage his sexuality had done? We didn't talk about this much. As long as I'd known him there had been many things Charles was tight-lipped about. Still in half sentences and meaningful looks we communicated this question in our minds. During his thirty-year marriage to Leslie he'd given her decades of grief. And sometimes this charming man had seduced married women, alienating them from their husbands and poisoning their marriages.

Before Charles came to know me, he hadn't believed in an afterlife but as his earthly end approached, I saw fear in his eyes. I kept assuring him that death was only a passage; whatever grievous sins he'd committed, they'd happened long ago and he'd atoned for them—in part through his commitment to the World Equity Budget. Still, even as I tried to soothe him, that look of dread didn't leave his face.

Until early one morning, as I hovered near him, he burst out with words that seemed wrenched from somewhere deep inside him, "I love you, I love you." I didn't answer. It came to me that as year after year, I'd showered him with endearments, never before had he said he loved me. I guess he felt he owed me this—he seemed relieved that he'd finally said it.

At last I welcomed a caregiver that I felt I could trust. Elizabeth had been busy with another patient and hadn't been able to help us until then. Together we set out to change Charles's pad and his sheets. He reached up to the trapeze to lift himself—but for the first time he couldn't do it. A look of surprise came over his face, by now cadaverously thin and saintly looking.

"Don't worry," said Elizabeth with a gentle smile, "we'll manage." And in fact, together, we did.

With her on duty I could take a nap or go out for a walk without worrying about Charles. But she only worked days. That night I dozed beside him on the couch and roused myself around 2:00 in the morning to give him his medicines for pain. Recently at the suggestion of the hospice nurse, he'd started taking a powerful sedative as well. I wished I could take a sedative myself but I didn't dare. I drank a little wine to help me relax. At last I fell into a deep slumber; it ended when summer sunlight worked its way through the curtains and blinds.

I checked on Charles, he was still breathing. He woke, blinked, said good morning. I asked him about his pain levels, gave him his meds, then he fell quickly back to sleep. Half awake, I managed to dress and have a bit of breakfast before Elizabeth arrived and I could relax. Leaving her in charge, I went out for a walk. I didn't walk far, I didn't walk long. When I came back, Elizabeth glanced up. "He's gone," she said calmly. Charles looked at peace.

A week later, a photo of Charles, twenty years younger, smiled confidently out of vending machines all over town. His odyssey was the cover story of *The Eugene Weekly*: "CHARLES GRAY: His lifelong fight for a better world ends."

Afterword

WE'D FELT THAT TOGETHER WE COULD stay young forever. Together we felt immune to the onslaughts of time. After he died, I grieved, I reeled, I struggled to regain my balance. Gradually I started to work again, to go through his office and pull his papers together. Charles would have wanted that—he was such a public man, concerned about his image, his impact on the world. But some of his files were empty that used to be full. In those last few months that he could climb the stairs to his office under the eaves, he must have weeded through them, discarding things he wanted left unseen.

I riffled through folders, saved a few keepsakes. Then I donated his papers and a few oddments he'd created—political banners, posters, an old shirt whose worn spots he'd camouflaged with skillful embroidery—to the library at the University of Oregon, just a couple of miles away. They were glad to get them. But once the staff at their Archives division had sorted through them, they said this collection was unusual because it contained so little personal correspondence, so few clues to his private life. Especially the colorful, complicated life Charles had had long before I met him.

So in 2008 I started compiling an oral history to flesh out his story,[1] getting on tape the memories of people who'd known him far longer than I did, or had known him well for a time, many years before. They themselves were growing old and maybe frail, some were far more forthcoming than others. As I probed and bantered and added observations of my own, we sketched out the world he'd inhabited and his way in the world. Soon the rambling recollections of thirteen people plus their interviewer would fill over 300 pages. The *Oral History of Charles Gray* would sit on the shelves of a few research libraries. And eventually authors on two continents[2] would draw on materials in the Archives for books of their own.

I MOVED FROM MY LITTLE HOUSE by the river to an apartment high in a 12-story building near the center of town. Down the street was a small abortion clinic where protestors marched or stood outside with placards. The desperate girls and women who went there had some tiny thing growing within them that they weren't able to love and nurture as every child deserves.

I've always believed that on our crowded planet, no child should be born that isn't wanted. And I'm convinced that no spark of the divine enters the fetus until quickening at the earliest—that extraordinary time when, midway through her pregnancy, a woman first feels some living thing kick within her. People have assumed this for thousands of years.

Most of all, I believe with all my heart in a woman's right to choose. How could I not? I've always loved my freedom and my right to follow the dictates of my conscience. So almost every week for years—until the doctor retired and a big new Planned Parenthood opened just outside of town—I would step inside that clinic and pass through its quiet waiting room. The receptionist would greet me cheerfully and open a door to an alcove where I helped myself to a flimsy cotton vest hanging on a hook. It was bright orange with big black letters that proclaimed PRO-CHOICE CLINIC ESCORT. I'd put it on and for a couple of hours I'd stand outside between the clinic's entering patients and those protestors who might otherwise badger them or force on them pamphlets full of frightening lies.

After a while someone would come along to relieve me. One day it was a jaunty young woman, less than one-third my age, who'd shown up unexpectedly some months before, carrying a sign she'd made to stage her own protest against the protestors. That's when I recruited Kayla to be a clinic escort. She reminded me of Eugene's cheeky activists who fight to save Oregon's old growth forests. She reminded me of those wonderful young people who demonstrated with Charles and me in Seattle and rode with us on the Zapatista caravan.

I took off my orange vest and passed it to Kayla. She put it on. And as I walked home, I thought that for the crises our nation faces, I pass the torch to her and the vanguard of her generation.

∽

Acknowledgments

This book has evolved over many years. Along the way, a wealth of people and organizations have played a role in that process.

Those who read early drafts of the manuscript include Marti Black, Tree Bressen, Daniel Goldrich, Madronna Holden, Helen Park, Carol Melia, Sonja Moseley, Lou Roberts, Sara Stewart, Mara Thygesen and Rustin Wright. I learned much from their comments, positive or negative, and for that I'm grateful. Of particular value were the comments of several professional editors and writers on sections of my memoir-in-progress. These include Anne Cherry, Mary DeDanan, Elizabeth Lyon, Anne Shapiro and Kristi Wallace. Medea Benjamin gave my morale a boost when she said my report on the 1999 demonstrations against the WTO in Seattle, where I'd met her briefly, was "beautifully written" and "brought back so many memories." Larissa MacFarquhar read a long section of my manuscript for research she was doing on Charles Gray. When out of the blue she expressed enthusiasm for my writing, I was thrilled and delighted.

I owe a double debt to Olivia Taylor-Young. Not only did she read my manuscript and give me trenchant feedback, she also led the writers group at the Osher Lifelong Learning Institute where for years I was a faithful attender. My thanks to her and to my fellow writers in that group.

As a researcher as well as a writer, I have lots of people, groups and institutions to acknowledge for providing me with data laid out in *Activist Odyssey*. Knight Library at the University of Oregon and the Eugene Public Library—especially their Interlibrary Loan services—have given me access to all manner of books and articles. My thanks to Eddy Portnoy at the YIVO Institute for Jewish Research for confirming the meaning of the Yiddish expression *hoykhe fenster* and telling me how to spell it. My gratitude, also, to Lou Roberts for transcribing numerous interviews.

For my portrait of Robert Martinson and his work, I relied not only on my old correspondence with him and personal recollections but on interviews I did with several men, some now no longer alive, who'd been his friends or professional associates. Most notable were Bogdan Denitch, Fritjof Thygesen, Arthur Lipow and Douglas Lipton. A former prison warden, David Winett, described the inner workings of the criminal justice system. Confirmation of the international impact of Martinson's work came from an unexpected source when David Sligar contacted me from Australia where he was working on an honors thesis about him at the University of Wollongong.

Michael Martinson, Dr. Martinson's son, is supremely knowledgeable about his father's life and work. I'm indebted to him for years of informative email exchanges and for graciously supplying me with photos of his father. I'm also indebted to the library at the University of California, Berkeley, where I accessed Martinson's master's thesis, his doctoral dissertation, and a typescript of *Carola*, the Jean Renoir play in which he starred when it was produced on the Berkeley campus. More recently, it has been a pleasure to exchange data with the filmmaker Adam Humphreys and to be interviewed by him for his documentary-in-progress about Martinson.

For the chapter on abortion, conversations with Judith Arcana and Maureen Hudson enriched my understanding of women's experiences in Chicago and elsewhere before Roe v. Wade. I'm also grateful to my former roommate and longtime friend, Judi Bloch, for her observations on this subject. My thanks, too, to the Network for Reproductive Options—now part of the Northwest Abortion Access Fund—for letting me consult their collection of books on the history of abortion in America.

Acknowledgments

For my account of a visit to Kenya, I owe much to Todd Harris, the Peace Corps volunteer who invited me to tour with him there. Not only did his invitation prompt me to take off on an unexpected adventure, he also took remarkable photos of my experiences there, three of which are reproduced in this book. Laurie Staniak enabled me to date the photo of Charles Gray and me at Yosemite. I'm grateful also to Ted Taylor for his photograph of me at Peg Morton's memorial service.

Witness for Peace, a human rights organization in solidarity with the people of Latin America, has more than once earned my gratitude. Witness shepherded my visits to Nicaragua in 1990 and 1995. For this book, Pamela Fitzpatrick, a friend and one of their former delegation leaders, supplied useful details about conditions in Nicaragua.

Like Witness for Peace, Oxfam America, International Rivers, and the International Forum on Globalization have been trusted sources of information on the world financial institutions and related issues of the environment and corporate power. Ten years after the 1999 demonstrations in Seattle, several members of our affinity group—Ruth Beller, Peg Morton, Jan Spencer, Win Swafford, Stan Taylor, Sterling Wallach and Ruth Wrenn—joined me to reminisce about our experiences there. Their recollections helped me recreate that experience in Chapter 22. Kindler Stout, who participated elsewhere in the demonstrations that day, kindly provided me with a long list of slogans he saw displayed there.

With unwavering professionalism, Do Mi Stauber compiled this book's thorough and sharrply analytical index. Finally, my warmest thanks go to Eva Long of Long on Books for collaborating with me to put *Activist Odyssey* into print. My multi-talented mentor, always encouraging and wise, she has used her graphics skills and editorial expertise to launch it into the world.

Notes

Chapter 1. Taking Our Chances in Mexico

1. **The new president of Mexico.** Vicente Fox <https://en.wikipedia.org/wiki/Vicente_Fox>

2. **protective accompaniment.** Karen Ridd and Craig Kauffman (1997) "Protective Accompaniment" Peace Review, v. 9 (2), 215-219.

3. **Subcommander Marcos.** Subcomandante Marcos. <https://en.wikipedia.org/wiki/Subcomandante_Marcos>.

4. **liberation theology.** Christopher Rowland. (1999) *The Cambridge Companion to Liberation Theology.* New York: Cambridge University Press.

5. **Pope Francis ... voices its principles.** Pope Francis. Encyclical Letter Laudato Sí, on Care for Our Common Home. http://w2.vatican.va/content/francesco/en/encyclicals/documents/papa-francesco_20150524_enciclica-laudato-si.html

6. **pressure from world financial institutions.** On April 8, 2014, page B1, *The New York Times* published an article by Eduardo Porter—one of its leading journalists on economic issues— "In New Tack, I.M.F. Aims at Income Inequality." In it Porter commented on "the IMF's new emphasis" since it had to deal with the threat of bankruptcy in European countries like Greece and Spain rather than in relatively remote Third World countries, typically out of sight and out of mind for First World citizens.

"Mexico, where I grew up," Porter reported, "was run for much of the 1980s under the aegis of some agreement or other with the fund, aimed at restoring the country's finances and preventing a default on its foreign debt. It is a period known to Mexicans as 'the lost decade.' Public payrolls were culled. Unemployment soared. Wages collapsed. Poverty jumped. And Mexico's lopsided distribution of income got worse.... An analysis published last year by economists in the I.M.F.'s fiscal affairs department concluded that efforts to curb budget deficits increase inequality, especially if they take the form of spending cuts. It suggested that targeted government spending and progressive taxes could offset some of these effects."

Chapter 2. High Windows

1. **your veteran's bonus.** In 1936, after years of fierce and sometimes blood-soaked agitation during the Depression by impoverished veterans of the First World War, bonus bonds they'd received from the federal government for their military service were paid off nine years early. Most of them spent the proceeds immediately and this influx of money gave the national economy a temporary boost.

Chapter 4. A Peace Center and a Couple of Passions

1. **Both sides had stockpiled enough.** Arthur T. Hadley. (1961) *The Nation's Safety and Arms Control.* New York: Viking Press, p. 3. According to Hadley, "the weapons in the United States stockpile [had] an explosive power roughly equivalent to 35 kilomegatons (35 billion tons of TNT) ...enough bang to provide ten tons of explosives for everyone in the world" while experts claimed the Soviet Union had another 20 kilomegatons in its stockpile.

2. **I had a buddy in town named Donn Bayard.** Donn Bayard went on to earn a doctorate in anthropology at the University of Hawaii. He moved on from anthropology to study the archeology of Southeast Asia and became a leading scholar of the region's linguistics, learning to speak Thai and indigenous New Zealand dialects. After he died in 2002, his obituary in a scholarly journal (Karl L. Hutterer "*Donn Bayard* (1940-2002): Outstanding Southeast Asian Archaeologist and Much More." *Asian Perspectives*, vol. 43, no. 1:1-6) hailed him as "a remarkable man ... who maintained, throughout his life, a strong commitment to social equality and a genuine interest in the problems and rights of peasants, working people, cultural and racial minorities, and women."

Chapter 5. "I Have a Dream"

1. **The nation's one major black union leader.** A. Philip Randolph organized and headed the Brotherhood of Sleeping Car Porters. In those days, these servants in railroad sleeping cars made a better than average living from their salaries, boosted by tips from well-to-do passengers. Since good jobs for blacks were exceedingly hard to find, this one attracted many highly educated and overqualified men noted for their gentlemanly demeanor.

2. **The National Association for the Advancement of Colored People.** This cumbersome name is generally called "the N double A C P" or just "the N double A." Its head at this time was Walter White. Coincidentally, White *looked* white, although his heritage was black. This made it easier for him to operate in a segregated society.

Chapter 8. Panama: Introduction to the Third World

1. **a co-op to market the molas.** "Molas from the San Blas Islands of Panama" <http://www.molasfrompanama.com/index.html>

Chapter 9. Getting Back on My Feet

1. **Your old friend Martinson ... split with his wife.** Bob told me ruefully that during the Vietnam War, his wife Rita traveled with Jane Fonda when that outspoken critic of the war entertained troops stationed in Southeast Asia. He suggested that Rita was a hanger-on, part of Fonda's entourage. Decades later I learned differently when I saw a prizewinning documentary, *Sir, No Sir,* about campaigning against the war within the military. It shows scenes from Fonda's FTA show that entertained tens of thousands of "grunts" in Japan, Okinawa and the Philippines. (Its name was shorthand for Fuck the Army.) Beside her stands Rita Martinson, sassy and funny, the two of them tall and slender.

Notes

Rita sings a song she wrote. "I read that you took a stand and refused to kill in Vietnam…. Soldier, we love you…." The camera pans over a sea of young male faces, suddenly calmed and reassured. Toward the end of *Sir, No Sir,* an older Jane Fonda recalls, "I used to love to watch the faces of those GIs when Rita sang, "Soldier, We Love You." Obviously she wasn't just a hanger-on at all.

2. **The University Center SEEK Program.** The acronym SEEK stood for Search for Education, Elevation and Knowledge—but nobody ever chose to spell it out that way.

3. **For my last job … I wrote a book.** While working for the Institute for the Study of Crime and Delinquency, associated with the School of Criminology at UC Berkeley, Martinson, under the supervision of his then boss, William J. O'Brien, wrote almost all of a 343-page report, *Staff Training and Correctional Change: A Study of Professional Training in Correctional Settings.* O'Brien contributed a chapter to this volume, copyrighted in 1966.

Members of the UC Berkeley sociology department where he'd been a graduate student for many years arranged for him to get a grant that supported him briefly while, at their suggestion, he prepared a revised version of the earlier work. This is what he submitted as his dissertation, *Treatment Ideology and Correctional Bureaucracy: A Study of Organizational Change.* On the basis of this he received his PhD in December 1968.

4. **Things between Martinson and me started to sour.** Much later I'd learn that around this time he started an affair with a dainty and beautiful brunette, Lilly Afan, a sometime actress, who worked as a lighting technician for big Broadway shows. Her relationship with Bob ended after three or four years but, according to Bob's son, in retrospect he considered her the great love of his life. She went on to become the longtime partner of a noted actor and acting teacher.

Chapter 10. Jordan and My Favorite Black Panther

1. **Aijaz Ahmad.** After teaching in American and Canadian universities, Aijaz Ahmad returned to India where he had been born and moved on beyond poetry to become a respected Marxist literary theorist and political commentator. He is the author of several books published in India and the United States.

2. **My article for *Library Journal*.** Sylvia Hart Wright. (1970) "A pre-college program for the disadvantaged." *Library Journal,* 90,16: 2884-2887.

Chapter 11. Dave's Pet Panther

1. **Most of the Oakland cops were … notoriously brutal to people of color.** The explanation I heard for this was that, like Berkeley, Oakland required all candidates for its police force to be college graduates but, since the Oakland job was not very desirable, hardly any Northern whites applied and city officials barely considered hiring people of color. Eventually Southerners were in a position to hire more Southerners for jobs there.

2. **Fred Hampton.** Hampton was a brilliant organizer who had been reaching out to the predominantly white radicals of Students for a Democratic Society and to black

and Puerto Rican street gangs with thousands of members to build a class-conscious, multi-racial alliance. He organized weekly rallies, taught political action classes, and launched a project for community supervision of the police. My main sources for this report are three articles in *The New York Times* on the days following this incident [John Kifner. "Police in Chicago Slay 2 Panthers." (December 5, 1969) 1; John Kifner. "Inquiry Into Slaying of 2 Panthers Urged in Chicago." (December 6, 1969) 29; John Kifner. "Panthers Say an Autopsy Shows Party Official Was 'Murdered'" (December 7, 1969] and a more detailed follow-up article in *Guardian,* Clark Kissinger. "Top Illinois Panthers Murdered." (December 13, 1969) 3, 9, 11.

According to the *Wikipedia* article on Fred Hampton, on the night of the police raid, Hampton was drugged by an FBI agent, William O'Neal, who also provided the cops with a floor plan of Hampton's apartment. In 1976, Sen. Frank Church, acting as head of the Senate's Select Committee to Study Governmental Operations with Respect to Intelligence Activities, revealed the FBI agent's identity and what he had done. On Martin Luther King Day in 1990, the 40-year-old O'Neal killed himself.

Soon after the shooting in 1969, the families of Hampton and Clark filed a civil suit against the city, state, and federal governments. After more than a decade of litigation, the suit was finally settled for $1,850,000. The money was divided between the two families.

Chapter 12. The Man Who Changed the Criminal Justice System

1. **Schachtman's theory.** Wikipedia."Max Schachtman"https://en.wikipedia.org/wiki/Max_Shachtman. Michael Lind (2003) "The Strange Path of Neoconservatism" *The Globalist.* www.theglobalist.com/the-strange-path-of-neoconservatism/

In Martinson's sociology master's thesis, submitted to the University of California, Berkeley, in 1953, *The Role of the Communist Party in the Spanish Civil War,* he supported the same conclusion: that a totalitarian Soviet-style state could not successfully be fought from within. This theory underlay his support for the Vietnam War.

2. **The *New Republic* published a series of articles.** *The New Republic* published this four-part series in 1972, as "The 'dangerous myth,'" (April 1: 23-25), "Can corrections correct?" (April 8: 13-15), "The meaning of Attica," (April 15: 17-19) and "Planning for public safety" (April 29: 21-23).

3. **The percentage of people imprisoned more than doubled.** Martinson drew these data from *Struggle for Justice* which he described as a recent report prepared for the American Friends Service Committee. The AFSC is associated with the Quakers (officially, the Religious Society of Friends) who for centuries have worked to improve prison conditions.

4. **The library association of City University published my thesis.** Sylvia Hart Wright. (1975) *Black Youth, Black Studies and Urban Education: A Study of Use Patterns in Two Innovative New York Libraries.* City University of New York: LACUNY Occasional Papers, no. 3.

Notes

5. **The Effectiveness of Correctional Treatment.** Douglas Lipton, Robert Martinson and Judith Wilks. (1975) *The Effectiveness of Correctional Treatment; A Survey of Treatment Evaluation Studies.* New York: Praeger. Though the title page lists three authors, the book's preface ends with a curious statement, "The authors wish to note that by mutual agreement, their names are listed in alphabetical order. This ordering in no way reflects the level or quantity of contribution made by the individual authors." Martinson was generally acknowledged to be the actual author although all three had served as researchers. On page vii of the preface, the compiler of the bibliography is identified as "Mrs. Sylvia Wright."

6. **"What Works? Questions and Answers...."** Robert Martinson. (1974) "What works? Questions and answers about prison reform." *The Public Interest,* no. 35, 22-54. According to this article, "the document itself would still not be available to me or to the public today had not Joseph Alan Kaplan, an attorney, subpoenaed it from the state for use as evidence in a case before the Bronx Supreme Court.... Following this case the state finally did give its permission to have the work published in its complete form in a ...book by Praeger."

7. **Written up in *People* magazine.** "In his own words: Criminologist Bob Martinson offers a crime-stopper: put a cop on each ex-con." (1976) *People Magazine* 5, 7: 20-23.

8. **It issued a small book.** Robert Martinson, Ted Palmer and Stuart Adams. (1976) *Rehabilitation, Recidivism, and Research.* Hackensack, NJ: National Council on Crime and Delinquency.

9. **Responding to the criticisms of a former co-worker.** Stuart Adams. (1976) "Evaluation: A way out of rhetoric." (Adapted from a paper presented at the Conference on Evaluation of Community-Based Corrections, University of Washington, Seattle, December 18, 1975.) *In* Robert Martinson, Ted Palmer and Stuart Adams. *Rehabilitation, Recidivism, and Research*, Hackensack, NJ: National Council on Crime and Delinquency, p. 76.

Chapter 14. The Harder They Fall

1. **An article by Martinson and Wilks.** Robert Martinson and Judith Wilks. (1977) "Save parole supervision." *Federal Probation,* v. 41, 23-27. Unfortunately, when Martinson switched sides, only obscure professional journals like this one published his articles.

2. Page 106. **Responding to an article.** Robert Martinson. (1978) "Martinson Responds." *Federal Probation,* v. 42, 61.

3. **At a conference workshop.** "It has come to our attention." (1979) *Federal Probation,* v. 43, no. 1, 86. It's tempting to ask who set the criteria for the studies to be included in *The Effectiveness of Correctional Treatment.* Surely Douglas Lipton who had hired Martinson and Wilks and who, unlike them, was a full-time employee of New York State, must have had primary responsibility for such decisions. My guess is that faced with mountains of studies to evaluate, the three researchers—with Lipton in the lead—chose to abide by the accepted wisdom of the day regarding criteria for studies to include.

4. **"Tell him I was full of crap."** Robert Martinson. "New findings, new views: A note of caution regarding sentencing reform." (1979) *Hofstra Law Review,* 7, 2. 15. This story is cited on page 43 of: O.J. Keller. (1980) "The criminal personality or Lombroso revisited." *Federal Probation,* v. 44, 37-43. V15: 213.

5. **How he responded when** *Contemporary Authors.* Gale Literary Databases: Contemporary Authors Online, 2009.

6. **Martinson's findings are being reexamined.** John Tierney. "Prison population can shrink when police crowd streets," *The New York Times.* January 25, 2013, A1.

Chapter 15. A Book, Some Insights, and a Giant March

1. **Awards given by the AIA and the leading magazines.** The Pritzker Architecture Prize, comparable to a Nobel Prize for architects, did not yet exist; it was first awarded in 1979.

2. **When he had a check to cash.** Though Paul could no longer teach, he still had income: Social Security because he was blind and over 55, and veterans' benefits for injuries sustained in World War II.

3. **My grandfather's cousin, Morris Rosenfeld.** My mother's father, who came to the United States from Russia in 1876 at the age of 16, had been trained as a tailor. In New York he eventually ran a small garment manufacturing business, a "sweatshop." During much of Rosenfeld's life, when he worked at a normal job, he worked for his cousin, my grandfather. What other employer would put up with him?

Chapter 16. Surprises

1. **Apparent confirmation of this.** This observation matches one reported by the British physicist, Sir Oliver Lodge, whose discoveries and inventions played a significant part in the development of wireless telegraphy, spark plugs and radio. His deep interest in the paranormal began early in the 20th century; he and Sir Arthur Conan Doyle worked together on what was then called psychical research. Later, in his book, *Raymond; or Life and Death, with Examples of the Evidence for Survival of Memory and Affection after Death* (1916, New York: George H. Doran) he reported that one of his sons, who died in World War I, had been trained as a mechanical and electrical engineer. At a séance during which Raymond's spirit apparently communicated via letters spelled out by the tilting of a table, Sir Oliver asked, "Can you explain how you do this?

I mean, how you work the table?" The message spelled back, letter by letter, was YOU ALL SUPPLY MAGNETISM GATHERED IN MEDIUM AND THAT GOES INTO TABLE AND WE MANIPULATE.

In his best-selling book, *Talking to Heaven,* (New York: Dutton, 1997) the gifted medium James van Praagh listed "ways spirits let their loved ones know that they are around them *without* the use of mediums." Topping his list was "lights," followed by other electrically operated devices.

Notes

2. **A society he knew of in Manhattan.** The group he told me about was the American Society for Psychical Research. At the time it offered a fairly active program of talks and seminars but as of this writing, its activities are greatly diminished.

3. **Westinghouse Science Talent Search.** This competition is now known as the Regeneron Science Talent Search.

4. **National Association of Teachers of Science.** The current name of this group is the National Science Teachers Association.

Chapter 17. Bonanza in Panama—For Some

1. **See-no-evil, hear-no-evil government policies.** On June 12, 1986, *The New York Times* featured on its front page a long article, "Panama Strongman Said to Trade in Drugs, Arms and Illicit Money; U.S. Aides Also Assert Noriega Helps Leftist Rebels in Colombia." It alleged that Manuel Noriega, head of the Panamanian army and de facto head of its government, had long been a double agent, supplying information to both the U.S. and Cuba. It also reported that "Panama's banking laws [permit] secret accounts by individuals and corporations that are virtually free from scrutiny by American law enforcement officials.... Panama has become a world leader in the depositing of illegal profits from drug dealing and other activities."

2. **Torrijos had died in a plane crash.** In his revealing book, *Confessions of an Economic Hit Man,* (San Francisco: Berrett-Koehler, 2004: 66-75, 180-186) the author, John Perkins, strongly backs the theory that Torrijos was assassinated by the C.I.A. Shortly after Ronald Reagan became president, Jaime Roldós, the president of Ecuador who was demanding that his nation receive more from Texaco for its oil reserves, died when his small plane blew up. Two months later, Torrijos who, like Roldós, had stood up to Reagan died the same way.

3. **Early the next year, my new guide came out.** Sylvia Hart Wright (1989) *Sourcebook of Contemporary North American Architecture: From Postwar to Postmodern.* New York: Van Nostrand Reinhold.

Chapter 18. Nicaragua: A Rougher Taste of the Third World

1. **Blew open the back door of the residence of six Jesuit priests.** Much of this account comes from an article by Lee Hockstader and Douglas Farah, Washington Post Foreign Service, November 17, 1989, available online at
<http://online ministries.creighton.edu/CollaborativeMinistry/WPnov16.html>.

2. **She could hear them being brutalized.** When I saw Jennifer Casolo speak, I didn't take notes. Therefore, the quotes supplied here and some of the other material in this section come from an article by Ron Arias. "Her Salvador Ordeal Over, Jennifer Casolo Hits the Road to End the War She Left Behind." January 22, 1990. *People Magazine* vol. 33, no. 3.

3. **We reviewed Nicaragua's history.** The summary of Nicaraguan history that follows owes much to articles in Wikipedia plus others found at <www.moreorless: heroes and killers of the 20th century> and <www.countrystudies.us/Nicaragua>.

4. **Somoza fled to Paraguay.** Claribel Alegria and Darwin J. Flakoll. (1996) *Death of Somoza,* p. 132-134. Willimantic, CT: Curbstone Press.

5. **The Contras fought very dirty.** As described in the Wikipedia article on the Iran-Contra Affair, "A Human Rights Watch report found that the Contras were guilty of targeting health care clinics and health care workers for assassination; kidnapping civilians; torturing and executing civilians, including children, who were captured in combat; raping women; indiscriminately attacking civilians and civilian homes; seizing civilian property; and burning civilian houses in captured towns." Ample documentation of these and other atrocities can be found elsewhere.

6. **It faced an unpredictable future.** When the Sandinista leader, Daniel Ortega, was defeated in the 1990 election for president of Nicaragua and replaced by Violeta Chamorro, he vowed that the Sandinistas would "govern from below." He continued to lead an active political movement and, after two unsuccessful runs for the presidency, was reelected in 2006.

Chapter 19. The Man Who Gave Away a Fortune

1. **People fasting with us in Japan and France.** One of the main fasters was a Frenchwoman, Solange Frenex, a pacifist and environmental activist who in 1984 was a co-founder of the Green Party and later served for years in the European Parliament. Six members of the British Parliament did sympathy fasts of a week or more.

2. ***We Gave Away a Fortune.*** Christopher Mogil and Anne Slepian with Peter Woodrow. (1992) *We Gave Away a Fortune: Stories of People Who Have Devoted Themselves and Their Wealth to Peace, Justice and the Environment.* Philadelphia, PA: New Society Publishers.

Chapter 20. Living on Less

1. **A whimsical profile contrasting his lifestyle.** "In Search of Happiness: Money" Angus Deayton, interviewer. (1995) British Broadcasting Corporation.

2. **Structural Adjustment Programs all over the Third World.** Laura Renshaw. (April 1995) *The Impact of Structural Adjustment on Community Life: Undoing Development.* Oxfam America. For a gripping insider's report on this process, see John Perkins' best-selling memoir, *Confessions of an Economic Hit Man.* (2004) Penguin Books.

3. **Structural adjustment in Mexico.** Judith Adler Hellman (1997) *Structural Adjustment in Mexico and the Dog That Didn't Bark.* North York, Ontario, Canada: York University. CERLAC Working Paper Series, Centre for Research on Latin America and the Caribbean.

Notes

4. **Buyers of government assets obligingly kicked back millions.** Sam Dillon (August 8, 1995) "Ex-Airline Chief Says $8 Million Went to Mexican Party" *The New York Times.* This article centers on the sleazy doings of Geraldo de Prevoisin, former chairman of Mexico's largest airline.

5. **Oxfam International ... also set up an advocacy office.** Ian Anderson, "Oxfam, the World Bank and heavily indebted poor countries" in *NGOs as Advocates for Development in a Global World*, ed. Barbara Rugendyke, 96-124 (London: Routledge, 2007).

6. **An activist newsletter would report.** Sameer Dossani, 50 Years Is Enough Network (September 2005) "A fragile moment of hope: The IMF and World Bank threaten debt cancellation" *Economic Justice News* (50 Years Is Enough: U.S. Network for Global Economic Justice) vol. 8, no. 3: 1,7.

7. **As reported in *The New York Times*.** Eduardo Porter (April, 8, 2014) "In new tack, I.M.F. aims at income inequality" *The New York Times,* page B1.

8. **A long and thoughtful article by Peter S. Goodman.** Peter S. Goodman (November 2, 2018)   "Merkel's legacy, and the fallout of stoic, hard-line leadership" *The New York Times,* page B1.

Chapter 21. Helping the Homeless

1. **In July 1998 an article of mine appeared.** Sylvia H. Wright (1998) Experiences of spontaneous psychokinesis after bereavement. *Journal of the Society for Psychical Research* 62, 852: 385-395.

2. **A brief survey of books and articles.** W. D. Rees (1971) "The Hallucinations of Widowhood." British Medical Journal 4, 37-41; : R. A. Kalish and D. K. Reynolds (1973) "Phenomenological reality and post-death contact." Journal for the Scientific Study of Religion. 112 (2) 209-21; P. R. Olson, J.A. Suddeth, P. J. Peterson, and C. Egelhoff (1985) "Hallucinations of widowhood." Journal of the American Geriatric Association. 33, 543-47; E. Haraldsson (1988) "Survey of claimed encounters with the dead." Omega, 19 (2) 103-113; A. Grimby (1993) "Bereavement among elderly people." Acta psychiatrica Scandinavica 87 (1) 72-80; and T. C. Lindstrom (1995) "Experiencing the presence of the dead." Omega 31, 1, 11-21. Many books have also been written on this subject, including one by me: When Spirits Come Calling: The Open-Minded Skeptic's Guide to After-Death Contacts (Nevada City, CA: Blue Dolphin, 2002). A slightly earlier study in Japan, where survival of the spirit is customarily taken for granted, reported that 90% of widows whose husbands had recently died in car accidents sensed their presence afterward: J. Yamamoto, K. Okonogi, T. Iwasaki, and S. Yoshimura (1969) "Mourning in Japan." American Journal of Psychiatry. 125, 1660-65.

3. **A best-selling book by medium James Van Praagh.** James Van Praagh (1997) *Talking to Heaven: A Medium's Message of Life after Death.* New York: Dutton. Page 178.

4. **Another article, published in the same journal.** Sylvia Hart Wright (1999) Paranormal contact with the dying: 14 contemporary death coincidences. *Journal of the Society for Psychical Research* 63, 857: 258-267.

5. **A couple of publications printed articles.** Charles Gray (1999) Corporate goliaths: sizing up corporations and governments. *Multinational Monitor* 20, 6: 26-27. Gray's chart also appeared in an article in *The Peaceworker,* an Oregon publication.

Chapter 22. Solidarity in Seattle

1. **Guidelines proposed by a Seattle woman.** Cecile Andrews (1997) *The Circle of Simplicity: Return to the Good Life.* New York: HarperCollins.

2. **This organization had been formed just four years earlier.** Much of the information reported here was supplied in *A Citizen's Guide to the World Trade Organization; Everything You Need to Know to Fight for Fair Trade.* (1999) Published by the Working Group on the WTO/MAI, this 28-page booklet was endorsed by 15 cosponsors including Alliance for Democracy, Americans for Democratic Action, Defenders of Wildlife, 50 Years Is Enough, Friends of the Earth, the International Brotherhood of Teamsters, Public Citizen, District 11 of the United Steelworkers of America, the Women's Division of GBGM United Methodist Church, and the Women's International League for Peace and Freedom.

3. **Pointed back in the other direction.** Chris Dixon, "Five Days in Seattle: A View from the Ground," included in the invaluable book, *The Battle of the Story of the Battle of Seattle,* (Oakland, CA: AK Press, 2009) by David Solnit and Rebecca Solnit with contributions by Anuradha Mittal, Chris Dixon, Stephanie Guilloud, and Chris Borte. Pages 82-85.

4. **"Human chain to end world debt."** Information about events scheduled to lead up to the demonstrations on Tuesday and commentary on them appeared in the *Seattle Post-Intelligencer* on November 28, 1999. This was included as Section G, in the Sunday edition of *The Seattle Times,* which supplied a timetable of these events.

5. **Cancel the debt of the world's poorest countries.** Chris Dixon, op. cit., 86.

6. **Streets too dangerous for Secretary of State Madeline Albright.** Chris Dixon, op.cit., 90.

7. **GET YOUR PAWS OFF OUR LAWS.** Kindler Stout of Ashland, OR, kindly supplied me with a long list of slogans, including these, that he collected in Seattle. It's estimated that 80,000 participated that day in actions against the W.T.O. The majority, about 50,000, attended the labor union-sponsored march and rally and were not directly involved in nonviolent protest although, after the rally, thousands of them flooded into downtown streets.

8. **Access was banned to all the tall buildings.** Chris Dixon. op. cit., 103.

9. **An agenda in which they saw they had little voice.** Chris Dixon, op. cit, 103. Also at stake is the ability of farmers in wealthier nations, like those in the European Union, to provide their homelands with food security—self-sufficiency with respect to food. Given the frightening consequences of global warming and the possibility it raises

Notes

of massive crop failures in regions impossible to predict, it's better for all of us if basic foodstuffs are raised all over the world.

10. **"This was not unexpected,"** *The New York Times* observed…. "Global trade after Doha's failure" *The New York Times* (lead editorial, January 1, 2016, A18).

Chapter 23. On the Road with the Zapatista Caravan

1. **Front page news in all the Mexican papers and the biggest story on TV.** Clandestine Revolutionary Indigenous Committee. General Command of the Zapatista Army of National Liberation "An automobile accident enroute from El Tephé." (March 1, 2001) http://www.struggle.ws/mexico/ezln/2001/ccri_crash_mar.html; Juan José Arreola "So mofa? Marcos? del gobernador queretano" (March 2, 2001) http://archivo.eluniversal.com.mx/nacion/48943.html; Salvador Herrera "Accidente en Querétero, caravana Zapatista" (posted June 5, 2009, showing events of March 1, 2001) https://www.youtube.com/watch?v=ghONeu_w6QU.

2. **Managed to send the makings of an article.** Sylvia Hart [sic.] (In Eugene I generally just used my maiden name as my pen name, omitting "Wright," the name of a previous husband.) and Charles Gray (March 2001) "On the Zapatista Trail: Revolution in Chiapas" *The Other Paper* (Eugene, Oregon) 12-14.

3. **A conservative newspaper reported.** *The Mexico City News,* reporting in mid-March 2001. Cited in: Charles Gray and Sylvia Hart. "Caravan for justice: Zapatista leaders take their fight for indigenous rights on the road." (April 1, 2001) *The Register-Guard* (Eugene, Oregon,) 1F.

4. **According to** *Encyclopaedia Britannica.* "Rafael Guillén Vicente: Mexican leader" https://www.britannica.com/biography/Rafael-Guillen-Vicente.

5. **Mexico's citizens … elect a firebrand leftist.** Azam Ahmed and Pauline Villegas. "López Obrador, an atypical leftist, wins Mexico presidency in a landslide." (July 1, 2018.) https://www.nytimes.com/2018/07/01/world/americas/mexico-election-andres-manuel-lopez-obrador.html. This article appeared under a slightly different title in the paper edition of *The New York Times* the next day .

Chapter 24. Winding Down

1. **A fuller, more polished article.** Charles Gray and Sylvia Hart [sic]. (2001) "Caravan for justice: Zapatista leaders take their fight for indigenous rights on the road." *The Register-Guard,* April 1, F1-2.

2. **A book of mine … about everyday people who'd sensed contact with the dead.** Sylvia Hart Wright (2002) *When Spirits Come Calling; The Open-Minded Skeptic's Guide to After-Death Contacts.* Nevada City, CA: Blue Dolphin.

3. **Public opinion was changing.** *The Gallup Poll: Public Opinion 2001* (2002) George Gallup, Jr. Wilmington, Delaware: Scholarly Resources, Inc. Humphrey Taylor.

(2003) The Religious and Other Beliefs of Americans 2003. www.harrisinteractive.com/harris_poll/index.asp?PID=359.

4. **By 2015, a scholarly article would report.** Marc A. Eaton. "Give us a sign of your presence": paranormal investigation as a spiritual practice." (Winter 2015) *Sociology of Religion;* Washington 76.4: 389-412, p. 389.

5. **50% of Americans believed in ghosts.** Gregory McCarriston. "Belief in ghosts is on the rise." (October 10, 2017) *YouGov: Lifestyle.* https://today.yougov.com/topics/lifestyle/articles-reports/2017/10/10/belief-ghosts-rise.

6. **A Canadian publication would report....** Joseph Brean. "Millenials are more likely to believe in an afterlife than are older generations." (March 29, 2018) *National Post* https://nationalpost.com//news/canada/millennials-do-you-believe-in-life-after-life>.

Afterword

1. **An *Oral History of Charles Gray*.** *An Oral History of Charles Gray, April 20, 1925-July 8, 2006.* Prepared by Sylvia Hart [sic], his widow, for the University of Oregon Special Collections and University Archives. Eugene, Oregon, January 2009.

2. **Authors on two continents.** Two recent books have contained long sections about Charles Gray. The first, written by an Australian author, is: Kyle Harvey. *American Anti-Nuclear Activism, 1975-1990: The Challenge of Peace.* (2014) London: Palgrave Macmillan. p. 93-116. The second, by an American author, is: Larissa MacFarquahar. *Strangers Drowning: Grappling with Impossible Idealism, Drastic Choices, and the Overpowering Urge to Help.* (2015) New York: Penguin Press. p. 28-40.

Index

abortion, 168–172, 291–292
Afan, Lilly, 298*n*4
Agent Orange, 135
Ahmad, Aijaz, 118, 298*n*1
Albright, Madeleine, 262
Algerian Revolution, 136
Alhambra, 281, 282–284
All But Dissertation (ABD), 52, 72
Alliance for Democracy (Eugene), *163*, 256, 267.
   See also Seattle WTO protests
Allyson, June, 36
American civil rights movement, 62
American Friends Service Committee, 299*n*3
American Institute of Architects (AIA), 182
American Library Association, 112
American Society for Psychical Research, 241, 252, 302*n*2
Aminifu, 126–130, 131–132
AMLO (Andrés Manuel López Obrador), 277
anti-Vietnam War movement
   CCNY actions, 117
   Fonda and, 297–298*n*1
   and Free Speech Movement, 78
   Charles Gray's participation, 224, 254
   militant actions, 135–136
   and Republican National Convention, 72–73
   and Republican National Convention (1964), 73
   and Turn Toward Peace, 69
   University of Wisconsin, 78
   Vietnam Day Committee, 78–79, 80–83

Baez, Joan, 69
Balfour, A. J., 252
Batista, Fulgencio, 44
Battle in Seattle. *See* Seattle WTO protests (1999)
Bayard, Donn, 58, 59, 297*n*2
Bay of Pigs, 44, 45, *155*
Berkeley, California
   car rental trade association job, 47–48, 51, 60–61, 77
   culture of, 69–70
   Free Speech Movement, 76–77
   move to, 46–47

INDEX

Berkeley, California (*continued*)
    and move to Eugene, 206
    New Left, 77–78
    Republican National Convention (1964), 72–73
    Turn Toward Peace, 49–52, 69, 77, 109
Berry, John, 121
Biutiful, 280
Black Bloc, 263
Black Panthers, 124–137
    and Aminifu, 126–130, 131–132
    Hampton, 130–131, 298–299n2
    Hampton and Clark assassinations, 130–131
    Johnny Lightning operation, 132–133, 135, 136–137
    Panther 11, 130
    SHW's fantasies about assisting, 136
    and University Center SEEK Program, 114–115, 119, 124–125
Black Youth, Black Studies and Urban Education: A Study of Use Patterns in Two Innovative New York Libraries (Wright), 144, 299n4
Bolaños, Nicolas, 218
Branman, Irving, 110–112, 113, 117
Bring Recycling (Eugene), 221
Brockelbank, Leslie, 224, 225, 228, 274, 286, 288
Brotherhood of Sleeping Car Porters, 62, 297n1
Brown v. Board of Education, 62–63
Burroughs, William S., 44
Bush, George W., 140

Callenbach, Ernest (Chick), 57
"Caravan for justice: Zapatista leaders take their fight for indigenous rights on the road" (Gray and Hart), 278, 306n1
Cardoso, Anabela, 280–282
Carola (Renoir), 52, 55
Carter, Rita. *See* Martinson, Rita Carter
Carter administration, 208
Casolo, Jennifer, 205
Castro, Fidel, 43, 44, 45, 136
Center for Knowledge in Criminal Justice Planning, 148–151, 176–177
Center for Popular Education (Nicaragua), 218–219
Central America, 204–205. *See also* Witness for Peace
Chamorro, Pedro Joaquin, 207
Chamorro, Violeta, 209, 234, 303n6
Chiapas (Mexico). *See* Zapatista accompaniment trip

INDEX

City College of New York (CCNY)
    anti-Vietnam War movement at, 117
    Martinson's faculty position, 113, 138, 139, 140
    SHW's architecture school library position, 181
    SHW's library position, 117, 138, 139, 148–149
    SHW's promotions, 172, 186, 203
    SHW's retirement, 206
    See also University Center SEEK Program
Civil Rights Act (1964), 80
civil rights movement, 62–63
    Brotherhood of Sleeping Car Porters, 62, 297n1
    Civil Rights Act (1964), 80
    Freedom Riders, 52, 54, 139, 148
    Freedom Summer, 72
    Free Speech Movement and, 76–77
    March on Washington for Jobs and Freedom (1963), 62–68
    NAACP, 297n2
Clark, Mark, 130–131, 299n2
Clark, Ramsey, 205
Cleaver, Eldridge, 114–115
Cold War, 44
Committee for a Sane Nuclear Policy (SANE), 49–50, 51
Congress of Racial Equality (CORE), 73, 76–77
Contras, 208–209, 212, 217, 227, 303n5
CORE (Congress of Racial Equality), 73, 76
Corelli, Pete (pseudonym), 129, 298n1
Cornell University, 34, *154*
COSEP (Nicaragua), 217–218
Costa Rica, 202
criminal justice reform. *See* Martinson's criminal justice work
Cuba
    abortion trip (1956), 44–45, 171–172
    Bay of Pigs invasion, 44, 45, *155*

Deayton, Angus, 232
DeFazio, Peter, 164
Democratic Party, 139
Denitch, Bogdan, 147–148
Direct Action Network, 256–257
Doha Round, 266
Doyle, Arthur Conan, 301n1

INDEX

Ecotopia (Callenbach), 57
Effectiveness of Correctional Treatment, The (Lipton, Martinson, and Wilks), 145–146, 300*nn*1, 3, 5
El Salvador, 204–205
Eugene, Oregon (1991–present)
    abortion rights activism, 291–292
    Alliance for Democracy, *163*, 256, 267
    Homeless Action Coalition work, 250–251
    move to (1991), 206, 220, 223
    Packwood protest, *160*
    psychic phenomena research, 241–242, 251–252, 253–254, 304*n*2
    psychic phenomena writing, 252–253, 254, 279, 304*nn*1–2, 4
    Quaker Economics Group, 1, 222–224, 225
    settling in, 220–221
    simplicity circle, 255, 256
    U.S.-based Witness for Peace work, 233–234, 238–239
    See also Gray, Charles; Kenya trip (1997); Seattle WTO protests; Witness for Peace delegation (1990); Witness for Peace delegation (1995); Zapatista accompaniment trip
Eugene Friends Meeting, 221–223
Eugene Mission, 242–243
Europe on Five Dollars a Day, 54
"Experiences of spontaneous psychokinesis after bereavement" (Wright), 252–253, 304*n*1
EZLN (Zapatista Army of National Liberation), 6, 268, 276–277
    See also Zapatista accompaniment trip

fair trade, 256
Fantasticks, The, 44
Fast, Howard, 136
Fast for Life, 226–227, 286, 303*n*1
Feldman, Bernice Meyers (sister/cousin), 19, 23, 26, 79, 102, *153*, 186
Fifty Years Is Enough, 239
Film Quarterly, 57
Fitzpatrick, Pam, 210, 212, 217, 221–222, 233
Fletcher, Paul (husband, 1973–83), *157*
    and Center for Knowledge in Criminal Justice Planning job, 149
    death of, 190–192
    Legionnaire's disease, 189–190, 191
    marriage, 143–144
    psychic abilities, 166–167
    psychic messages from, 192–196, 231, 251, 252–253
    as punster, 167, 194, 231

Fletcher, Paul (husband, 1973–83) (*continued*)
  relationship with Rusty, 143, *157*, *158*, 167, 190
  vision problems, 172–173, 176, 183–185, 301*n*2
Fonda, Jane, 297–298*n*1
Fondersmith, John, 182–183
Ford, Gerald, 148
Fox, Vicente, 3, 7, 267–269
Francis (Pope), 7
Freedom Summer, 72
Free Speech Movement, 76–77, 78, 80
Freire, Paolo, 218
FSLN (Sandinista National Liberation Front) (Nicaragua), 207, 208, 237, 303*n*6

Ghost, 280
Ghost Hunters, 280
Gibran, Kahlil, 115
Goldstone, Herbert (husband, 1953–54), 34, 35–36, *154*
Goldwater, Barry, 72–73, 78
Goodman, Peter S., 240
Granada, Dorothy, 222, 226, 227, 228
Gray, Charles (husband, 1997–2006), *161*, *163*
  and anti-Vietnam War movement, 224, 254
  background of, 224
  celebration of life, 285–287
  corporate spending poster, 254
  end of life, 287–289
  and Fast for Life, 226–227, 286, 303*n*1
  first meeting, 221–222
  health issues, 280, 281–283, 284–285
  and Homeless Action Coalition, 242, 243, 249–251
  marriage (1997), *161*, 243, 244
  Oprah Show appearance, 227–228
  oral history on, 290–291, 307*n*1
  organic farm work, 279
  and psychic phenomena, 231, 241, 242
  Quaker Economics Group (Eugene Friends Meeting), 1, 222–224, 225
  relationship beginnings, 1, 16, 225–226, 228–229
  U.S.-based Witness for Peace work, 233–234, 238–239
  voluntary simplicity commitment, 224–225, 227, 230–231, 232–233, 243
  Witness for Peace delegation (1995), 236–238
  Witness for Peace long-term work, 222, 227
  WTO protests, 1–2

INDEX

Gray, Charles (husband, 1997–2006) (*continued*)
    See also Seattle WTO protests; Zapatista accompaniment trip
Great Society programs, 107, 109
Guevara, Che, 112
Gulf of Tonkin Resolution, 78
Gull Haven, 286

Hampton, Fred, 130, 131, 298–299*n*2
Harrington, Michael, 120, 121, 139
Harrison, George, 100
Hart, Bernice. *See* Feldman, Bernice Meyers
Hart, Hiram (brother), 19, 30–31, 79, *153*, *154*, *159*, 186
Hart, Max (father), *154*, *158*
    civil service job, 32, 185
    early life and education of, 18, 24, 185
    Jewish background, 20
    on Edna and Joseph Meyers, 21
    navy service, 17
    reaction to SHW's book, 185, 186
    second marriage, 102
    on SHW's birth, 22
    and SHW's separation from Howard, 94
    SHW's stay with (1967), 102
    social justice views of, 24, 25, 79, 94, 223
    stock market studies, 31, 223
    wife's relationship with, 18–19, 23, 29, 44
Hart, Ruth Meyers (mother), *153*, *154*
    childhood sexual abuse of, 18, 27, 28
    Christian Science conversion, 30
    death of, 79
    education of, 22–23, 27
    generosity of, 17
    health issues of, 26, 30
    housekeeping, 23–24, 34–35
    husband's business failures and, 18–19
    Jewish background, 20
    and Protestant ethic, 27–28
    relationship with husband, 18–19, 23, 29, 44
    on SHW's birth, 22
    and SHW's education, 32, *154*
    and SHW's first marriage, 35
    and social class, 18–19, 20, 29
    social justice views of, 25

INDEX

Hart Wright, Sylvia, *165*
abortion, 169–172
ACTIVISM: abortion rights, 168–169, 291–292; Alliance for Democracy, *163*, 256, 267; anti-Vietnam War movement, 78–79, 80–83; Bay of Pigs protest, 45, *155*; and civil rights movement, 80; Committee for a Sane Nuclear Policy, 49–50, 51; El Salvador, 204–205; Eugene simplicity circle, 255, 256; Free Speech Movement, 76–77; Homeless Action Coalition, 250–251; March on Washington (1983), 195; March on Washington for Jobs and Freedom, 62–68; New Left and, 77–78; nuclear freeze march (New York, 1982), 186–188; *Oakland Tribune* racial discrimination protests, 73; Packwood protest, *160*; Quaker Economics Group (Eugene Friends Meeting), 1, 222–224, 225; rally for Rep. DeFazio (Eugene), *164*; Republican National Convention (1964), 72–73; Turn Toward Peace, 49–52, 69, 77, 109; U.S.-based Witness for Peace work, 233–234, 238–239; Witness for Peace delegation (1995), 234, 236–238. *See also* Seattle WTO protests; Witness for Peace delegation (1992); Zapatista accompaniment trip
astrological sign, 119–120
drive to accomplish, 181–182
early life, 18, 22, 23–24, 25–26, 27–33, *153*
EDUCATION: childhood reading, 28–29; Cornell University, 34, *154*; high school, 32–35; junior high, 31; library science degree, 35, 37, 121–122, 170; sociology master's degree, 122–123, 143
EMPLOYMENT: car rental trade association (Oakland), 47–48, 51, 60–61, 77; CCNY retirement, 206; Center for Knowledge in Criminal Justice Planning, 148–151; City College of New York libraries, 138, 139, 148, 149, 181; criminal justice research project, 104–105, 106, 145, 300*n*5; New York junior high library, 107, 110; New York Public Library, 35, 112, 170; New York subscription agency, 103, 106–107, 182; Oakland Public Library, 77, 79; Sloan-Kettering Institute, 63; University Center SEEK Program, 109–113, 114–115, 117–120, 121–122, 137–138, 140, *157*, 298*n*2. *See also* University Center SEEK Program
family background, 17–23, 185–186, 296*n*1, 301*n*3
MARRIAGES. *See* Fletcher, Paul; Goldstone, Herbert (husband, 1953–54); Gray, Charles; Nadler, Robert; Wright, Howard
New York sojourn with Robert Nadler, 43–46
parenthood. *See* Wright, Rustin
Peace Corps and, 95
pregnancy, 81, 83, 85
Santa Barbara move, 81, 83–85
Spanish study, 88
TRAVEL: Cuba abortion trip (1956), 44–45, 171–172; Europe solo tour, 54, 55–56; Kenya (1997), *162*, 243–249; Mexico stay with Robert Nadler, 41–43

315

Hart Wright, Sylvia (*continued*)
    Mexico with Howard, 73–74; Panama with Rusty (1985), 198–202; solo Mexico tour, 37–40; Spain, 280–284. *See also* Panama
    Unitarian-Universalist Church attendance, 142–143
    WRITING: architecture guides, 181–183, 185, 202–203, 301*n*1, 302*n*3; fiction, 41, 43, 59; *Library Journal* article, 121, 122, 140, 298*n*2; and marriage to Robert, 41, 43; master's thesis, 144, 299*n*4; on psychic phenomena, 252–253, 254, 279, 304*nn*1–2, 4; rental car trade association newsletter, 48, 51; Turn Toward Peace newsletter, 50–51, 77, 109; Zapatista accompaniment trip articles, 273–274, 306*n*1, 2

Hereafter, 280
Highlights of Recent American Architecture (Wright), 181–183, 185, 203, 301*n*1
Homeless Action Coalition (Eugene-Springfield), 242–243, 249–251
Hudson Institute, 149
Hyde Amendment, 168

International Monetary Fund (IMF), 234, 256. *See also* World Bank
International Rivers Network, 239
Iran-Contra Affair, 209

James, William, 252
Jefferson Airplane, 46
Johnson, Lyndon, 78, 107, 109
Jonathan Livingston Seagull (Bach), 192, 193
Journal of the Society for Psychical Research, 252–253
Jubilee 2000 campaign, 239
Juilliard School of Music, 32

Kahn, Herman, 149
Kennedy, John F., 44, 120
Kenya trip (1997), *162,* 243–249
King, Martin Luther Jr., 67, 68, 80, 91, 108, 109
Knowland, William Fife, 73

Lawrence, D. H., 44
liberation theology, 7
Library Journal, 121, 122, 140, 298*n*2
Lipton, Douglas, 104, 300*nn*3, 5
Lisle Fellowship, 275
Lodge, Oliver, 192–193, 301*n*1
López Obrador, Andrés Manuel (AMLO), 277
Lyndon Johnson's War on Poverty, 120

Mailer, Norman, 45
Man of La Mancha, 108–109
March on Washington (1983), 195
March on Washington for Jobs and Freedom (1963), 62–68
Marcos, *Subcomandante,* 7, 11–12, 268, 273, 276
marijuana, 46, 96
Martinson, Rita Carter, 57–59, 60, 61, 148, 297–298*n*1
Martinson, Robert M. (Bob)
    Berkeley mayoral campaign, *156*
    and Center for Knowledge in Criminal Justice Planning, 148–151
    City College position, 113, 138, 139, 140
    correspondence with, 70–72
    critiques of, 147
    dissertation, 113, 298*n*3
    early life, 105–106
    Freedom Riders participation, 52, 54, 139, 148
    and King assassination, 108–109
    marriage of, 57–59, 60, 61, 297–298*n*1
    mental instability of, 107, 151–152, 176, 179
    New Left and, 77
    relationship with SHW in Berkeley, 53, 54–55, 57, 59–61
    relationship with SHW in New York (1967–79), 103–104, 107–109, 113–114, 115–116, 121, 142, 174–176
    and Schachtmanism, 139–140, 299*n*1
    SHW's's marriage to Paul and, 143–144
    son of, *156*, 174–175
    suicide of, 176–177
    support for Vietnam War, 139, 147, 299*n*1
    and Turn Toward Peace, 51–52
    See also Martinson's criminal justice work
Martinson's criminal justice work
    Center for Knowledge in Criminal Justice Planning, 148–151
    current re-examination of, 179–180
    The Effectiveness of Correctional Treatment, The, 145, 300*nn*1, 3, 5
    New Republic articles, 140–142, 299*nn*2–3
    People magazine article, 146
    Rehabilitation, Recidivism, and Research, 147, 300*n*8
    research project, 104, 105, 107, 176–178
    right-wing support for, 148, 177–178, 300*n*1
    SHW's bibliography job, 104–105, 106, 145, 300*n*5
    Sixty Minutes interview, 144–145
    Treatment Ideology and Correctional Bureaucracy: A Study of Organizational Change, 298*n*3

Martinson's criminal justice work (*continued*)
    "What Works? Questions and Answers about Prison Reform," 145–146, 147, 178, 300*n*6
McCarthy era, 45, 49
McDaniel, Joseph (pseudonym). *See* Yusef
McKenzie Free affinity group, 256–257, 258. *See also* Seattle WTO protests
McKenzie River Gathering Foundation (MRG), 225, 286
Meade, Bill (pseudonym), 109, 126–130
Medium, 280
Merkel, Angela, 240
Mexico
    Howard's sojourn, 72, 73–74, 275–276
    SHW's solo tour of, 37–40
    SHW's stay with Robert Nadler, 41–43
    structural adjustment programs, 235
    See also Zapatista accompaniment trip
Mexico Solidarity Network, 2, 5, 6–7, 267, 274. *See also* Zapatista accompaniment trip
Meyers, Arthur (uncle), 27
Meyers, Harold (uncle), 25–26
Meyers, Joseph (uncle), 18, 19–20, 21–22, 29, 32
Miller, Henry, 44
Montgomery Bus Boycott, The, 63
Morton, Margaret "Peg," 165
Movement for a New Society, 224
MRG (McKenzie River Gathering Foundation), 225, 286
Myers, Walter, 95

Nadler, Robert (husband, 1960–62), *155*
    Berkeley sojourn, 46–47
    courtship, 40–41
    Mexico stay, 41–43
    New York sojourn, 43–46
    separation, 52–53
NAFTA (North American Free Trade Agreement), 9, 268
NARAL (National Abortion Rights Action League), 168–169
National Abortion Rights Action League (NARAL), 168–169
National Association for the Advancement of Colored People (NAACP), 62, 63, 65, 297*n*2
National Council on Crime and Delinquency, 147
neoconservatives, 140
New Frontier, 120
New Left, 77–78, 122

New Republic, 140–142, 299*n*2
Newton, Huey, 112
New York (1967–91), *159*
  architecture guides, 181–183, 185, 202–203, 301*n*1, 302*n*3
  CCNY architecture school library position, 181
  Center for Knowledge in Criminal Justice Planning job, 148–151
  City College of New York library position, 117, 138, 139, 148, 149, 172
  criminal justice research project job, 104–105, 106, 145, 300*n*5
  Jordan Smith relationship, 119–120, 123–124, 130, 136–137
  junior high library job, 107, 110
  marriage to Paul, 143–144, 166–167, 172–173
  move to (1967), 101
  nuclear freeze march, 186–188
  relationship with Martinson (1967–79), 103–104, 107–109, 113–114, 115–116, 121, 142, 174–176
  Rusty's childhood, 106, 107, 118, 126, *157*, *158*
  sociology master's degree studies, 122–123, 143, 144
  stay with father, 102
  subscription agency job, 103, 106–107, 182
  University Center SEEK Program job, 109–113, 114–115, 117–120, 121–122, 137–138, 140, *157*, 298*n*2
  Upper West Side apartment (1969–91), 118, 120–121
  Washington Heights apartment (1967–69), 102–103
New York Public Library, 35, 112, 170
New York University, 122
Nicaragua
  history of, 206–209, 303*nn*5–6
  post-Cold War conditions, 222
  and World Bank/IMF, 234–236
  See also Witness for Peace
Nike, 263–264
9/11, 278
Nixon, Richard M., 139
Noriega, Manuel, 200–201, 302*n*1
North American Free Trade Agreement (NAFTA), 9, 268
nuclear freeze march (New York, 1982), 186–188
nuclear weapons, 49–50, 55, 297*n*1

Oakland Tribune, 73
Oil Shock, 234
O'Neal, William, 299*n*2
"On the Zapatista Trail: Revolution in Chiapas" (Hart and Gray), 274, 306*n*2
Oral History of Charles Gray (Hart), 290–291, 307*n*1

INDEX

Ortega, Daniel, 303*n*6
Orwell, George, 136
Other America, The (Harrington), 120
Oxfam International, 239

Packwood, Bob, 160
Panama, 87–101
    early parenthood, 91–92
    encounter with Ramon, 98–100
    friendship with Felicia, 94–95
    Howard's conference trip, 90–91, 92
    Howard's fellowship plans, 81, 85–86
    legal separation, 101
    move to, 87–89
    Peace Corps office volunteering, 95–96, 100–101
    politics (1980s), 198–202, 302*nn*1–2
    Rusty's babyhood, 91–92, 93–94
    Rusty's birth, 90–91
    separation plans, 89–90, 93–94, 96, 98, 100
    trip with Rusty (1985), 198–202
    visit to Marge, 96–97
paradox of prison reform, 140
"Paranormal contact with the dying: 14 contemporary death coincidences" (Wright), 254, 304*n*4
Partido Revolucionario Institucional (PRI) (Mexico), 9
Pax Christi, 51
Peace Corps office (Panama), 95–96, 100–101
People magazine, 146
People's Songbook, The, 59
Perkins, John, 302*n*2
Pickus, Robert ("Pick"), 50, 51, 69, 77–78
Porter, Eduardo, 296*n*6
poverty. *See* social class
Praagh, James van, 253, 301*n*1
"Pre-college Program for the Disadvantaged, A" (Wright), 121, 122, 140, 298*n*2
prison reform, 141–142
Prophet, The (Gibran), 115
protective accompaniment, 2–3. *See also* Zapatista accompaniment trip
Protestant ethic, 27–28
psychic phenomena
    after-death contacts from Paul, 192–196, 231, 251, 252–253
psychic phenomena (*continued*)

Paul's psychic abilities, 166–167
public opinion on, 279–280
SHW's research on, 241–242, 251–252, 253–254, 304*n*2
SHW's writing on, 252–253, 254, 279, 304*nn*1–2, 4
Spain conference, 280–282
study of, 192–193, 301*n*1, 302*n*2
Public Interest, The, 178, 300*n*6

Quaker Economics Group (Eugene Friends Meeting), 1, 222–224, 225

racial equality
    and Jordan Smith relationship, 123, 124
    and University Center SEEK Program, 114–115, 117–118, 124–125
    See also Black Panthers; civil rights movement
Rainforest Action Network, 258
Ramparts, 122
Randolph, A. Philip, 62, 297*n*1
Reagan administration, 195, 204, 208, 209, 226, 302*n*2
Realist, The, 122
Reed, Donna, 36
Rehabilitation, Recidivism, and Research (Martinson, Palmer, and Adams), 147, 300*n*8
religion
    Eugene Friends Meeting, 222
    and family background, 20
    Paul's attitude toward, 184–185
    and psychic phenomena, 252
    Unitarian-Universalist Church, 142–143
Renoir, Jean, 52
Republican National Convention (1964), 72–73
Ricardo (pseudonym), 95
Richet, Charles, 252
Roe v. Wade, 168
Roldós, Jaime, 302*n*2
Role of the Communist Party in the Spanish Civil War, The (Martinson), 299*n*1
Roosevelt, Eleanor, 49
Roosevelt, Franklin Delano, 62
Rosenfeld, Morris, 185–186, 301*n*3
Rustin, Bayard, 91

Sababa, 132–133, 137
Sacramento Bee, 48
San Andres Accords, 7–8

Sánchez, Celia, 136
Sandinista National Liberation Front (FSLN) (Nicaragua), 207, 208, 237, 303*n*6
Sandino, Augusto, 207
Santa Barbara, California, 81, 83–85
Sartre, Jean-Paul, 136
"Save Parole Supervision" (Martinson and Wilks), 178, 300*n*1
Savio, Mario, 80
Schachtmanism, 120, 139–140
Scranton, William Warren, 73
SDS (Students for a Democratic Society), 298–299*n*2
Seattle WTO protests (1999), 1–2, 3–4, 8, 255–266
    background of, 255, 305–306*n*9
    Black Bloc actions, 263–264
    blocking tactics, 260–261
    impact of, 264–266
    McKenzie Free affinity group, 256–257, 258
    police violence, 261–262, 263
    preparation for, 257–259, 305*n*4
    signs and chants, 262
    size of, 305*n*7
    union rally, 264, 265
SEEK Program. *See* University Center SEEK Program
September 11, 2001 terrorist attacks, 278
Servas, 54, 55
simple living. *See* voluntary simplicity
simplicity circles, 255, 256
Sir, No Sir, 297–298*n*1
Sixth Sense, The, 280
Slick, Grace, 46
Smith, Jordan, 119–120, 123–124, 130, 136–137
Smithsonian Tropical Research Institute, 81
SNCC (Student Nonviolent Coordinating Committee), 76
social class
    and draft, 78
    and SHW's education, 31
    SHW's father on, 24
    SHW's mother on, 18–19, 20, 29
    Third World comparisons, 42, 74, 215–216, 246
Socialist Party USA, 120, 139, 140
Society for Psychical Research, 252, 253
Somoza Garcia, Anastasio, 207, 208, 217–218
Soul on Ice (Cleaver), 114–115

Sourcebook of Contemporary North American Architecture: From Postwar to Postmodern (Wright), 202–203, 302*n*3
Space Shuttle Student Involvement Project, 196–197, 302*n*4
Spain trip, 280–284
Spanish Civil War, 139
Spock, Benjamin, 69
Stevenson, Adlai, 44
Stevenson, Ian, 252
Stiglitz, Joseph, 240
structural adjustment programs, 234–236, 240. *See also* World Bank
Student Nonviolent Coordinating Committee (SNCC), 76
Students for a Democratic Society (SDS), 298–299*n*2

The Nation, 51
"They Call the Wind Mariah" (Grace Slick), 46
Torrijos, Omar, 200, 302*n*2
Treacy, Stephen, 101
Treatment Ideology and Correctional Bureaucracy: A Study of Organizational Change (Martinson), 298*n*3
Turn Toward Peace (TTP), 49–52, 69, 77, 109

Unitarian Church (Eugene), 220–221
United Nations Association, 51
United World Federalists, 51
Universalist Church (New York)
    and nuclear freeze march, 187–188
    Paul's memorial service at, 191–192
    Paul's volunteer work at, 173, 176
    and psychic messages from Paul, 193, 194–195
    SHW's abortion rights testimony at, 169
    SHW's attendance, 142–143
    SHW's Witness for Peace testimony at, 238–239
University Center SEEK Program, *157*
    black activist protests, 117–119
    and Black Panthers, 114–115, 119, 124–125
    closing of, 137–138
    job acceptance, 112–113
    job interview, 110–112
    and library science degree, 121–122
    meeting Jordan, 119–120
    and racial equality, 114–115, 117–118, 124–125
    SHW's article about, 121, 122, 140, 298*n*2
University of Wisconsin, 78

INDEX

USAID (U.S. Agency for International Development), 88, 236

veteran's bonuses, 19, 296n1
Vietnam Day Committee, 78–79, 80–83
Vietnam War
    Martinson's support for, 139, 147, 299n1
    See also anti-Vietnam War movement
VISTA (Volunteers In Service To America), 109
voluntary simplicity
    Charles' commitment to, 224–225, 227, 230–231, 232–233, 243
    simplicity circle (Eugene), 255, 256

War on Poverty, 120
War Resisters League, 51
We Gave Away a Fortune (Mogil, Slepian, and Woodrow), 228, 303n2
Weinberg, Jack, 76
Westinghouse Science Talent Search, 196, 302n3
"What Works? Questions and Answers about Prison Reform" (Martinson),
    145–146, 147, 178, 300n6
When Spirits Come Calling: The Open-Minded Skeptic's Guide to After-Death
    Contacts (Wright), 279, 304n2, 306n2
White, Walter, 62, 297n2
Wilks, Judith, 104, 148, 150, 177, 178, 300nn1, 3, 5
Williams, Edna Meyers (aunt), 18, 19–21, 22, 32–33
Witness for Peace
    Charles Gray's participation, 222, 227
    U.S.-based work for, 233–234, 238–239
    See also Witness for Peace delegation (1990); Witness for Peace delegation
        (1995)
Witness for Peace delegation (1990), 209–219
    building project, *159*, 212–213
    Condega stay, 216–217
    invitation to, 205–206
    organization meetings, 217–219
    piñata party, 215–216
    stay with Maria Rosa, 210–212, 214–215, 216, 219
Witness for Peace delegation (1995), 234, 236–238
World Bank, 234–236, 239–240, 256
World Equity Budget, 230, 232–233, 243, 255, 288
World Trade Organization. *See* Seattle WTO protests (1999)
World War II, 62

Wright, Howard (husband, 1964–68), *155*
    affair with Sally, 90, 92–93, 98
    courtship, 70
    dissertation, 72, 77, 81
    legal separation, 101
    living together, 71–72
    marital tensions, 83–85
    marriage, 74–75
    Mexico sojourn, 72, 73–74, 275–276
    move to Eugene, 206
    Panama fellowship, 81, 85–86
    Panama sojourn, 87–91, 92–94
    and Peace Corps office staff, 96, 101
    Santa Barbara teaching position, 81, 83
    separation plans, 89–90, 93–94, 96, 98, 100
    Vietnam Day Committee office bombing, 82–83
Wright, Rustin (Rusty) (son)
    as adult, *160*, 220, 278–279
    babyhood, 91–92, 93–94
    birth, 90, 91
    childhood, 106, 107, 118, 126, *157*, *158*
    education, 166, 196–197
    Panama trip (1984), 198–202
    Paul's relationship with, 143, 154, *158*, 167, 190
    and psychic messages from Paul, 192, 193
    and September 11, 2001 terrorist attacks, 278
    Space Shuttle Student Involvement competition, 196–197
Wright, Sylvia Hart. *See* Hart Wright, Sylvia
WTO protests (Seattle, 1999). *See* Seattle WTO protests

Ya Basta, 5, 12, 14, 270
Yusef (Joseph McDaniel, pseudonym)
    and Aminifu warning, 130, 131–132
    and Johnny Lightning operation, 133, 137
    police shooting boast, 134–135, 136, 137
    and University Center SEEK Program, 114, 115, 124, 125

Zapata, Emiliano, 10, 13, 275
Zapatista accompaniment trip (2001), 1–16, *164*, 267–276
    delegation group, 6, 8
    and memories of past Mexico travel, 274–276
    Morelia stay, 273–274
    paramilitary threats, 3, 8, 11, 12

INDEX

Zapatista accompaniment trip (2001) (*continued*)
    planning for, 1–4, 267–269
    Puebla rally, 11–12
    Querétero incident, 13–16, 269–273
    San Cristobal de las Casas embarcation, 3, 4–5, 269
    writing about, 273–274, 278, 306nn1, 2
    Ya Basta, 5, 12, 14, 270
    Zapatista movement background, 7–10, 268, 296n6

www.ingramcontent.com/pod-product-compliance
Lightning Source LLC
Chambersburg PA
CBHW030303080526
44584CB00012B/425